WALL STREET
FOR GLOBAL INVESTORS

A Practical Guide to the World's Largest Stock Market
+ SMIGRM Method: Tactical Timing Based on Risk Threshold

- 1st Edition -

Sidney Shauy, MBA
Rodrigo Bittencourt Shauy

PALLAS VESTA
PUBLISHING CO. LLC

Published by Pallas Vesta Publishing Company LLC, New Jersey, USA

Limitation of Liability/Disclaimer of Warranty: Although the publisher and the author have made their best efforts in creating this book, they make no representations or warranties regarding the accuracy or completeness of its content. The publisher and the author expressly disclaim any implied warranties for a specific purpose, including those made by third parties or in sales materials. The advice and strategies contained herein are purely educational in nature and may not be suitable for everyone's particular circumstances. Neither the publisher nor the author shall be liable for any loss or damage of any kind incurred as a result of using this book. You should always consult a competent licensed professional whom you trust, as appropriate for your unique situation.

PALLAS VESTA
PUBLISHING CO. LLC

Pallas Vesta Publishing Company LLC
New Jersey, NJ – United States of America

Volume discounts are available.

SIDNEY
SHAUY

Stock Market Investing
Guided by
Risk Management

ISBN: 978-1-960691-19-4 (e-book/PDF)
ISBN: 978-1-960691-18-7 (paperback)
ISBN: 978-1-960691-20-0 (hardcover)

First edition: 2025

www.Engineering-Finance.com

Printed in the United States of America. Cover design and part of the content assisted by ChatGPT, CoPilot (artistic conception).

SPECIAL THANKS

To my family, for all their love and unconditional support, always

To my parents and grandparents, my eternal gratitude

To my mentors, for their wisdom and inspiration

GENERAL LEGAL NOTICE

Although great care has been taken to provide accurate, informative, and useful material on the subjects covered in this book, neither the publisher nor the author is responsible for any errors or omissions, or for the results obtained from the use of this information. The book contains the author's ideas and opinions. The strategies described in the book may not be suitable for everyone under any circumstances, and are not guaranteed or warranted to produce any specific results. The book is intended to provide general information for educational purposes only. The book is sold with the understanding that neither the author nor the publisher is engaged in providing legal, business, financial, investment, tax, accounting, securities, or any other professional advice. The author is not a licensed advisor. The reader should always consult their own trusted and licensed professional advisors before adopting any of the strategies suggested in the book or drawing inferences from them. The content of this book is provided "as is," without any warranties of accuracy, completeness, or timeliness regarding the results obtained from its use. The reader assumes full responsibility for the use of this information and uses it at their own risk. Neither the author nor the publisher shall be liable for any direct, indirect, special, incidental, consequential, or punitive damages of any kind. Under no circumstances shall the author, Sidney Shauy, or the publisher, Pallas Vesta Publishing Company LLC, its affiliates, partners, agents, employees, associates, service providers, or their employees be liable to readers or any person for any decision or action taken based on the content of this book and its consequences. The information and all figures in this book, which were accurate at the time of writing, may become inaccurate or outdated over time and due to changes in the economy and markets. New laws and taxes may be enacted. The figures, including prices and rates, and assumptions are not guaranteed and are subject to change at any time. Any disrespect toward individuals, groups, organizations, or companies is unintentional. The models used in the book are based on assumptions, which may or may not apply to everyone, and are subject to errors, omissions, and changes. All models are simplifications of reality and should be understood as such. As with all models, assumptions, and numerical examples in the book, it has been emphasized repeatedly that individual results vary based on a wide range of factors related to each person's unique set of circumstances, needs, goals, and quality of strategy execution, as well as uncontrollable factors such as the timing and state of the economy and markets.

Clarification regarding references to the S&P 500®: **S&P 500® is a registered trademark of S&P Global**. It has nothing to do with the RISP 500™, which is a stock market risk metric developed by the authors based on data related to the S&P 500®, using a proprietary algorithm from Risk Scientific LLC.

About the Author

Sidney Shauy is the founding CEO of Risk Scientific LLC (U.S.), creator of the RISP 500™, a risk indicator used by equity managers, and the SMIGRM Method based on Contextual Dynamic Allocation. He was a trader and risk manager with over 30 years of combined experience in international financial markets at Citigroup, Morgan Stanley, Lloyds Bank, ABN Amro, and Bilbao Vizcaya, in New York, Hong Kong, and São Paulo. The author successfully managed multibillion-dollar portfolios for these banks during multiple financial crises since the 1990s. In recent years, he has worked with high-net-worth clients, helping them create investment strategies and portfolios; served as *a subject matter expert* for Deloitte Consulting; and currently provides trading and consulting services to wealth managers and investment funds in the U.S. An expert in financial derivatives across various asset classes—stocks, currencies, interest rates, commodities—including hybrid and exotic derivatives, he is constantly testing market data, new strategies (including experimental ones in the Chinese market, the next frontier), and developing/refining new algorithms.

An automation engineer by training and a quadrilingual, Sidney Shauy earned an MBA from the Wharton School at the University of Pennsylvania.

帥 SIDNEY SHAUY

Stock Market Investing
Guided by
Risk Management

Website: www.Engineering-Finance.com (in English)

Blog: engineering-finance.medium.com (in English)

Summary

Preface

Dear Reader and [Future] Global Investor:

Whether you already invest in Wall Street or not, congratulations! You are very special because it is not every day that someone decides to step out of their comfort zone and challenge their own boundaries to explore new possibilities that can transform their life. Just by being here, reading these words, you are already demonstrating your courage, your willingness to expand boundaries, and your growth mindset—both personal and financial. This is the first step in a journey that could be decisive in your quest for much faster wealth accumulation and a more secure and promising financial future.

The simple act of wanting to learn something new also puts you ahead of most people. After all, it takes vision to see opportunities and determination to seize them. You are about to explore a new world: **the powerful financial market of the United States**, also widely known as **Wall Street—the largest and most sophisticated capital market on the planet**. A market that offers a range of possibilities far beyond what we are used to in most countries around the world—and which today can be accessed simply and directly, without even leaving your home. But to take advantage of the opportunity, it is essential to have the right knowledge and mindset.

Wall Street: A Life-Changing Opportunity

Thanks to 21st-century globalization and technological advances, investing in the American market has become a real and accessible opportunity for all global investors, regardless of social class or level of experience. Today, all you need to get started is a computer or cell phone, an internet connection, and a few clicks. That's right: you can become a global investor with tools that are already in your hand, right at your fingertips.

But, of course, there is a crucial difference between simply investing and **investing the right way, with security, strategy, and real results in your pocket**. And this is where this book comes into your journey. We will guide you along the path of knowledge, teaching you everything you need to know to not only access the American market, but **also to avoid fatal mistakes and make the most of the opportunities it offers with great security**. What lies before you is not just a possibility to invest in U.S. dollars, but a chance to **accelerate the formation of your personal and family wealth in a solid and consistent way**.

The Powerful But Forgotten Time Factor

Think about it with me: what is the most valuable asset in your life? It is certainly not your money, nor your investments, nor any material asset. **It is your time**. We are all born with a clock counting down. We are all born with an expiration date, regardless of social class. We can always earn or recover money, but each of our times is finite, regardless of wealth or economic status. Lost time cannot be recovered. Since life is finite, the faster we accumulate wealth, the more time we will have in life to enjoy it, right? A young person in their twenties has a huge financial advantage over a senior citizen in their sixties. **The time factor is crucial because it allows compound returns to have "time" to effectively accelerate the formation or growth of wealth.** And there's more! Consider the central formula of any investment:

$$Future\,Value \;=\; Present\,Value \;\times\; (1 + Retorn\;Rate)^{Time}$$

In the formula for the future value of an investment, the time factor appears in the exponent and is often overlooked or neglected by investors. Why? Because we are always focused on the search for better returns. Isn't that true? What do all investors and their financial advisors discuss all the time when planning new investments, if not rates of return or profitability? No one remembers that little factor (Time) hidden in the exponent of the formula. We want a higher rate of return to accelerate asset growth, but we have to consider the time factor as well! The more time you have to grow an investment, the better.

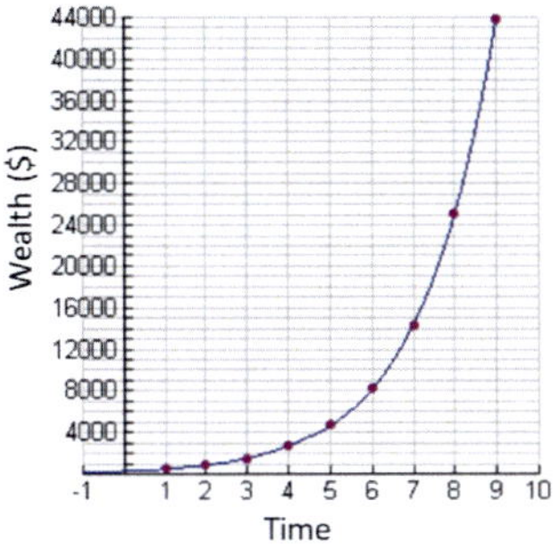

Wealth accumulation is the same concept as compound interest. The graph of the formula above is exponential (see figure on the right). Notice how in the early years, the curve is flatter, meaning your wealth grows slowly (because the base is still small). Notice that as time passes, the curve slopes upward and the speed of wealth growth increases dramatically. Everyone wants this final phase of accelerated wealth formation, when gains accumulate quickly, but to get there, what do we need? TIME. To reach the final phase, we must necessarily go through the initial phase. So, the big lesson is this: don't procrastinate on investment decisions. Start the journey as soon as possible. Time is money, especially if you live in a country with a certain amount of persistent inflation or relatively high interest rates. The money lost through procrastination (which is money you fail to earn and that is also a loss) accumulates quickly. Think about it this way: every time you don't embrace time as your best ally in building your wealth, you are antagonizing it so that it becomes your worst enemy, making you poorer and future wealth less likely. So don't procrastinate. Make every minute of your life count, because I assure you that it is very precious and worth a lot of money in itself.

The Time is Now

Thousands of investors around the world have already taken this step—ordinary people who decided to broaden their financial horizons. Many started small but reaped surprising results over time. And if they can do it, so can you. But there is one crucial difference. Most of them went into battle in a rush, but not you: you are preparing yourself, acquiring the right knowledge. This will make a crucial difference in terms of results, guaranteed.

What will really **set your trajectory apart is the knowledge you will acquire here**. This book was written to give you a practical and an absurd advantage that they never had—**the SMIGRM Method**—and to show you **how to navigate with confidence and, above all, navigate safely in the world's largest stock market**. We are here to transform complexity into clarity and equip you with everything you need to achieve your goals more easily, more quickly, and more safely, above all else.

An Important Revelation

Over the years, you have probably heard of a multitude of methods for investing in the financial markets. Terms such as fundamental analysis, macro, *valuation*, technical analysis (charting), diversification, balanced portfolios between stocks and fixed income (60/40), etc. are often promoted as the **traditional methods** to guide you in the stock market. Business schools mass teach these concepts enthusiastically, and financial experts repeat them tirelessly in the media. But here's the truth that no one likes to admit: none of these methods work consistently in the long run. And although they are theoretically logical, they are not very easy to execute in practice and your results will hardly be consistent.

The reality is that all of these methods have their moments—they work in some situations and fail in others. During periods of market bull runs, when stocks rise almost universally, anyone can look like a genius. But it is in times of crisis, when the market collapses or becomes volatile, that these methods reveal their true limitations. And it is precisely at these times that you need something that works! It's like having your GPS signal cut off just when you arrive at an unfamiliar place with many forks in the road.

As a professional trader and risk manager with decades of experience on Wall Street, responsible for managing hundreds of millions to billions of dollars for international banks, I have experienced this reality firsthand. I tested, applied, and saw these strategies fail repeatedly at the worst moments when confusion and uncertainty in the markets were increasing. The feeling of helplessness in those moments is something I have never forgotten—and that is what motivated me to seek a truly resilient solution, capable of adapting to different market conditions: knowing how to respond when no one knows what to say, what to expect, or what to do!

But here's what makes this revelation even more powerful: this solution—**the SMIGRM Method**—has proven over the years that it is not only effective in market ups and downs, but also **incredibly simple to use**. You don't need years of experience or a PhD to know how to use it. It only takes 2 to 3 minutes of your time per day to implement! That's right, in just a few minutes a day, as quick as reading an email, checking a dashboard of key indicators, and clicking a few times (if necessary), you can make investment decisions with confidence, knowing that you are maximizing your returns and keeping risks under control in the U.S. stock market.

Don't believe it? Every method has an Achilles heel. The secret to success lies precisely in the combination of tools. **The SMIGRM Method will make traditional methods work better and more robust, filling an important blind spotin modern finance: market *timing***.

A Powerful Method at Your Fingertips

After years of testing and refining the model in the day-to-day market under real conditions (up, down, sideways, volatile, directionless, etc.), and using it in my own personal investments, I decided to share the SMIGRM method with the general public, as well as wealth managers and financial professionals (CFPs, fund managers, family offices, etc.). For you, dear global investor, my goal is to ensure that when you take your first steps in the US stock market, you can do so with greater ease, confidence, and strategy. It's not just about investing; it's about **investing intelligently and adaptively, even during the most challenging conditions**.

This book will be your guide. Here, you will learn **how to turn the largest financial market on the planet into your greatest opportunity for wealth acceleration in an easy, fast, and safe way**. And with the method I am going to present to you, you will be equipped with the most valuable and indispensable tool to explore this new world.

Marcelo's Story: A Journey of Discovery and Transformation

Marcelo R. is 51 years old and is a senior IT manager at a large multinational company in Brazil. Always disciplined, with the analytical mindset of an engineer, he sought to stay up to date, both in his professional field and in the management of his personal finances. Coming from a middle-class family in São Paulo, with a good academic background, Marcelo is married and has two children: one in college and the other preparing for college entrance exams. Since the age of 19, Marcelo has been working and saving, always thinking about his family's future, prioritizing his children's education and keeping an eye on his own future retirement.

Despite all his efforts, accumulating wealth in Brazil has never been an easy task. He faced the typical challenges of an unstable economy: frequent changes in monetary policy, persistent inflation, high interest rates, and a currency in constant devaluation against the dollar. Like many Brazilians, Marcelo has tried everything: stocks, fixed income, CDI, investment funds. But the fluctuations of the Brazilian market always kept him on alert, especially with stocks. He felt that, no matter how hard he tried, there was always something beyond his control, and it would be very difficult to realize all his dreams and aspirations for himself and his family—while he was still alive—and then have a peaceful retirement and, if possible, leave valuable assets to his children.

The Turning Point

During the pandemic in 2020, Marcelo sent me a message on WhatsApp. It was an informal conversation that lasted less than 15 minutes, but it ended up completely changing his financial trajectory. Knowing his difficulties, I asked him why he didn't invest in the US stock market. Marcelo said he had always admired companies like Amazon, Apple, Microsoft, and Google, but never thought that world was accessible to him. The idea of opening an online account with an American brokerage firm seemed exciting, but the initial excitement soon gave way to a lot of doubts about his real ability to pull it off.

He began to wonder: how could he invest without the necessary knowledge? Where were the "banana peels"? Would the methods he used on the Brazilian stock market apply equally to the American stock market? Although he knew the big American companies by name, he had never analyzed them in depth. How could he know if they were really promising for the future? And how about market timing, how could he know when to enter and when to exit? Wasn't the price already too high (or too late to jump in now)? These persistently recurring questions always discouraged him.

It actually took another chat to break down his paralysis. I showed him how I had not only avoided losses during the pandemic crash, but also returned to the market at the right time to capture the subsequent upturn. Marcelo was intrigued. How on Earth you or any sane person would invest in stocks in the middle of the pandemic? I told him there is a lot more going on below the surface of what is broadcast by major news media. For instance, nobody was talking about the liquidity the Federal Reserve was injecting in the economy. Such amounts of money intended to stimulate the economy largely exceeded productive uses of it and made its way to the stock market, pumping up prices. Marcelo started to realize that he had a lot to learn but he could only really learn by doing and by adopting a solid risk management methoid based on data, not expert opinions. He decided to give it a try. Still skeptical, he invested R$ 10,000.00 on September 17, 2020, dividing the amount into two simple strategies: R$ 5,000.00 in Strategy A and R$ 5,000.00 in Strategy B.

Jaw-dropping results

The first few months were already revealing. Marcelo quickly began to realize something he had never experienced before: a method that really worked, with consistent and clear results. The impact of the SMIGRM Method was so positive that he allocated more and more money to the two strategies applied to the US market, and never withdrew a single cent until the moment I am writing this book (early 2025). But for simplicity's sake, just for the purposes of analyzing his performance, let's assume that Marcelo did not increase the size of his investments and kept the same R$5,000.00 in each strategy until the end of 2024. See the table below for a summary of his two strategies (A and B) compared to a simple and direct investment in the S&P 500 index and another in his home country's stock index, the Bovespa index (through the ETF called BOVA11 in Brazil) of the same initial value:

RATES OF RETURN

	Strategy A SPY or cash	Strategy B SSO or cash	S&P 500	Ibovespa BOVA11
17 Sep 2020				
31 Dec 2020	5.08%	8.40%	-1.48%	19.4%
31 Dec 2021	12.22%	21.54%	26.61%	-12.1%
31 Dec 2022	0.53%	-5.19%	-19.64%	5.1%
31 Dec 2023	33.13%	59.21%	26.29%	23.1%
31 Dec 2024	23.51%	47.87%	23.31%	-10.1%
Return in USD:	**94.9%**	**194.1%**	**56.1%**	**22.2%**

MARCELO'S INITIAL INVESTMENT 10,000.00 BRL

	Strategy A SPY or cash	Strategy B SSO or cash	S&P 500	Ibovespa BOVA11	BRL/USD Exchange rate
Investment (R$)	5,000.00	5,000.00	5,000.00	5,000.00	
	(USD)	(USD)	(USD)	(BRL)	
17 Sep 2020	946.97	946.97	946.97	5,000.00	5.28
31 Dec 2020	995.10	1,026.51	933.00	5,971.35	
31 Dec 2021	1,116.70	1,247.63	1,181.27	5,250.00	
31 Dec 2022	1,122.61	1,182.87	949.27	5,518.23	
31 Dec 2023	1,494.54	1,883.25	1,198.83	6,791.15	
31 Dec 2024	**1,845.90**	**2,784.77**	**1,478.28**	**6,107.81**	6.20
Currency Conversion	(BRL)	(BRL)	(BRL)	(BRL)	
31 Dez 2024	**11,444.59**	**17,265.56**	**9,165.31**	**6,107.81**	
Return in BRL:	**128.9%**	**245.3%**	**83.3%**	**22.2%**	

Marcelo started investing on September 17, 2020. The dollar exchange rate at the time was 5.28. In other words, R$ 5,000.00 was equivalent to US$ 946.97. As we said, he allocated this amount to each of the two strategies. We are simplifying things here because the unit prices of SPY and SSO assets are not identical, but it makes it easier to compare the results, which is what really matters in this example. Let's examine how much Marcelo's assets grew in the United States until December 31, 2024 (a period of 4 years and 3 months), and compare it with what would have happened if he had simply bought SPY (equivalent to the S&P 500 in the US) and waited for time to pass ("buy & hold") and also what would have happened if he had simply invested in BOVA11 in Brazil (equivalent to the Bovespa index).

First, note that Strategies A and B yielded 94.9% and 194.1% in US dollars, respectively. If Marcelo had simply invested in the S&P 500 index, he would have earned 56.1% in US dollars. In other words, both strategies beat the S&P 500 by a wide margin! What if Marcelo had not invested in the US but had invested in the Bovespa Index? He would have had a return of only 22% in Brazilian reais over the same period. Note that we have not even included the 17.4% appreciation of the dollar (from 5.28 to 6.20 during the period)! Let's include it and redo the calculations to see how they turned out.

Converting the results of the investments in US dollars to Brazilian reais to compare on the same basis with the hypothetical investment in Ibovespa, here are the final results sorted by outcome (assuming that Marcelo invested the same R$ 5,000.00 in each):

Investment	Final value (R$)	Gain (%)
Strategy B	R$ 17,265.56	245.3%
Strategy A	R$ 11,444.59	128.9%
S&P 500	R$ 9,165.31	83.3%
Ibovespa (BOVA11)	R$ 6,107.81	22.2%

Isn't the difference jaw-dropping?

The S&P 500 alone yielded 50% more. But:

Strategy A yielded 87% more than the Bovespa Index. The return was 5.8x faster.

Strategy B yielded 183% more than the Bovespa Index. The return was 11.0x faster.

This was only possible thanks to **the SMIGRM Method** based on risk management. We will explain the two strategies in more detail in **Chapter 8**, but just to give you a heads up, Strategy A uses the SPY ETF that replicates the S&P 500 but follows a risk indicator called **RISP 500** by **the SMIGRM Method** to avoid sharp market losses when they occur. Strategy B is the leveraged equivalent of Strategy A. But we will detail these strategies and many others in **Chapter 8** of the book.

Now, entering 2025, Marcelo says he is more confident and happier than ever. He believes that his plans and dreams for his financial future are finally on track. The worries that had plagued him for years have been replaced by a sense of control and optimism. He sees the achievement of his goals as something entirely possible within his reach.

Connecting with You

Marcelo's story could be your story. Like him, you may be facing the challenges of investing in your country or even feeling unsure about exploring new markets. But, as Marcelo discovered, there is a practical and effective way to overcome these obstacles. This book is here to show you how to turn this opportunity into reality. And if he could do it, like so many others, why couldn't you?

The U.S. Stock Market Attracts Investors from Around the World

The U.S. stock market is the largest and most liquid in the world, characterized by its vast market capitalization, significant number of listed companies, and high daily trading volume.

Market Capitalization and Number of Listed Companies:

The New York Stock Exchange (NYSE) and Nasdaq are the two main stock exchanges in the US. In 2022, the NYSE had approximately 2,584 listed companies, totaling a market capitalization of US$ 25.8 trillion. Nasdaq, known for hosting many technology companies, surpassed the NYSE in number of listings for the sixth consecutive year in 2024, with 160 initial public offerings (IPOs) raising approximately $22 billion. Daily trading volume on the NYSE is significant, with a monthly average of $1.452 trillion in 2021. These figures reflect the depth and liquidity of the U.S. stock market.

The U.S. stock market is composed of a diversity of investors, including institutional and individual investors. It is estimated that more than 60% of the U.S. population owns stocks in their investment portfolios. Institutional investors, such as pension funds, insurance companies, and mutual funds, also play a significant role in the market.

In terms of **the origin of foreign investors**, the main countries investing directly in the US include Japan, Germany, Canada, the United Kingdom, and Ireland.

Foreign Investors Resident and Non-Resident in the United States

Whether or not you reside in the United States will not affect any of the principles of finance and investing that you will learn in this book. As you already know, investors residing anywhere in the world today have access to the U.S. financial market. However, operationally, the experience will be quite different for those who live in the United States and those who do not, so we need to provide some guidance so that you can make the most of your opportunities without major difficulties.

Opening Accounts

The first notable difference is in the form of access, which begins with the process of opening an account with an American brokerage firm. Those who live in the US will have a wider range of choices, but this difference has been diminishing over the years as more brokerage firms are opening up to international investors. The requirements for opening an account are greater for those who do not live in the US, but they vary from brokerage firm to brokerage firm. Just as an example, bearing in mind that I have no commercial association with any of these brokers, there are several: Avenue, Nomad, Inter, XP, etc., including Charles Schwab, but this one requires a minimum investment of US$ 25,000 today (2025). However, Schwab itself, for example, does not impose any minimum limit for US residents. Ultimately, the choice of brokerage firm will be based on account opening requirements, minimum contributions, and fees charged.

In the past, before Robinhood came along, US brokerages used to charge brokerage fees per trade (buy or sell) executed. They even charged monthly maintenance fees and other junk fees. Today, due to increased competition, many of these fees have disappeared. But some may persist, especially for non-resident foreigners. So, pay close attention when choosing a broker before signing the membership agreement. Avoid brokers that charge monthly fees or fees per trade on basic instruments such as stocks and ETFs.

Impact of the Exchange Rate

U.S. residents who have lived their entire lives in dollars will not be affected by currency exchange rates, but foreign investors outside the U.S. will. When exchanging currency, they may be getting a bad deal on the conversion rate if they are not careful. See Chapter 18 about Currency Risk and ways to hedge it.

Also be careful with the costs of executing the exchange. Here they can be expensive in the currency conversion rate or in fixed fees per transaction, or both. It is a good idea to check this as well before deciding.

Do you need to open a checking account at a U.S. bank? For investment purposes, not necessarily, but it is a very personal decision. If you also buy real estate or other assets in the U.S., it is advisable to have a checking account at a bank. Large chain banks such as Citi, Chase, Wells Fargo, and Bank of America, as well as regional U.S. banks, require the account holder to be present at the branch to open a checking account.

Taxation Effects

U.S. residents only need to worry about U.S. taxation, but non-U.S. resident investors will also have to report their earnings to their countries. International taxation is a complex topic that is beyond the scope of this book and requires clarification by specialized accounting professionals.

Taxation is never a very popular topic, but it is important for investors to have a good understanding of it so they can be strategic and **minimize their tax obligations**. Always remember that taxes are generally levied only on profits earned on investments. This means that **if you receive a tax bill, it means you have made a profit, which is something to celebrate**. And with the possibility of high returns on US stocks, taxation may end up being a mere detail, but you have to be smart and avoid paying unnecessary taxes. It is always worth investing some time to find ways to pay as little tax as possible.

Knowing When to Enter and Exit (Timing) is Even More Important than Knowing What to Invest In

Timing is more important because passive index investors generally achieve better results than most active investors, and they don't even have to choose stocks. But **both active and passive investors** need to know how to execute timing accurately.

Just like those who invest directly in the U.S., global investors who access U.S. stock indices and sectors of the economy need a method. Especially when it comes to the *timing* of their purchases and sales. Access and the ability to buy and sell is only the first step. Even knowing what to buy is only half the battle. To make a profit, you need to sell to realize that profit and put it in your pocket. Knowing the best time to enter and exit the market is the key to profitability.

This book will teach you the **SMIGRM method – "Stock Market Investing Guided by Risk Management"** – to masterfully determine *timing*: **when it is worth entering the market and when it is not worth staying in it from a risk vs. potential return perspective**.

I'll prove it to you why in one paragraph. Let's go back to basics, the beginning of it all. First of all, why are you thinking about investing in stocks? Why do you invest in stocks? You take a risk when buying stocks because you expect to receive a return and nothing else, right? So, the relationship between risk and return is crucial for you. And for all investors. You will maximize your return when the relationship between risk and return is favorable to you. The big problem for the vast majority of investors is exactly this: when they lose a lot of money, **the diagnosis is usually because they are not being properly rewarded financially for the risks they are taking**. In other words, their risk vs. return ratio is misaligned or unfavorable to them, usually without them even realizing it. The SMIGRM method corrects this exact problem. Its RISP 500 risk indicator will measure the current risk in the context of the last 15 years to give you this parameter to help determine when it is worth entering the market (buy) and when it is no longer worth staying in the market (sell).

This concept is so important that we will make an analogy for you to understand it well. Imagine that you are at a card table. It is your turn and you have two options: bet your hand or pass. When should you decide one way or the other? A card game is a probabilistic environment, just like the stock market. In a probabilistic environment, there are no certainties, only probabilities. You make decisions under uncertainty (like almost everything in life, right?), but there is method and logic in decision-making under uncertainty. Thus, your decisions may prove to be right or wrong, because there are no certainties. So, to maximize your chances of success, you need to weigh the probabilities. At the gaming table, what are your chances by risking your hand? If the risk is not favorable to call, don't risk it: pass the round. In the stock market, the same logic applies: if the risk has risen to the point where it is not worth calling, get out of the market. And only return to the table when the risk has normalized again to healthy and acceptable levels – for you.

If you understand this logic, you are halfway to understanding the SMIGRM Method. The RISP 500 risk indicator will give you this information – every day and in real time.

Almost all existing methods help investors determine what to buy – stock X or Y, etc. – but they stop there, without teaching how to *time the market*, or they teach it in a very *sloppy* way. They usually say that it is impossible to *time* the market, so you are free to *guess* the timing you want. Isn't it? The truth is that none of the well-known market experts, nor the financial and fund industry in general, have the slightest idea how to *time the* market well, so they give this kind of recommendation that doesn't help anyone. SMIGRM has proven that they are all wrong, I'm sorry to say, without any arrogance on my part. Just look at the evidence we will present. So when you read this book, you are in the right place. That is why I can say without being pretentious or arrogant that with the

SMIGRM Method, you will have the unique chance to beat 90% of the hedge fund (multimarket) industry out there.

How to Use This Book: Differentiated Study Sequences

We know that many investors prefer to be active and others passive. There is no right or wrong, just personal preferences. Active investors have the chance to make big moves and earn a lot of money if they choose the right stocks. This usually requires identifying extremely promising stocks before most investors even think about them, meaning they can be purchased very cheaply. This is very difficult to do, especially consistently. Even Warren Buffett, considered the greatest master of all time in the art of choosing winning stocks, agrees that it is extremely difficult to get it right consistently. That is why many investors choose to be passive and buy index ETFs instead of trying their luck by choosing stocks. But there is absolutely nothing wrong with being active or passive. Both are great choices, as long as you know how to execute them masterfully. And there are those who are hybrid investors, meaning they make both active and passive investments. In fact, this is an important group, especially among the wealthiest investors, who invest in both: hand-picked individual stocks and ETFs that track stock market indices.

That is why, in this book, we give readers two different study sequences. We have marked [Active] and [Passive] in brackets in the chapter titles to make your study sequence easier.

Differentiated Study Sequence for Active and Passive Investors

Active Investor Sequence	Passive Investor Sequence
Chapters 1 - 9	Chapters 1 - 9
Chapter 10: Fundamental Analysis, Valuation, Technical Analysis Chapter 11: Active Allocation and Stock Portfolio Construction Chapter 12: MPT - Modern Portfolio Theory	Chapters 13: Passive Investing with Index ETFs
Chapters 14 - 20	Chapters 14 - 20

As you read this book, you will notice that we cover a wide range of important topics and knowledge, but we do not go into too much depth on each topic, meaning that they can be expanded upon. The reason is that the intention in writing the book is to give the reader the opportunity to take their first steps toward Wall Street to begin accelerating their wealth formation more easily, quickly, and safely. If we were to delve deeper into each topic, the book would have to become an encyclopedia with a total of 10,000 pages! You will also notice that the topics covered in the book have a more practical than theoretical goal or character. This is intentional because we want you to be able to execute the techniques you learn and achieve your financial goals. We want to help you quickly and easily implement your idea of accelerating your wealth with the full power of Wall Street.

[CHECKLIST] STEP-BY-STEP IMPLEMENTATION GPS

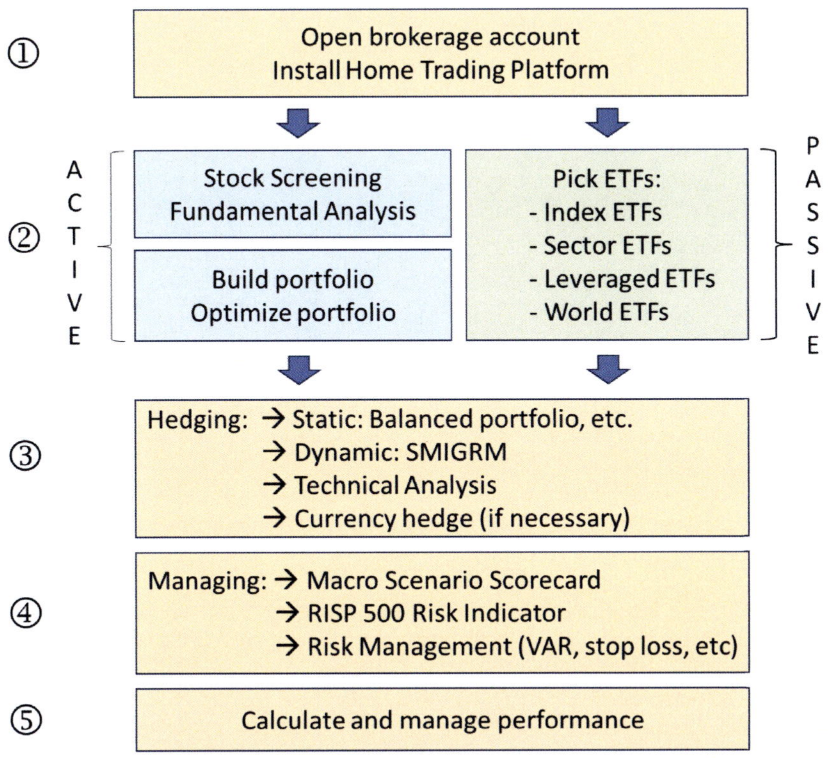

Chapter 1. Success on Wall Street Begins with Preparation

The Super Promise

Investing on Wall Street is the dream of many global investors who seek to diversify their investments and accelerate the growth of their wealth in a strong currency, the US dollar. However, they encounter many obstacles, such as lack of knowledge, fear of the unknown, and even the English language barrier, among others. But let's pause for a moment... What if I told you that it is possible **to** do this **easily and safely, outperforming the S&P 500 index and 90% of professional fund managers?** Sounds too good to be true, doesn't it?

Even without a crystal ball — which, let's face it, no one has — we have developed a risk measurement system so calibrated to the US market that it allows us to have something extraordinary: a true "Early Crash Detector." It works like a mine sweeper. This system, developed in the form of a computer algorithm, gives us the agility to detect and avoid crashes in the stock market early before they become serious and difficult to recover from. As a bonus, it also boosts results, **delivering <u>more</u> return with <u>less</u> risk**. This means that **it is possible not only to avoid devastating losses, but also to consistently outperform the S&P 500 index** — a task considered very difficult to do consistently.

But here we don't just talk the talk. We walk the walk. See the table below for the performance tables of eight strategies that have been operationalized (and updated) live every single day since January 1, 2022. The table on the left refers to performance in 2024, and the table on the right shows performance from the beginning on January 1, 2022, to December 31, 2024 (3 years of continuous results). Note that in the long term, all 8 strategies beat the S&P 500 index, and by a landslide!

2024 Return Ranking

Asset/Strategy	YTD Return
ST4-2L-Nasdaqx2	54.46%
ST3-2L-SP500x2	47.87%
ST7-3L-Nasdaq	35.77%
ST6-3L-SP500	32.71%
ST2-2L-Nasdaq	28.21%
ST1-2L-SP500	23.51%
SPY (S&P 500)	23.30%
ST5-2L-Volatility	10.51%
ST8-3L-Volatility	8.45%

Published every day after the close
Since 01 Jan 2024

2022 - 2024 Performance Ranking 31-Dec-2024

Asset/Strategy	Cum. Return	CAGR	Max DD	RoMaD
ST7-3L-Nasdaq	221.47%	46.75%	-22.78%	9.7x
ST4-2L-Nasdaqx2	206.30%	44.44%	-37.18%	5.5x
ST6-3L-SP500	192.15%	42.21%	-15.75%	12.2x
ST5-2L-Volatility	192.04%	42.19%	-36.40%	5.3x
ST8-3L-Volatility	184.14%	40.92%	-14.88%	12.4x
ST3-2L-SP500x2	148.43%	34.84%	-18.86%	7.9x
ST2-2L-Nasdaq	87.24%	22.88%	-14.52%	6.0x
ST1-2L-SP500	65.30%	17.95%	-8.72%	7.5x
SPY (S&P 500)	23.40%	7.15%	-25.51%	0.9x

Max DD: Maximum Drawdowns, RoMaD: Return over Maximum Drawdowns
Since 01 Jan 2022. Cumulative return is compounded daily.

These tables are updated every single day after the market closes on Facebook https://www.facebook.com/risp500 and X https://x.com/Risp500 to provide **complete transparency and allow the public to follow our performance live**. Note that the returns in the table are expressed **in US dollars**!

You can also achieve these results!

My Motivation for Sharing SMIGRM and Publishing This Book

My career on Wall Street was a dream come true. Over 30 years of experience gave me a level of professional and personal fulfillment that few have had the opportunity to achieve. I worked at large institutions, international banks in São Paulo, Hong Kong, and New York, where I traded millions to hundreds of millions of dollars for clients or for the banks' own portfolios. I had the opportunity to experience the global financial market at its most intense, including during numerous financial crises and market crashes. Now, at my age, it is inevitable to reflect on what really matters in life. At a certain age, we begin to realize that we will not be here forever. For me personally, what gives meaning to life is the legacy we leave to others, the way we will be remembered.

The knowledge I have acquired during my journey will be of little use to me when my time here is up. Neither will money. However, if I can share this knowledge and benefit others, my experience will have been invaluable. That is why I decided to share the method, write this book, and mentor students.

Investing abroad, especially on Wall Street, has never been easier than it is today. Technology and globalization have opened doors for anyone with internet access to explore the world's largest financial market. But there is a huge difference between accessing the market and actually making money in it. And this is precisely where the danger lies. A real danger that many people ignore and end up getting hurt, turning dreams into nightmares.

A Minefield for Beginners

Wall Street is a minefield for the unprepared. I'm sorry to say it, but it's the plain truth. Dreams can easily turn into nightmares when you don't have the right knowledge or the right methods and tools. Investing without preparation can result in catastrophic losses due to factors such as:

Misreading the market: Understanding the nuances of a foreign market is much more complex than it seems.

Currency exchange losses: Unfavorable exchange rate fluctuations can occur at any time and erode your profits.

Market crashes: Without a robust strategy, it is easy to be caught off guard by a sudden drop, especially if you do not monitor your investments as often as necessary.

Inappropriate investment methods: Strategies, shortcuts, and "tricks" that worked in the market of your country that you are used to do not necessarily work in the American market.

These factors not only put your invested capital at risk, but can also destroy wealth and dreams built over a lifetime. **The market is unforgiving to those who make mistakes.**

The Greater Purpose

But it doesn't have to be that way. I deeply believe that **with the right knowledge, the right tools, and proper preparation, it is possible to avoid the mistakes** that so many make. And more than that: it is **possible to prosper, even in times of turmoil**. My goal with this book is to share what I have learned in over three decades of experience—mistakes and successes—and offer you a clear path, or at least a smoother and less thorny one, to success on Wall Street.

If I can help you avoid the pitfalls I faced myself, and put you on the path to building a more secure and prosperous financial future, I will feel that my life journey has had even greater meaning. After all, true success lies in empowering people to achieve their goals and exceed their expectations.

Ready to take the first steps on the journey? This book will be your guide with the potential to turning a great opportunity into an even greater reality than you had ever imagined.

My Own Journey – And Who is the Author

You may be wondering who I am, how I acquired so much knowledge in my career, and how we developed the RISP 500™ algorithm, the driving force behind the SMIGRM Method that has given so many of us, like Marcelo, such solid and surprising results. Recently, while speaking to an audience of professional investors in New York, I received praise for my ability to navigate turbulent markets, but I can assure you that it wasn't always like that. My journey was very difficult, extremely hard, and full of ups and downs, to say the least.

Modest Origins

I was born in Taiwan, and my family emigrated to Brazil when I was only 5 years old, in the 1970s. Like many other middle-class immigrant families, we faced difficulties, especially during the decades of hyperinflation. Younger readers have never experienced it, but to give them an idea of what it was like, in March 1990, inflation reached 3% per day. That's right: per day! In the 1990s, the annualized inflation rate reached an unbelievable 150,496%!

You may be wondering how people survived in such an extreme situation. The answer is that people adapt and find solutions. I remember my father sending me to the bank every day with a bag of cash from his sales for the day to invest in an "overnight" deposit (basically, a one-day deposit backed by government bonds that returned interest the next day——which covered losses due to inflation). My father had a small business (difficult to manage in such an environment!), and every day we had to rush to invest the money received from customers immediately in the overnight deposit, or it would lose 3% of its value the very next day.

That was one of my first lessons about money in life. Later, when I started my career in *trading rooms* at international banks, I learned a lot more, especially from the numerous financial crises I experienced firsthand, managing extreme risks in an emerging market (Brazil) during times of extremely high volatility.

Forged in Fire and Iron by the Financial Crises from 1990 to 2020

In about 30 years, facing the challenges of so many financial crises around the world, it is impossible not to learn something really relevant. For me, it all started with the Mexican currency crisis of 1994, just three years after I graduated from college (I obtained a bachelor degree in engineering). Although the crisis originated in Mexico, we felt the contagion effects directly in the Brazilian markets. I had just been hired as *a trainee* by Lloyds Bank in Brazil to start as a junior systems analyst to provide IT support to *traders*. It was my first contact with a trading floor. Amazed by what I saw, I knew immediately that this was where I wanted to be. I wanted to be a derivatives *trader* because I knew I was very *nerdy* and loved numbers and complicated formulas. The more complex, the better, because that's where my competition would be less, I thought. And in my mid 20s, I was hungry for the action!

To improve my chances, I started attending the same graduate program (IBMEC) where *traders* received training, to prove that I could be as good as them. I ended up with higher grades than even the senior *traders* at Lloyds! But without the right connections (which, unfortunately, counted for more than skills), Lloyds' treasurer refused to give me a fair chance as a *trader* on the trading desk, not even as a junior assistant. I heard the treasurer, head of the department, say "*you don't fit the profile*." In other words, he meant I didn't have "backing." But that's okay; I will take care of my own destiny. For example, even my humble origins did not prevent me from getting where I am today. Persistent, I looked for opportunities outside that bank and was hired by ABN Amro Bank as *a trader* for their trading desk. I started *trading* swaps, forward contracts, and options on interest rates and foreign exchange (BRL/USD trading). Over time, I realized that clients wanted protection against interest rates and exchange rates simultaneously in a single product, so I developed a new product for the bank, calling it "Bi-indexed." It was my first creation, as I have always believed that if something is needed and does not exist, create it. Over time, other products were also developed and launched on the market.

Then came 1997, and we were hit by the contagion of the Asian crisis. In 1998, we faced the consequences of the Russian debt and currency crisis. In 1999, Brazil itself was at the center of the turmoil. During those years of successive crises in emerging markets, I was already managing billions of dollars for my new employer, Citibank Brazil, as a risk manager.

Saving My Dreams Amid Chaos

On a personal level, I was planning to pursue an MBA at a top school in the United States, buying US dollars and saving to pay for two years of tuition and expenses. A massive devaluation of the Brazilian real could not have come at a worse time for me! It could have completely destroyed my savings efforts and canceled my educational plans. I acted quickly and decisively. I bought as many dollars as I could on the first day of the devaluation. The cashier said he had no more cash dollars, but he could sell me *traveler's checks*. I bought everything he had and the rest the next day. Not only did I save my MBA plans, but I also managed to successfully manage the bank's risk portfolios. The lessons here were: be hyper-vigilant and aware of risks, especially when you have a lot to lose; stay mentally focused to think clearly and act quickly and decisively, without hesitation. Critical decisions cannot wait and are made under uncertainty and without all the facts.

The following year, in 2000, I embarked on a two-year educational journey in the MBA program at the Wharton School, University of Pennsylvania, at the time considered the number one school in the world in finance (it still is today). The course was very expensive, but I was able to pay for it thanks to my agility and cool head when necessary in the eye of the hurricane of a financial crisis centered precisely in Brazil.

Lessons from Global Crashes and Crises

Later, as *a trader* and risk manager also in the US, I continued to be tested by successive global financial crises, in addition to emerging markets. The most notable include the bursting of the internet bubble in 2000-2001, the Great Financial Crisis of 2008-2010, *Volmageddon* in 2018, the Coronavirus Crash in 2020, and the *Everything* Bubble in 2022. With each crisis, I learned more and more because none of them were exactly the same, even though they shared many similarities. New questions also arose. I think this is a sign of progress.

Why am I highlighting my experience with financial crises? Because it is in difficult times that we build the most wisdom and character. People who have never experienced hyperinflation will find it difficult to imagine what it is like, because certain things that happen during this period would never occur in normal times. The same is true for every financial crisis and stock market crash. With social media, we see new "experts" in the market popping up every day on YouTube, claiming to be stock investment experts. But have any of them really been tested enough in difficult times? Do they have the proper educational credentials? What was their track record during times of difficulty? Some are not even old enough to have had experience on the real battlefield. Think about this before following the advice of anyone who pops up with a smooth talk. Remember, not every thing that sounds logical is true. And not every thing that sounds absurd is necessarily false.

Everyone is a genius in bull markets, and everyone has good stories to tell. But it is challenging and unusual times that reveal the true nature of how things work. For example, neuroscience researchers learn more about the brain by studying mental illness. In aviation, aircraft engineering and safety design improve every time there is an accident or air disaster after the NTSB investigates its causes. Similarly, we learn how things work in our daily lives when they break down, forcing us to figure out how to fix them so they work again. Peaks in learning tend to occur during challenging times. Anyone who has never experienced and survived stock market crashes should not claim to be a stock market expert because they are not. It's amazing, but we learn more about the inner workings of things not during normal times, but when they stop working.

A Vision Born from Successive Crises

You may be wondering how we came to develop this new SMIGRM Method solution and the RISP 500 algorithm that resulted in the performance presented above. In fact, it all started about 15 years ago! Until the Great Financial Crisis of 2008, few financial market professionals could claim to have predicted what was coming. The crash decimated markets, destroyed countless investment portfolios, devastated lives, and then a disturbing question arose: how did such a huge risk go unnoticed by so many experienced experts?

After all, looking back, it is clear that the 2008 crisis did not happen overnight. The descent from the top of the market took several months to reach rock bottom. So why did so many people still lose so much money in the crisis?

For those who work in wealth management, responsible for their clients' portfolios, the consequences were particularly disastrous. The main objective of any manager was to protect and grow their clients' wealth. But 2008 proved how vulnerable these portfolios were, even the most diversified and well-planned ones, in the face of systemic risk.

For me, this crisis marked a turning point. My mission became clear: to develop a reliable and proactive system capable of anticipating sharp market declines like this before the worst happens, even if it was just one day or even hours before. But that was easier said than done. Early attempts to develop an algorithm failed; the techniques and data available at the time were simply not sufficient to provide the necessary predictive power. However, the seed had been planted. It was only after nearly 10 years of obsessive testing, study, and model refinement that a framework we believed could transform wealth management by redefining how we understand and manage risk began to emerge.

My Journey to SMIGRM: Risk-Guided Tactical Investment Decisions

After the 2008 crisis, a small group of *traders* and quantitative experts, including myself, began to think and debate ways to prevent another financial disaster. At the time, I was *trading* interest rate derivatives for an international bank in New York while taking evening classes at the master's program in Mathematical Finance at New York University's Courant Institute in the evenings. With 15 years of experience in *trading* and risk management at the time, I devoured research papers, learned from market tacticians, and began developing models to detect small changes in data that could provide early warnings of market declines. Despite numerous attempts and collaborations with various colleagues, none of the models met the minimum acceptable standards for an effective early warning system, and our small informal testing lab was eventually shut down and the group disbanded.

However, I never gave up. Traditional tools I used, such as technical, fundamental, and macroeconomic analysis, which can work well in normal situations, often failed to provide useful answers during times of market turmoil—the very moments when reliable tools were most needed. This glaring gap fueled my determination to find a solution.

In fact, I am no stranger to financial crises. I grew up in Brazil during a period of hyperinflation that reached 3% per day, astronomical interest rates, and a currency that was constantly devaluing against the US dollar. Having experienced several crises firsthand while managing billion-dollar portfolios for my employers, I learned countless lessons (the hard way) and knew that much more robust *timing* and risk management tools were desperately needed.

After years of trial and error, progress came with new insights into VIX products, new ideas, and better data. I also learned from the work of extremely intelligent people in the field. Leveraging this knowledge, I built and refined new models that incorporated data from multiple markets and macroeconomic variables. Still, it took more than 10 years of trial and error to perfect several algorithms capable of delivering consistent and robust results in live trading.

Our efforts led to the development of SMIGRM, a customizable solution designed to help investors optimize the balance between return and risk. In other words, we want to maximize return while minimizing risk. **In finance, higher-return assets always equate to higher risks. So simply swapping one asset for another or combining different assets in a balanced portfolio—as is done in financial advisory and the fund management industry—cannot change this reality.** No matter how inventive they may be, the return on the resulting portfolio is always the weighted average of the returns on the component assets, and the risk of the portfolio is also an "average," but calculated in a way that considers the correlation between the assets. So, you might say, "Aha! Correlation." Yes, correlation (I mean low correlation and especially negative correlation with stocks) has always been the wild card of Modern Portfolio Theory.

Theoretically perfect, but in practice, there is a huge problem. You will never hear this from financial professionals, but the reality is that **almost all assets in the economy have a correlation that is not very low with stocks, and negative correlation with stocks rarely exists**. Worse still, **correlation is not constant**. Fixed-income securities such as bonds, which are traditionally paired with stocks, have correlations that vary over time. We will discuss this further ahead, but the best solution is not to rearrange assets in a portfolio like everyone does. Portfolios are built on the flawed correlation assumption that it's relatively constant or stable. But in reality, correlations converge to +1 when they are needed the most: right during market crashes. I realized this problem very early in my career. I knew I had to change the way we understood and made investments. In other words, **the solution was not in the pieces of the puzzle itself, but in how we handled the pieces**. This realization was the beginning of the SMIGRM Method, with an idea I called "**Context-Dependent Dynamic Asset Allocation**."

On January 3, 2022, we launched live trading of eight strategies using our best SMIGRM algorithm prototype, which produces the RISP 500—a risk indicator for the S&P 500—to prove its effectiveness to the public with maximum transparency. More than just a crash detector, our goal evolved to create a risk management solution and *timing* tool that investors could easily customize to achieve their goals according to their own risk tolerance. This innovation now serves as a powerful tool for preserving wealth and achieving returns superior to the S&P 500 index itself but most importantly: with less risk.

Your Success Will Depend on the Decisions You Make Now

You now know my background and how I have traveled my journey. When planning yours, you will have to make some important decisions that will determine the results you will achieve. I hope to offer you some ideas based on what I have learned over the years. So many mistakes and successes made us grow, and the best we can do is share the lessons with others so that their path can be less traumatic and smoother, enabling them to achieve success faster.

In this book, I will teach you the basics of finance in the United States so that you can have a broad and decent introduction to the largest financial market on the planet and the center of world capitalism. I will also comment on the most popular and widespread methods and ways of investing in stocks, adopted by both professional and amateur investors. However, I will also introduce the SMIGRM method, which I personally believe to be far superior, so that you have the opportunity to learn about it and compare it with other methods. SMIGRM is based on risk management, treating investment decisions from a unique, different, and innovative perspective. I am certainly not the only one to invest with this philosophy; there are others who have developed or follow methods similar to SMIGRM, based on the same principles. But I believe I may be the only one to organize the concepts into a theoretical formulation.

In your opinion, what do you consider to be the most important characteristics for an ideal investment method? If you could choose, would you choose a method based on which characteristics:

1. (A) Objective data **or** (B) Subjective opinions?

2. (A) Information from data measured in the present **or** (B) Future projections?

3. (A) Adjusting between risky and safe assets when the market changes (dynamic allocation) **or** (B) Maintaining risky and safe assets in a fixed proportion regardless of whether the market is up or down (fixed allocation)?

If you answered (A) for all of the above, SMIGRM is probably the best choice for you. But it is up to you to decide which method to adopt. Make your decision calmly and wisely, as it will determine your results, from failure to success. Keep in mind that there is no perfect method. All have pros and cons. All work well in many situations, but not in all. No one has a crystal ball. However, you can use more than one method at the same time! This way, you can build your own comparative experience. SMIGRM, for example, works very well in conjunction with most other methods.

The Limitations of Traditional Investment Methods

As professional *traders* with decades of experience at the world's largest banks, many of us have realized that existing and widely used methods, based on variations of fundamental and technical analysis, although they have evolved over the years, have not fundamentally changed the way investors make decisions. Both methods analyze the past and attempt to make inferences about the future.

Fundamental analysis, widely used for stock picking, examines companies' financial data and assesses their competitive strength in their respective markets and sectors. With this information, fundamental analysts generally perform a *valuation* of the company and its stock price. Based on various *assumptions*, they project price targets for the stocks over different time horizons and issue a recommendation (buy, sell, or hold).

Technical analysis, or chart analysis, used mainly for **market timing** purposes (seeking the best entry and exit points), is based on historical stock price behavior, pattern formations, and indicators derived from that behavior to predict its next major movement.

These tools have guided investors for generations, since the 18th century, with mixed results. Some people have built fortunes, while others have lost everything, and the rest have had mixed results. Like any tool, these methods have their pros and cons. Because they involve future predictions, such as stock price projections, fundamental analysis requires making many *assumptions* about the future, such as projections of sales, expenses, competitiveness, market trends, among other factors inside and outside companies, including macroeconomic factors such as inflation, interest rates, aggregate demand, etc. Technical analysis, on the other hand, is based more on observations and assumptions and has little proven scientific basis to support them. In addition, the conclusions of these analyses are highly dependent on the analyst. Two different people analyzing the same set of data and graphs can easily interpret them differently and reach completely different conclusions.

Questioning the Effectiveness of Traditional Tools

We began to wonder if we were really using the BEST tools available to navigate the markets. If we weren't, then it was necessary to develop new tools. We saw colleagues in the industry and investors facing these very common problems (and you will probably identify with some if you have experienced something similar yourself):

The stock market is more volatile and less predictable. It is increasingly more difficult to navigate markets or interpret the signals from the methods used. There are long-term structural changes gradually taking place and altering the post-war world order paradigm. Since 2018, US market volatility has increased considerably. Corrections and crashes are becoming more frequent, and for many of us, traditional tools are becoming increasingly inadequate to deal with the challenges of this new reality.

There is an excess of conflicting information, conflicting opinions, and unfounded analysis. We live in the age of social media and "gurus" who appear overnight. This has led to an overload of news and information, causing more confusion in the public's mind than ever before. There is also the government machine manufacturing narratives and often "cooking" economic data. Sometimes it is very difficult to distinguish facts from myths and untruths. And it is precisely in periods of uncertainty that more divergent and conflicting opinions (even from renowned experts) take center stage, creating enormous confusion among investors and leading them to make the wrong decisions.

Difficult decision-making moments are more frequent. With increased volatility, it has become even more complicated to identify the right time to enter or exit the market. Many investors end up feeling lost in these situations, but again, this is not their fault. The real issue is the lack of adequate tools to deal with these challenges.

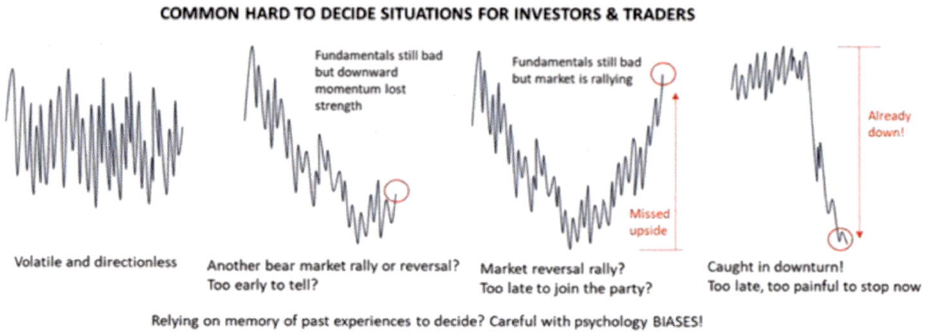

What if you are caught off guard by a sudden crash like the Coronavirus Crash in 2020?

Imagine being caught off guard by a sudden and unexpected market crash, such as the one caused by the Coronavirus in 2020. Initially, the outbreak was relatively contained at its epicenter, but it quickly turned into a global pandemic. By the time you finally realized the gravity of the situation, you had already accumulated significant losses in the stock market. What would you do at that moment? The price has already plummeted, and you are already at a loss. Would you buy more, taking advantage of the moment because "now it's cheap"? Or would you sell immediately, triggering a stop-loss, cutting your losses, and seeking refuge in safety?

All of these situations create confusion in investors' minds about how to react. It's no wonder that many investors and even professional portfolio managers don't like *trading*! Making decisions under so much uncertainty and pressure, requiring quick responses in difficult market situations, is not for everyone. We believe that no one should make hasty decisions under pressure, as this is how mistakes and misjudgments occur. What people really need is an objective and more appropriate tool, especially in ambiguous situations.

The Limitations of Traditional Risk Management Tools

Traditional risk management tools are limited to risk control and reduction, which are usually triggered when risks have already risen and significant losses have already occurred. They are not designed to anticipate and guide important decisions, nor to take the initiative to produce any advantage that improves returns. These tools exist to ensure that you do not lose too much (beyond the limits you have predefined), but not to help you profit by taking calculated risks. It is no coincidence that risk managers generally occupy support roles within banks and investment funds (in the *middle* and even *back-office* roles), rarely assuming leadership and strategy-setting positions in these institutions.

Common Sense and Shortcuts Can Be Dangerous

Common sense, popular beliefs, generic rules, "rules of thumb", or shortcuts can easily lead to underperformance or, in the worst-case scenario, financial disaster. Here are some examples:

"Buy the dips, sell the rips": this is the immediate impulse to buy whenever a stock price falls or sell when it rises, as if stock prices always needed to self-correct to a supposed "average" to which they were destined to return. Contrary to this popular belief, stock prices do not have a natural "mean reversion" characteristic. There is simply no mean to revert to. To prove this, just look at the S&P 500® chart over an extended period. Can you identify any mean to which it reverts to? In markets with a defined trend (consistent uptrend or downtrend), this practice can generate some profit, but as soon as the market regime changes and you are caught off guard, this strategy can backfire disastrously. The practice of buying every time the price falls is usually equivalent to "catching a falling knife" because you don't know if it has already hit rock bottom. This expression comes from "*buy the dip or catch a falling knife*." It is an extremely risky practice that I have seen fellow professional *traders* do at the banks where I worked, and I noticed that they lost most of the time and the losses were usually very large.

"Buy cheap (undervalued) stocks, sell expensive (overvalued) stocks": this idea seems obvious, but it is much easier said than done. This is because value assessment is highly subjective. What is undervalued to some may be overvalued to others — and that is exactly why a market exists! On its own, this principle is useless from a practical standpoint, but many people use it to make (or justify) investment decisions. Generally, there is a reason why asset prices fall, which does not mean that the asset has become cheaper. Furthermore, cheap and expensive are relative concepts. Instead of comparing with the “fair” price, people usually compare with the previous price. Instead of looking to the future, doing so is equivalent to focusing on the past, and can lead to misguided conclusions. Furthermore, what constitutes a “fair” price is also highly debatable. So, ultimately, the whole idea doesn’t really help investors.

"Stocks always go up in the long run": this is a very common myth. There is no concrete evidence to support this claim, but many people still believe it. The same myth is often applied to real estate prices, also without solid and irrefutable evidence. Take a look at the chart showing 150 years of historical data for the S&P 500® index, which represents the U.S. stock market. As you can see at , the U.S. stock market really took off after World War II. It is worth noting that this growth is even more impressive than the chart suggests, as it is on a logarithmic scale. What explains this impressive and explosive growth?

After World War II, the US became the largest hegemonic economic power on the planet. The US created the world's leading economic bodies, such as the World Bank, the IMF, etc., to serve its own interests. The dollar was established as the hegemonic currency, which all countries use for trade and as a store of value. Initially, the US convinced the world to adopt its currency because it was backed by gold and they had the largest reserves in the world. Then, President Nixon abandoned the gold standard. From then on, the currency could be printed without restriction, giving the US unique power on the planet. Imagine being able to pay for purchases of products or services without having to give anything in return (such as gold), simply by turning on the dollar printing machine. In this way, the US has always exported its inflation and crises to the rest of the world to foot the bill. When they need money, they raise interest rates and suck dollars out of developing countries, generating a cascade of financial crises in those countries (yes, the same crises I have experienced since the 1990s). That is the power of the US dollar. Later, the US further strengthened the power of the dollar with the famous "petrodollar," which was nothing more than a deal with oil producing countries in the middle east to only accept the dollar in oil sales that every country on the planet needs. But what does all this have to do with US stocks? Everything! Look at the S&P 500 chart over the last 80 years, which shows impressive growth. Despite frequent crashes, overall it has been a long *bull market* spanning multiple decades.

Because of this prolonged growth, most people alive today do not know what the market was like before World War II, when the hegemonic power on the planet was not the US, but the UK, and the most powerful currency was the pound sterling. So people today have the impression that, in general, the stock market always goes up. This is a mistaken impression, as there is no reason for the word "always." Let's look at the case of Japan, which, despite being an economic powerhouse, is nowhere near the hegemonic position of the US. See in the graph how the Japanese stock market lost its peak in the late 1980s with the end of the "Japanese Miracle" and how it took 40 years to recover to the same level as before. Imagine someone who was invested in the Japanese stock market at that time. What if they also believed in this myth and decided to wait for the stock market to recover? So, it is dangerous to believe in this myth.

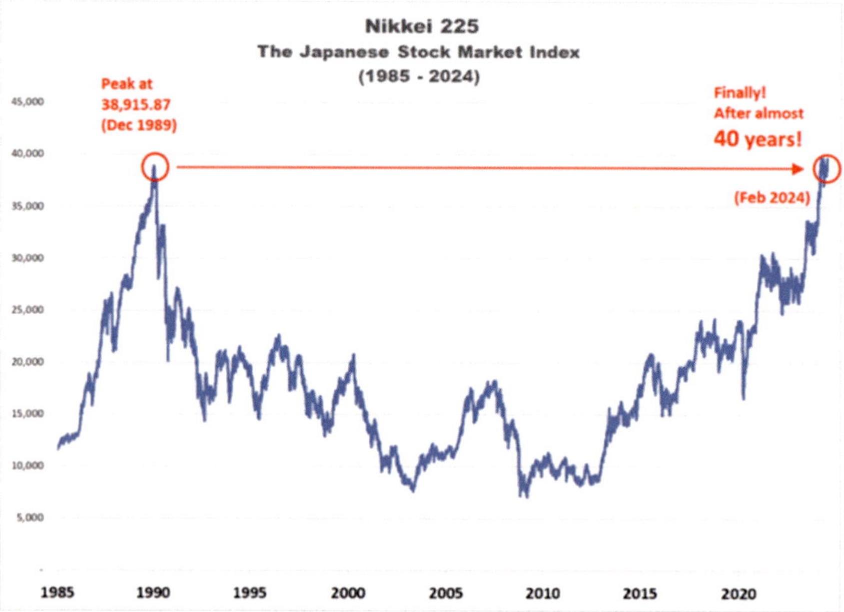

Dangers of Common Sense and Investor Mentality

"Double your bet if you're losing": Some investors take aggressive and irresponsible actions by doubling down on a losing position simply because they cannot tolerate losses (which is ironic and contradictory to the point of being bizarrely absurd). It is irrational to try to recover from a loss amid so much uncertainty. Based on what evidence and why would the market recover at exactly the moment of your choice? It's the same analogy as trying to catch a falling knife! In psychology, this behavior is known as **regret aversion bias**. Putting more money into an investment that is already at a loss in an attempt to reverse the situation can inevitably lead to financial ruin faster with twice the size of the loss.

"Guess, hope, and pray": This behavior is more common among retail investors, but it affects all of us because we are human. There is a high degree of subjectivity when investing in stocks, which opens up room for behavioral biases that easily result in poor outcomes. Neuroscience has already discovered how humans make purchasing decisions. According to research conducted by Harvard Business School professor emeritus **Gerald Zaltman**, 95% of our decisions are guided by subconscious mental processes. We like to believe that we make decisions based on reason and logic, but in reality, according to neuroscientists, our decisions are based on subconscious emotions and only later justified rationally. In other words, we find justifications for decisions we have already made emotionally, often without realizing it.

And that is where the danger lies. Many investors become so passionate about an idea or the name of a stock (or a famous brand) that they do everything they can to justify holding on to it, even when it is already generating losses. This is a problem common to all of us as human beings.

That is why we need objective tools to protect us from ourselves! We need a tool based on concrete data, free from bias or illusory thinking. The SMIGRM Method's RISP 500™ was created for this purpose. It is entirely based on hard data, which is collected, filtered, processed, and interpreted in a completely cold and objective manner. The resulting actions can be taken quickly, even automatically, based on data, not opinions subject to biases, prejudices, and psychological factors.

Chapter 2. Investor Mindset and Psychology

Data-Driven Decisions vs. Dangers of Investor Psychology

As we have already discussed, human psychology can cause serious problems for investors, resulting in below-potential performance in the long term. The human mind, as powerful as it is, has limitations when it comes to decision-making and is easily influenced by various behavioral biases. We have already talked about some of them, but one of the most common in the financial market is the **self-attribution bias**.

Self-attribution bias causes us to attribute the merits of a successful investment to ourselves, while blaming external factors or other people when an investment goes wrong. This behavior easily leads to **overconfidence** (unsupported by real evidence) and **excessive risk-taking**. Who has never heard someone bragging about having made a small fortune by investing in a particular stock, implicitly or explicitly attributing this success to their own abilities? Everyone seems to be a genius during bull markets. But wait until the market turns bearish or becomes volatile and confusing to see if these so-called geniuses continue to perform in the same way.

Another very common bias is the **negativity bias**. This behavior probably arose during human evolution as a survival mechanism to protect us from imminent dangers. This bias often causes us to attach more weight to negative experiences than to positive or neutral ones, affecting our judgment and behavior, such as risk-taking, for example.

Think about how you reacted during the **Coronavirus Crash in 2020**, which appeared almost out of nowhere, catching everyone off guard and lasting just over a month, from February 20 to April 7, 2020. What followed was an impressive recovery that continued for the rest of 2020 and throughout 2021. If you sold your shares during the crash, how long did it take you to return to the market? Incredibly, a large number of investors, including experienced professionals, were so frightened by what happened that they did not return to the market even months after the crash ended. This episode caused many to miss out on a great opportunity for gains. The mind attached so much weight to the negative side of the crash that investors missed the positive side of the recovery.

There are many psychological biases that affect the long-term performance of investors. Here is a list of the 10 most common psychological biases that affect rational judgment and important decision-making by investors:

Overconfidence Bias

Description: Overestimating one's own knowledge or ability to predict market movements.

Example: An investor believes they can consistently outperform the market based on their personal analysis, which leads them to trade excessively and potentially accumulate losses.

Confirmation Bias

Description: Seeking information that confirms pre-existing beliefs and ignoring data that contradicts them.

Example: Focusing only on positive news about a favorite stock and disregarding negative reports, resulting in a distorted view of the investment.

Loss Aversion Bias

Description: Feeling the impact of losses more intensely than the satisfaction of equivalent gains.

Example: Holding on to a falling stock to avoid realizing a loss, even when selling would be the more rational decision.

Herd Mentality Bias

Description: Following the decisions of the majority or other people, or internet gurus, without your own analysis, which can lead to irrational decisions.

Example: Investing in a stock that is on the rise just because many people are buying it, without conducting a detailed analysis to understand the reason for that movement. One example was the rise and crash of the now-defunct Gamestop stock, led by posts on a forum or social media.

Anchoring bias

Description: Giving excessive weight to the first piece of information received (the "anchor") when making decisions.

Example: Basing the value of a stock on the initial purchase price, influencing buying or selling decisions, even if market conditions have changed. Instead of looking to the future, the person remains anchored to the purchase price because they refuse to accept that they made a mistake in choosing the stock or the timing of the purchase.

Recency Bias

Description: Giving more importance to recent events and ignoring historical data.

Example: Assuming that a stock will continue to rise because it has performed well in recent months, ignoring long-term indicators.

Familiarity Bias

Description: Preferring investments in familiar or well-known assets, which can result in poor diversification.

Example: Investing mainly in companies in your country or shares in the company where you work, neglecting international opportunities.

Status Quo Bias

Description: Preferring to keep everything as it is and resisting change.

Example: Maintaining an outdated portfolio allocation, even after changes in financial goals or market conditions.

Regret Aversion Bias

Description: Avoiding decisions that may cause regret, often leading to inaction.

Example: Not investing in higher-risk assets for fear of potential losses, even when these investments are compatible with long-term goals.

Disposition Effect

Description: The tendency to sell assets that have appreciated and hold on to those that have depreciated.

Example: Selling a stock shortly after a small rise to "lock in profits," but holding on to a falling stock in hopes of a recovery. In other words, getting rid of your "winners" and holding on to your "losers." Think about it: is this rational?

One word about the Disposition Effect Bias above: it's incredible but a very common advice, which even became a method, called **Stock Portfolio Rebalancing** - involves "*selling high-performing assets and buying underperforming ones*". If you are constantly getting rid of your winners to load up with losers, where do you think you will arrive at?

Best Practices for Maintaining a Winning Mindset

To nullify or mitigate the harmful effects of psychological biases, there are some best practice tips you can adopt. See the list below. Pay particular attention to the last one, as it can completely nullify biases.

- **Set Clear Financial Goals**

Set specific goals to guide your investment decisions, such as retirement, buying a home, or your children's education. Constantly refreshing your memory of your long-term goals helps you focus on what is most important instead of getting distracted by details whose effects will be diluted in the long run, such as small short-term losses.

- **When in Doubt, Diversify Your Portfolio**

Whenever you are not entirely confident about an investment decision, don't put all your eggs in one basket. Spread your investments across different asset classes and sectors to minimize risk.

The same applies with your methods. Diversify your methods too. Try and experiement new methods and new ideas. Don't be so hung up on old ideas and rigid beliefs.

- **Stay Patient and Disciplined**

Avoid impulsive reactions by focusing on long-term goals. Remember that you don't have to win every time the market moves. If you missed a high, don't worry, as there will always be new opportunities to profit. You will often find that the market is not doing what you thought it would and is causing you losses. There is no problem in admitting your mistake and cutting your losses. Don't be stuck in a losing position. Remember: a great warrior can always withdraw from the wrong battles and preserve himself to fight again the next day.

- **Continuously Educate Yourself**

Seek knowledge about finance and investing to make informed decisions and adapt to market changes. Investing is an activity that demands a lot from your brain. The more prepared you are with the right information and experience to face both highs and lows, and stay mentally strong, the greater your chances of success. Read books by authors who have had real-world experience to share their acquired wisdom. Take courses from qualified people who have been through these experiences. Nothing against young instructors, but if they have never experienced a real crisis in their time in the market, how can they pass on that expertise to you? Some people love to play tennis with those who play less than them because they win every match. But that doesn't help them evolve or improve their own game. If you are going to take a course or seek mentoring, make sure it is with someone who has really been through the test of fire!

- **Periodically Reassess Your Portfolio**

Regularly review your investments to ensure they are aligned with your goals and make adjustments as necessary. Incredibly, many experts recommend that investors not check the status of their investments or the market too often. The reason, according to them, is to prevent investors' emotions from causing them to make rash decisions at the wrong time when checking the market and its results. In my opinion, this recommendation is another serious mistake the industry makes. First, because it disregards the investor's intelligence. Second, because it aims to keep the investor in the dark so that they will never learn to make decisions. And third, because it is the **ostrich syndrome**: just because you are not looking does not mean that the problems, dangers, risks, and accumulated losses will cease to exist.

- **Control Your Emotions**

Recognize and manage emotional biases that can negatively influence your investment decisions. This recommendation is easier said than done. It is extremely difficult to separate the emotions and biases that we all carry with us. It is what makes us human. The best way to prevent emotions and psychological biases from affecting our investment decisions is the next recommendation below.

- **Use an Objective Data-Based Tool**

A tool that is 100% data-driven would guide investors objectively, eliminating room for subjectivity, opinions, and psychological biases. Imagine you are flying a plane. The instruments will give you clarity and information such as speed, altitude, pressure, air temperature, distances, weather conditions, etc., so you can control the aircraft by making good decisions based on this data. Imagine that you lose one of these instruments, such as speed, for example. You would then have to guess the speed visually, which is highly inaccurate and dangerous. Your co-pilot could easily disagree with you, as both of you would be giving your opinions on the speed of the aircraft, making it difficult to make decisions. In investing, it's the same thing. The best way to avoid subjectivity and opinions, which can be biased, debatable, or simply wrong, is to use objective, data-driven tools such as SMIGRM.

Investor Personality and Impact on Results

Another important factor that has been studied in investor psychology is the personality resulting from your psychological profile as an investor. Sam Phoem, author of the book *"Personality Driven Portfolio,"* identified four major groups and assigned an animal to each personality type. We all fit into one of these groups. To find out which group you belong to, just answer two very simple questions:

1. Imagine you have a stock that is generating a good profit. What would you probably do?

(A) I would continue to hold the stock and let the profits accumulate for as long as possible.

(B) I would sell the stock, pocket the profit, and then evaluate my next move.

2. Imagine that your investment is generating a loss. What would you probably do?

(A) Continue to hold the stock until the price returns to its original purchase price, or wait until it at least generates a profit before selling.

(B) I would sell the stock, take the loss, and then evaluate my next move.

If you answered:

1A and 2A → Egoistic Elephant
1A and 2B → Diligent Deer
1B and 2A → Cagey Crab
1B and 2B → Busy Bee

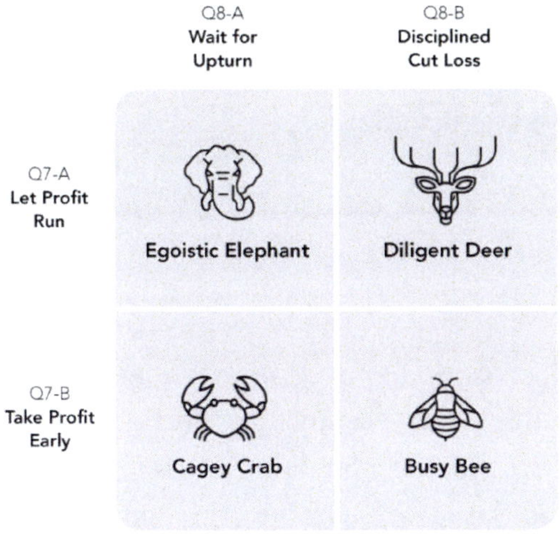

Now let's take a look at the main characteristics of each investor profile.

The Egoistic Elephant (1A and 2A)

You are probably an investor with strong convictions and are willing to weather major market fluctuations while waiting for your expectations to materialize. Alternatively, you may also be a long-term investor who does not closely monitor your investments and tends to invest with a very long-term perspective. Either way, you believe that your opinions and projections will prevail and would be unlikely to accept cutting losses if the market moves in the opposite direction, unless you are forced to do so. Your unwavering confidence and ego come from past successes in which you made large profits. However, you need to understand that no one is right 100% of the time, and your eventual mistakes could result in losses as large as, or even greater than, your successes. As such, you will likely be subject to large fluctuations in results, with large gains and large losses over time, since you do not usually limit or cut losses or gains, firmly focused on the scenario you envision and firmly believe will occur.

Investments best suited to this personality profile: Stocks that pay dividends or are more focused on income.

The Diligent Deer (1A and 2B)

You are a disciplined investor focused on risk management and closely monitor your investments to ensure they do not cause major problems. Any investment that exceeds a predefined loss level (*stop loss*) will be sold immediately without mercy. On the other hand, when your investments are doing well, you let the profits accumulate, unless there is a significant change in the reasons for holding the asset. Your diligent nature ensures that no wrong decisions compromise your portfolio, while your patience with good investments allows for significant gains from time to time. This is a highly desirable style, as it tends to generate small losses (limited on purpose) and large gains (unlimited on purpose) over time.

Most suitable investments: Stocks with high long-term appreciation potential.

The Cagey Crab (1B and 2A)

You are similar to many non-professional investors: you don't like to accept losses when an investment goes wrong, preferring to wait for the price to recover to at least your purchase price. But when an investment starts to turn a profit, you tend to take the profit quickly. This behavior usually results in small gains (when you're right) but large losses (when you're wrong) — and you're reluctant to acknowledge this, holding on to falling stocks until you have no choice but to sell. This strategy is not sustainable in the long run, as losses on just a few bad investments can easily wipe out gains made on good investments. Unlike the Diligent

Deer, who limits losses and does not limit gains, the Cagey Crab limits gains and does not limit losses. In the long run, this behavior is not sustainable.

If you have this personality, this is probably why you often feel frustrated with your investments. But don't worry. There's no reason to despair because change is possible. Adopting an objective, data-driven tool is one of the best solutions. Recognizing problems is the first step toward solving them.

More suitable investments: Fixed income, avoid investing in stocks. (See our final comments below.)

The Busy Bee (1B and 2B)

You tend to take profits when investments are doing well and also cut your losses when something goes wrong. You are an active investor who closely follows the market, managing and trading your positions or constantly rotating your portfolio, almost like a *day trader*. Because you are always attentive to the market, you will likely make many trades and do so frequently, accumulating small gains and small losses because you limit both sides, not allowing them to grow over time.

Most suitable investments: Stocks with good prospects for short-term gains.

Knowing Your Investor Personality is the First Step to Long-Term Success

Each person is born with a different personality, and this should be respected. There is nothing wrong with that. However, some profiles are more suited to long-term investment success than others, and it is important to be aware of this. The **Diligent Deer** is the most recommended profile for long-term success in the stock market.

On the other hand, the **Cagey Crab** is the profile least likely to achieve sustainable success in risky investments, such as the stock market.

The SMIGRM Method, being based on risk management through the RISP 500 risk indicator, signals to the investor when to limit losses when the risk rises above an acceptable threshold level defined by the investor himself. **By using the SMIGRM Method, investors naturally adopt the personality of the Diligent Deer, as it allows them to always cut losses in a disciplined manner, not letting them grow and accumulate in any way. On the other hand, SMIGRM never limits investors when the market is moving in their favor, allowing profits to accumulate over time.** After all, isn't that what we all want?

Why Data-Driven Decisions Are So Imperative

The point I want to make is that if we rely solely on our own judgment as investors, we can easily become **overconfident** or **overly suspicious**, and at precisely the wrong moments. Concrete, cold, and objective data extracted from the market itself reveals the truth about the real risks of the market, guiding us to make rational and informed decisions.

These and other psychological bias issues have hurt investors and the financial industry for years. The result is consistently underperforming investors and investment managers, who could potentially have earned much better returns if they had more appropriate tools for making important decisions.

As you can see, this really shouldn't be the case. Something is clearly wrong. Many other *traders* and I were also dissatisfied with traditional tools and methods, so we decided to look for solutions. We tested many models with great dedication, but we didn't make any significant progress in this search for years... until the **Great Financial Crisis of 2008** opened Pandora's box for us! The initial seed that would result in the SMIGRM (*Stock Market Investing Guided by Risk Management*) philosophy over the course of 10 years was planted due to this crisis, when we finally said enough was enough.

Chapter 3. The U.S. Stock Market

The U.S. stock market is a pillar of the global financial system, providing a platform for capital formation, investment opportunities, and economic growth. On July 1, 2024, the total market capitalization of U.S. public companies was approximately $55.2 trillion, representing a significant portion of the global stock market. It is simply the largest stock market on the planet. Here is the list of the top 10 largest in terms of market capitalization:

1. **New York Stock Exchange (NYSE)** - US, $25.5 trillion
2. **Nasdaq** - US, $23.4 trillion
3. Shanghai Stock Exchange (SSE) - China, $7 trillion
4. Euronext - Europe, $6.9 trillion
5. Japan Exchange Group (JPX) - Japan, US$ 6 trillion
6. Shenzhen Stock Exchange (SZSE) - China, US$ 4.8 trillion
7. Hong Kong Exchanges (HKEX) - China, US$ 4.6 trillion
8. National Stock Exchange of India (NSE) - India, US$ 3.7 trillion
9. London Stock Exchange (LSE) - England, US$ 3.3 trillion
10. Toronto Stock Exchange (TSX) - Canada, US$ 3 trillion

Major Stock Exchanges in the US

The US is home to several prominent stock exchanges, with the New York Stock Exchange (NYSE) and Nasdaq being the most notable:

New York Stock Exchange (NYSE): Established in 1792, the NYSE is the world's largest stock exchange in terms of market capitalization, with over 2,400 listed companies and a combined market capitalization of over $25.5 trillion.

Nasdaq: Known for its high concentration of technology companies, Nasdaq has a market capitalization of approximately $23.4 trillion.

Liquidity and Key Participants

The U.S. stock market is known for its high **liquidity**, allowing investors to buy and sell securities with ease. This liquidity is supported by a diverse group of participants, including institutional investors (such as mutual funds, pension funds, and insurance companies), individual retail investors, and foreign investors. Foreign participation is significant, with international investors attracted by the depth of the market, transparency, and the robust U.S. economy.

Evolution of Stock Prices since the 1900s

Since the early 20th century, U.S. stock prices have experienced substantial growth, punctuated by periods of volatility. The Dow Jones Industrial Average (DJIA), a key indicator of market performance, rose from approximately 68 points in 1900 to over 42,000 points in December 2024, reflecting the market's long-term upward trajectory.

The S&P 500 index was launched in 1957, but its historical data series begins in 1927. In December 1927, the value of the S&P 500 index was approximately 17.66 points. On February 22, 2025, it closed at 6,013.13 points.

This growth was driven by factors such as industrialization, technological innovation, and economic expansion. However, the market also faced challenges, including the Great Depression, the dot-com bubble of 2000, and the financial crisis of 2008, each contributing to periods of decline and recovery.

Major Stock Market Indices and Corresponding ETFs

S&P 500 Index: Comprises 500 of the largest U.S. companies, representing approximately 80% of the market capitalization of U.S. stocks.

- **ETF**: SPDR S&P 500 ETF Trust (Ticker: SPY)

Dow Jones Industrial Average (DJIA): Includes 30 large publicly traded companies from various sectors.

- **ETF**: SPDR Dow Jones Industrial Average ETF (Ticker: DIA)

Nasdaq Composite Index: Covers more than 3,000 stocks listed on the Nasdaq, with a significant emphasis on technology companies.

- **ETF**: Invesco QQQ Trust (Ticker: QQQ)

Russell 2000 Index: Measures the performance of approximately 2,000 small-cap companies, providing insights into the small-cap segment of the market.

- **ETF**: iShares Russell 2000 ETF (Ticker: IWM)

MSCI EAFE Index: Tracks the performance of large- and mid-cap stocks in developed markets outside the US and Canada.

- **ETF**: iShares MSCI EAFE ETF (Ticker: EFA)

The US stock market's long history, substantial market capitalization, and diverse participant base underscore its fundamental role in the global economy. Its evolution over the past century reflects broader economic trends and technological advances, offering investors a dynamic environment for capital growth and investment opportunities.

Growth Stocks, *Value Stocks*, Blue Chips

Growth investing and *value investing* are two distinct stock investment strategies, each catering to different investor preferences and market conditions.

Growth Investing

Growth investing focuses on companies that are expected to increase their revenues, profits, or market share at above-average rates. These companies generally reinvest profits to fuel expansion rather than pay dividends. Growth stocks, which are generally "young," are often found in dynamic sectors such as technology or biotechnology.

Characteristics of Growth Stocks

- High price-to-earnings (P/E) and price-to-book (P/B) ratios.
- Low or no dividend payments.
- Potential for significant capital appreciation.

Examples:

- **Amazon.com (AMZN)**: Known for its rapid growth in e-commerce and cloud computing.
- **Tesla (TSLA)**: Leader in electric vehicles and clean energy innovation.

Performance:

Growth stocks typically benefit from periods of economic expansion and low interest rates. For example, during the 2010s, the technology-heavy Nasdaq significantly outperformed other indices, driven by growth stocks.

Value Investing

Value investing focuses on companies considered undervalued relative to their fundamentals, such as earnings, dividends, or book value. Value stocks often belong to traditional, mature industries with stable cash flows and are attractive during market downturns for their perceived safety.

Characteristics of Value Stocks:

- Low P/E and P/B ratios.
- They often pay dividends.
- Stable and mature businesses.

Examples:

- **Berkshire Hathaway (BRK.A)**: Focused on acquiring undervalued companies.
- **Johnson & Johnson (JNJ)**: Leader in healthcare and pharmaceuticals.

Performance:

Value stocks tend to benefit from economic recoveries and periods of high interest rates. For example, in the early 2000s, value stocks led the market recovery after the dot-com bubble burst.

Investing in Blue-Chip Stocks

Blue-chip stocks represent large, well-established, and financially stable companies with a history of strong performance and reliability.

These companies often dominate their industries, providing consistent returns and dividends.

Examples:

- **Apple (AAPL)**: Global leader in consumer electronics.
- **Coca-Cola (KO)**: Dominant in the beverage industry.
- **Procter & Gamble (PG)**: Known for its wide range of consumer goods.

Contribution to the U.S. Market

Blue-chip stocks have been instrumental in the growth of the US stock market and economy since the 1930s. They have provided stability during turbulent times, including the Great Depression and several recessions, while driving innovation and economic expansion. Their consistent dividends and robust business models make them popular with conservative investors.

US Market Performance Since the 1930s

Since the 1930s, the U.S. stock market has experienced remarkable growth, driven by industrialization, technological advances, and globalization. Blue-chip companies have played a key role in this trajectory:

- **Post-Depression Recovery**: During the 1930s and 1940s, blue-chip companies helped restore investor confidence with steady returns and dividends.
- **Technological Boom**: In the 1980s and 1990s, companies such as IBM and Microsoft led the US market into a new era of technological innovation.
- **Resilience in Crises**: During the 2008 financial crisis and the COVID-19 pandemic, blue-chip stocks such as Johnson &

Johnson and Procter & Gamble offered investors greater relative stability.

Conclusion

Growth and value investments serve different objectives: growth for capital appreciation and value for stability and income. Blue-chip stocks exemplify reliability and innovation, contributing significantly to the evolution of the US stock market. Together, these investment strategies and assets highlight the diversity and resilience of the American financial system.

Economic Cycles and Their Effects on the U.S. Stock Market

Economic cycles, comprising periods of expansion and contraction, significantly influence the U.S. stock market. Understanding these cycles is crucial for investors seeking to navigate market volatility and take advantage of investment opportunities.

Phases of Economic Cycles

- **Expansion**: Characterized by increased economic activity, GDP growth, rising employment, and consumer confidence. During this phase, businesses invest and consumption accelerates.
- **Peak**: The height of economic activity where growth rates stabilize. Indicators such as inflation may rise, signaling possible overheating.
- **Contraction (Recession)**: Marked by a decline in economic activity, reduced consumption, increased unemployment, and decreased industrial production.
- **Bottom**: The lowest point of economic activity, setting the stage for recovery and the next phase of expansion.

Impact on the U.S. Stock Market - The stock market often reflects these economic phases, with investor sentiment and corporate earnings driving market performance.

Expansion: During economic booms, corporate profits generally increase, leading to higher dividends and stock appreciation. Investor optimism prevails, often resulting in bull markets. For example, the expansion of the 1990s, driven by technological advances and a robust economy, led to a prolonged bull market, with the S&P 500 advancing 582.1% in approximately 12 years.

Contraction: Recessions typically lead to a decline in corporate profits, reduced consumption, and increased investor anxiety, culminating in bear markets. The global financial crisis of 2008 exemplifies this, where the S&P 500 experienced a significant decline, losing approximately 57% from its peak, reflecting the severe economic contraction.

Historical Examples

- **Great Depression (1929-1939)**: The stock market crash of 1929 preceded a severe economic recession. The Dow Jones Industrial Average (DJIA) plummeted nearly 90% from its peak, taking more than two decades to fully recover.
- **Internet Bubble (Late 1990s - Early 2000s)**: An era of excessive speculation in internet companies led to inflated stock prices. The subsequent market correction resulted in significant losses, with the Nasdaq Composite Index losing approximately 78% of its peak.
- **COVID-19 Pandemic (2020)**: The rapid economic shutdown caused by the pandemic led to a sharp market decline. However, unprecedented fiscal and monetary interventions facilitated a rapid recovery, with major indices reaching new highs within a few months.

Sector Performance Across Cycles - Different sectors exhibit varying performance across economic cycles:

- **Early Expansion**: Cyclical sectors such as consumer discretionary and industrials often excel due to increased consumption and industrial activity.
- **Late Expansion**: Energy and materials sectors can benefit from rising commodity prices.
- **Recession**: Defensive sectors such as utilities (electricity, water, gas, internet, etc.), healthcare, and essential consumer goods tend to be more resilient, as demand for essential services remains stable even during recessions.

Understanding these patterns can help investors with sector rotation strategies, aligning portfolios with prevailing economic conditions.

The **interaction between economic cycles and the stock market** highlights the importance of macroeconomic awareness in investment decision-making. Recognizing the phases of economic cycles and their impact on various market sectors allows investors to make informed choices, potentially increasing returns and mitigating risks.

Long-Term Investing vs. Short-Term Investing

1. Long-Term Investing Long-term investing involves holding investments for years or even decades, often focusing on fundamental analysis and growth potential over time.

Common Methods:

- **Buy & Hold**: Investors purchase stocks or assets and hold them regardless of market fluctuations.
- **Dollar-Cost Averaging (DCA)**: Investors regularly invest a fixed amount, buying more shares when prices are low and fewer when prices are high.

Pros:

- Less time-intensive, more suitable for passive investors.
- Beneficial tax treatment due to long-term capital gains rates.
- Compound growth over time reduces the need to time the market.
- Easy to execute.

Cons:

- Requires patience and tolerance for short-term volatility.
- May miss opportunities to capitalize on market swings.
- Psychological difficulty in maintaining during downturns.
- Declines can be significant (crashes have become more common and the market more volatile since 2018), which means it takes even longer to achieve the desired profits, which is not good for those who want to accelerate their wealth growth.

2. Short-Term Investment - Short-term investment focuses on capitalizing on price fluctuations over days or weeks.

Common Methods:

- **Day Trading**: Involves buying and selling securities on the same day to profit from intraday price movements.
- **Swing Trading**: Targets price movements over several days or weeks, typically based on technical analysis.

Pros:

- Potential for quick profits.
- Allows for frequent reallocation of capital.
- Profits in both rising and falling market trends.

Cons:

- High transaction costs due to frequent trading.

- Taxes on short-term capital gains are higher.
- Requires significant time, skill, and emotional discipline.
- More difficult to execute.

Short Selling and Leveraged Investments in the US Stock Market

Short Selling

Concept: Short selling involves borrowing someone else's shares and selling them on the market with the expectation that their price will fall. The investor aims to repurchase the shares at a lower price, return them to the lender, and pocket the difference as profit.

When it is used:

- **Bearish Market Conditions**: Short selling is employed when investors anticipate a decline in stock prices or market indices.
- **Hedge**: It is also used to offset potential losses in other long positions during downturns.
- **Speculation**: Traders with strong convictions about a company's overvaluation or adverse developments may sell its shares short.

Risks: Short selling is inherently riskier than normal stock trading because:

Unlimited Loss Potential: The maximum loss is theoretically infinite, as stock prices can rise indefinitely.

Margin Calls: Short selling requires a margin account, and rising stock prices can lead to margin calls, forcing investors to cover their positions at a loss.

Short Squeezes: A rapid increase in a stock's price, often driven by high demand, can force short sellers to exit their positions, exacerbating losses.

Leveraged Investments

Concept: Leveraged investments involve the use of borrowed capital or financial derivatives to amplify potential returns. Common forms include margin trading (borrowing money to buy more shares) and leveraged ETFs (exchange-traded funds that use derivatives to amplify daily market movements, such as 2x or 3x the returns of an index).

When It Is Used:

- **Bullish Market Conditions**: Leveraged investments are typically used when investors expect a significant upward momentum and want to maximize returns.
- **Short-Term Speculation**: Traders use leverage for short-term opportunities, as leverage compounds both gains and losses.

Risks: Leveraged investments carry high risks due to their amplified exposure:

Magnified Losses: While leverage increases potential gains, it also exacerbates losses. A 10% loss on a 2x leveraged position equates to a real loss of 20%.

Margin Risk: Using borrowed funds means that investors may face margin calls if the value of the asset falls, potentially leading to forced liquidation of positions.

Why These Activities Are Riskier Than Normal Stock Trading

- **High Sensitivity to Volatility**: Both short selling and leverage increase exposure to price fluctuations, increasing risk.
- **Potential for Rapid Losses**: Unlike traditional stock investments, where losses are limited to the amount invested, short selling and leverage can result in losses that exceed the initial investment.
- **Dependence on Market Timing**: Success in short selling and leverage requires precise market *timing*, which is notoriously

difficult even for experienced traders. Our RISP 500 risk indicator based on the SMIGRM Method masters *timing*.

- **Psychological Pressure**: The potential for rapid and significant losses creates immense stress, often leading to poor decisions under pressure.

Short selling and leveraged investments offer tools to capitalize on specific market conditions or expectations, but their high risks make them suitable only for sophisticated investors. Proper risk management, a clear understanding of strategies, and careful market analysis are essential to mitigate the substantial disadvantages inherent in these approaches. Our RISP 500 risk indicator based on the SMIGRM Method solves this problem.

Chapter 4. Federal Reserve (Fed), Economic Cycles, and Indicators

The U.S. federal government employs a combination of economic and fiscal policies to steer the nation's economy toward a path of sustainable growth, price stability, and full employment. These policies encompass government spending, taxation, and borrowing strategies designed to influence economic activity.

Implementation of Fiscal Policy

Fiscal policy involves adjustments in government spending and taxation to influence the economy. During economic downturns, the government may implement expansionary fiscal policies, such as increasing public spending or reducing taxes, to stimulate demand and job creation. On the other hand, in periods of rapid economic growth, contractionary policies—cutting spending or raising taxes—and raising interest rates can be used to curb inflation.

The implementation of fiscal policy follows a structured process:

- **Policy Formulation**: Economic advisors and policymakers assess current economic conditions to recommend appropriate fiscal measures.
- **Legislative Process**: Proposed fiscal measures are debated and must be approved by Congress, which can be time-consuming and subject to political negotiations.
- **Execution**: Once enacted, government agencies execute the policies, adjusting spending and taxation as legislated.

The effectiveness of fiscal policy is influenced by *timing*, magnitude, and the specific economic context. Delays in legislative approval and implementation can reduce the impact of the policy, especially if economic conditions change during the process. In addition, the fiscal health of the government, including debt levels and budget deficits, can constrain policy options.

For example, during the COVID-19 pandemic, the federal government enacted substantial fiscal stimulus packages to mitigate economic contraction. These measures included direct payments to individuals, expanded unemployment benefits, and support for businesses. While these actions provided immediate economic relief, they also significantly increased the federal debt, raising concerns about the long-term fiscal sustainability of the US.

The Federal Reserve's Dual Mandate

The Federal Reserve (the Fed), as the central bank of the United States, has a dual mandate: to promote maximum employment and ensure price stability. To achieve these goals, which are often antagonistic, the Fed uses various monetary policy tools to influence financial conditions in an effort to find a healthy balance between the two objectives of its mandate.

- **Price Stability**: The Fed aims to maintain a low and stable inflation rate, with a long-term goal of 2%. Stable prices facilitate economic planning and preserve the purchasing power of money.
- **Maximum Employment**: The goal is to achieve the highest level of employment without triggering inflation. Although the Fed cannot directly control employment levels, it influences the economic conditions that affect job growth.

Monetary Policy Tools and Implementation

To fulfill its dual mandate, the Fed employs several instruments:

- **Open Market Operations (OMOs)**: Buying and selling government securities to regulate the money supply and influence short-term interest rates.
- **Federal Funds Rate**: Setting the target for the interest rate at which banks lend to each other *overnight*, which serves as a benchmark for other interest rates in the economy. It functions as an "American Selic."
- **Reserve Requirements**: Determining the minimum reserves that each bank must maintain, influencing banks' ability to create loans.
- **Discount Rate**: The interest rate charged to commercial banks for short-term loans directly from the Fed.

The Federal Open Market Committee (FOMC) meets regularly to assess economic conditions and set monetary policy. Decisions are based on various economic indicators, including GDP growth, unemployment rates, and inflation metrics.

For example, if inflation exceeds the 2% target, the Fed may implement a contractionary monetary policy by raising the federal funds rate, making borrowing more expensive, reducing spending and investment, and thus easing inflationary pressures. On the other hand, to combat high unemployment, the Fed may lower interest rates through the Fed Funds to stimulate economic activity.

The Fed's monetary policy decisions are communicated through statements and press conferences, providing transparency and guiding market expectations. However, the effectiveness of monetary policy can be influenced by factors such as global economic conditions, fiscal policy actions, and financial market responses.

In summary, the federal government and the Federal Reserve play key roles in managing the U.S. economy through fiscal and monetary policies. While the government adjusts spending and taxation to influence economic activity, the Fed uses monetary tools to promote price stability and maximum employment, striving to create a balanced and sustainable economic environment.

FOMC Meetings and Communication of Fed Decisions

The Federal Open Market Committee (FOMC) is a key decision-making body within the Federal Reserve System, responsible for setting monetary policy. The committee is composed of 12 members: the seven members of the Federal Reserve Board of Governors and five regional presidents of the Federal Reserve Banks, with the president of the New York Fed serving as a permanent voting member. The remaining four voting positions rotate annually among the other regional bank presidents.

FOMC meetings are held eight times a year, approximately every six weeks. Special meetings may be called during periods of economic uncertainty or crisis. Meetings typically last two days and follow a structured format:

- **Economic Assessment**: Federal Reserve economists present detailed reports on domestic and global economic conditions, including data on inflation, employment, GDP growth, and financial markets.

- **Discussion**: Committee members discuss economic forecasts and assess potential risks to achieving the Fed's dual mandate of price stability and maximum employment.

- **Policy Decisions**: Members debate and vote on monetary policy actions, such as adjustments to the federal funds rate, asset purchases, or forward guidance.

- **Communications Planning**: The committee prepares public statements to announce decisions and justify the rationale behind them.

Communication of FOMC Decisions - After each meeting, the FOMC releases a statement summarizing its decisions, usually at 2:00 p.m. on the last day of the meeting. Key elements of the statement include:

- The target range for the federal funds rate.
- The committee's assessment of current economic conditions.
- Guidance on the future direction of monetary policy.

In addition to the statement, the Fed chair holds a press conference to detail the decisions and answer questions from the media. The FOMC also publishes the minutes of the meetings three weeks later, providing a detailed account of the discussions and the range of opinions among members.

Market Reaction to FOMC Decisions

Financial markets closely monitor FOMC meetings and decisions, as they directly influence borrowing costs, investment strategies, and economic activity. Fed decisions on interest rates, quantitative easing, quantitative tightening, or forward guidance can trigger immediate and significant market reactions:

- **Interest Rate Adjustments**: An increase in rates generally leads to higher borrowing costs, causing stock markets to fall and bond yields to rise. Conversely, rate cuts tend to boost stock markets and reduce bond yields.
- **Future Guidance**: Markets also react to subtle changes in language or tone, as investors analyze the statement and press conference for clues about the future path of interest rates. Phrases such as "moderate increases" or "data-driven approach" can alter expectations.

- **Volatility**: Unexpected policy actions or ambiguous statements can increase market volatility as investors reassess their outlook.

For example, a *hawkish* statement indicating possible interest rate hikes could cause stocks to fall and the dollar to strengthen. Conversely, a dovish tone suggesting accommodative policies could boost stocks and weaken the dollar.

The Federal Reserve's FOMC Policy and Its Impact on Stock Prices

The Federal Reserve's Federal Open Market Committee (FOMC) plays a crucial role in formulating monetary policy, which directly influences economic conditions and financial markets, including stock prices. The FOMC's two main tools—setting interest rates and managing the money supply (M1 and M2)—affect investor sentiment, corporate profitability, and overall market valuations.

1. Setting Interest Rates - The FOMC sets the target range for the federal funds rate, which is the interest rate that banks charge each other for *overnight* loans. This rate serves as a benchmark for other interest rates, influencing borrowing costs throughout the economy.

Effects on Stock Prices:

- **Higher Interest Rates**:
  - **Corporate Earnings**: Increased borrowing costs reduce profit margins for companies dependent on debt financing.
  - **Impact on Discount Rate**: Higher rates increase the discount rate in valuation models, decreasing the present value of future earnings and, therefore, stock prices.
  - **Sector Impact**: Growth sectors such as technology, which rely heavily on future earnings, and young

companies that generally rely heavily on financing, are particularly sensitive to interest rate increases.

- **Lower Interest Rates**:
  - **Stimulus Effect**: Cheaper borrowing promotes corporate investment and consumer spending, boosting economic activity and stock prices.
  - **Market Liquidity**: Lower interest rates encourage risk-taking, directing funds toward stocks.

2. Money Supply (M1 and M2) - The FOMC indirectly influences the money supply through tools such as open market operations, reserve requirements, and interest on excess reserves. Sometimes, expansion of the monetary base is informally referred to as "turning on the printing press."

- **M1**: Represents liquid forms of money, including cash and demand deposits.
- **M2**: Includes M1 plus less liquid assets, such as savings accounts and money market funds.

Effects on Stock Prices:

- **Expansion of the Money Supply**:
  - Increases liquidity in the financial system, allowing for more investment in stocks.
  - Boosts consumer spending, driving corporate profit growth.
- **Contraction of the Money Supply**:
  - Reduces available liquidity, potentially leading to tighter financial conditions and lower returns.

The Fed's aggressive monetary expansion during the COVID-19 pandemic (2020–2021) drove up stock prices by injecting liquidity into the economy and keeping interest rates near zero.

FedWatch Tool and Insights for Investors

Investors closely monitor the CME's FedWatch Tool, which provides probabilities for future changes in the federal funds rate as predicted by Fed Funds futures market participants. This tool offers insights into market expectations and helps investors anticipate FOMC actions.

How It Works:

- It tracks futures contracts linked to the federal funds rate to calculate the implied probabilities of rate changes for upcoming FOMC meetings.
- Displays these probabilities in easy-to-interpret charts and tables.

Why It's Useful:

- It helps investors gauge market sentiment and adjust their portfolios ahead of FOMC announcements.
- It provides a consensus view of how monetary policy may evolve, reducing uncertainty.
- Since this is a market where participants bet on the future direction of Fed Funds rates, it is a more reliable measure, as they "put their money where their mouth is" rather than just giving opinions based on guesswork.

Access the Tool: Investors can visit the CME FedWatch Tool to explore real-time forecasts on rate setting. Visit the website: https://www.cmegroup.com/markets/interest-rates/cme-fedwatch-tool.html.

The FOMC's interest rate and monetary policy decisions are key determinants of stock market performance. By influencing borrowing costs, corporate profitability, and liquidity, these policies shape investor behavior and market valuations. Tools such as FedWatch empower investors to anticipate and adapt to these policy changes, enhancing their ability to navigate market fluctuations and make informed decisions.

Implications for the Future Path

FOMC decisions and indications for future policy provide critical guidance to market participants. Indicators such as the Fed's Summary of Economic Projections (SEP), dot plots showing rate forecasts, and economic data emphasized in discussions shape expectations. Clear and consistent communication from the Fed's helps reduce uncertainty and allows markets to effectively price in anticipated policy changes. However, changes in economic data or unexpected external events can still lead to deviations from the Fed's projected trajectory.

History: Federal Reserve Chairmen

The Federal Reserve (Fed) has been led by several notable chairmen since the late 20th century, each guiding U.S. monetary policy through different economic scenarios. Here is an overview of their terms, policy approaches, and implementation of Quantitative Easing (QE) and Quantitative Tightening (QT) measures:

1. **Paul Volcker (1979–1987)**
    - **Monetary Policy Approach:**
        - **Anti-Inflation Measures:** Volcker is known for combating high inflation in the late 1970s and early 1980s by significantly raising interest rates, which reached over 20%. This restrictive monetary policy successfully reduced inflation but led to a recession in the early 1980s.

- **Quantitative Measures:**
    - During Volcker's tenure, the Fed did not use QE or QT as monetary policy tools.

2. **Alan Greenspan (1987–2006)**
    - **Monetary Policy Approach:**
        - **Market-Oriented Strategy:** Greenspan's tenure was marked by a focus on controlling inflation while supporting economic growth. He skillfully managed monetary policy during events such as the 1987 stock market crash and the bursting of the Internet bubble in 2001.
    - **Quantitative Measures:**
        - QE and QT were not used during Greenspan's leadership.
3. **Ben Bernanke (2006–2014)**
    - **Monetary Policy Approach:**
        - **Crisis Management:** Facing the 2008 financial crisis, Bernanke implemented unprecedented measures to stabilize the economy, including lowering interest rates to near zero.
    - **Quantitative Measures:**
        - **Quantitative Easing (QE):** Under Bernanke, the Fed launched several QE programs to inject liquidity into the financial system:
            - **QE1 (2008–2010):** The Fed purchased $1.75 trillion in mortgage-backed securities and Treasury securities.

- **QE2 (2010–2011):** An additional $600 billion in Treasury securities were purchased.
- **QE3 (2012–2014):** The Fed conducted open market purchases, acquiring $40 billion in mortgage-backed securities monthly, later increasing t to $85 billion, until tapering began in 2013.

4. Janet Yellen (2014–2018)

- **Monetary Policy Approach:**
  - **Gradual Normalization:** Yellen focused on gradually raising interest rates and normalizing monetary policy after extensive QE measures, emphasizing improvements in the labor market and inflation targets.
- **Quantitative Measures:**
  - **Quantitative Tightening (QT):** In 2017, the Fed began reducing the Fed's balance sheet by not reinvesting all maturing securities, effectively initiating QT to unwind post-crisis asset purchases.

5. Jerome Powell (2018–Present)

- **Monetary Policy Approach:**
  - **Adaptive Strategy:** Powell's tenure has been characterized by flexibility in response to economic conditions, including the COVID-19 pandemic, where swift action was taken to support the economy.
- **Quantitative Measures:**
  - **Quantitative Easing (QE):** In response to the pandemic, the Fed launched a substantial QE program in

2020, purchasing a wide range of assets to ensure market liquidity and support economic recovery.

- **Quantitative Tightening (QT):** In June 2022, the Fed began QT by reducing its balance sheet to address rising inflation, a process that is ongoing.

Each Fed chair has navigated unique economic challenges, employing a variety of monetary policy tools to maintain economic stability. The use of QE and QT has been particularly prominent in recent years, reflecting the Fed's evolving strategies in response to financial crises and economic fluctuations.

Understanding Economic Cycles

Economic cycles, or business cycles, represent the natural fluctuations in economic activity over time, characterized by periods of expansion (growth) and contraction (recession). These cycles are influenced by various factors, including consumer behavior, business investment, government policy, and external shocks. A typical economic cycle comprises four phases:

- **Expansion:** A period of increased economic activity, GDP growth, rising employment, and higher consumption.
- **Peak:** The height of economic activity, where growth rates are at their maximum before a slowdown begins.
- **Contraction (Recession):** A decline in economic activity, marked by a decrease in GDP, increased unemployment, and reduced consumption.
- **Trough:** The lowest point in the cycle, where the economy hits bottom before entering a new phase of expansion.

Understanding these cycles is crucial for policymakers, businesses, and investors to make informed decisions and implement strategies that mitigate economic volatility.

The U.S. Economy Post-Pandemic 2020

The COVID-19 pandemic precipitated a sharp economic contraction in 2020, with GDP plummeting and unemployment rates soaring due to widespread *lockdowns* and disruptions in the production of goods and services across the U.S. economy. In response, the U.S. government and the Federal Reserve implemented unprecedented fiscal and monetary measures to stabilize the economy.

In 2021, these interventions facilitated a robust recovery, with GDP growth rebounding and unemployment rates declining. The U.S. economy has demonstrated remarkable resilience, outperforming many other advanced economies in its recovery trajectory. This rapid recovery can be attributed to substantial fiscal stimulus, rapid vaccine rollout, and adaptive behaviors by consumers and businesses.

However, the rapid recovery also led to challenges, notably rising inflation rates driven by disruptions in production chains, increased consumer demand, and tightening labor market conditions. The Federal Reserve responded by adjusting monetary policies, including raising interest rates, to curb inflationary pressures.

Current Situation: Strengths and Challenges for the Next Decade

Strengths:

- **Technological Innovation:** Advances in technology, particularly in artificial intelligence and automation, are being leveraged to increase productivity and drive economic growth. An AI-driven productivity boom could lead to unprecedented growth rates, significantly altering economic projections.

- **Resilient Labor Market:** The U.S. labor market has shown resilience, with unemployment rates returning to pre-pandemic levels. This strength supports consumption and overall economic stability.
- **Energy Independence:** The U.S. has become a net exporter of petroleum products, increasing energy security and contributing positively to the trade balance.

Challenges:

- **Inflationary Pressures:** Despite recent declines, inflation remains a concern. Persistent inflation can erode purchasing power and savings, posing challenges for consumers and policymakers.
- **Fiscal Sustainability:** Substantial fiscal stimulus measures have led to an increase in the national debt. Ensuring fiscal sustainability while supporting economic growth will be a critical balancing act for policymakers.
- **Geopolitical Risks:** Global tensions, including trade disputes and geopolitical conflicts, could disrupt stability and economic growth. For example, tariffs proposed by Trump could impact inflation and economic performance.
- **Demographic Changes:** An aging population can strain public resources and impact labor market dynamics, requiring policy adjustments to support an evolving demographic landscape.
- **Climate Change:** Environmental challenges pose risks to economic infrastructure and require investments in sustainable practices, which may influence economic planning and resource allocation.

In conclusion, although the U.S. economy has demonstrated significant resilience and adaptability in the wake of the 2020 pandemic, it faces a complex landscape of opportunities and challenges in the coming decade. Strategic policy decisions, technological advances, and effective management of emerging risks will be critical in shaping the economic trajectory and ensuring sustained growth and stability.

Economic Indicators

Here is a list of the top 10 essential economic indicators that every investor should monitor, along with a brief description of each:

1. Inflation (*Consumer Price Index – CPI*) - The CPI measures the average change in prices paid by consumers for goods and services. It provides insights into purchasing power and changes in the cost of living. High inflation usually leads central banks to raise interest rates, impacting the stock and bond markets.

2. *Fed Funds* Rate - The interest rate at which banks lend to each other *overnight*, set by the Federal Reserve. It influences borrowing costs, consumption, and investment. It functions as the US equivalent of the Selic rate. Changes in this rate often have broad implications for financial markets.

3. 10-Year Treasury Note Yield - The yield on the 10-year Treasury note reflects investor sentiment about future economic growth and inflation. It serves as a benchmark for mortgage rates and corporate borrowing costs, affecting sectors such as real estate and banking. It is the benchmark rate in the US.

4. Employment Report (*NFP – Non-Farm Payrolls*) - A monthly report that measures job creation in the US, excluding the agricultural sector. Strong NFP numbers signal economic expansion, while weak numbers may indicate a slowdown in growth. Markets often react to this report because of its implications for Fed policy. It is by far the most closely watched economic indicator in the U.S. financial market! When the NFP surprises the market, all markets tend to move violently—both for better and for worse.

5. U.S. Dollar Index *(DXY)* - The DXY tracks the value of the U.S. dollar against a basket of major currencies. A strong dollar affects international trade, corporate profits for exporters, and the prices of commodities such as gold and oil, which are denominated in dollars.

6. *Gross Domestic Product* (*GDP*) Growth Rate - The GDP growth rate measures the expansion or contraction of the economy over a period of time. Positive growth indicates economic health, while negative growth may signal a recession. Investors use GDP data to assess market potential and corporate earnings prospects.

7. *Unemployment Rate* - The percentage of the labor force that is unemployed but actively seeking reemployment. A low unemployment rate suggests a strong economy, while a high rate may point to economic challenges. It often complements the NFP report in assessing the health of the labor market.

8. *Initial Jobless Claims* - This weekly report tracks the number of individuals filing for unemployment insurance benefits for the first time. It provides a timely view of labor market trends and can indicate early signs of economic stress or recovery.

9. Retail Sales - This report measures the consumption of goods and services, representing a significant portion of GDP. Consumption in the US accounts for 2/3 of the country's GDP; it is a consumerist country. Strong retail sales indicate robust consumer demand, while weak numbers may suggest an economic slowdown or reduced consumer confidence.

10. Manufacturing Purchasing Managers Index (*PMI*) - A monthly survey of manufacturing sector activity, including production, employment, and new orders. A reading above 50 signals expansion, while below 50 indicates contraction. It offers insights into the health of the industrial sector and overall economic momentum.

Let's add five more important indicators to the list. These additional indicators provide deeper insights into the structural health of the economy, inflationary trends, consumer behavior, and global trade dynamics. Together, these metrics complement the core indicators and help investors refine their market strategies and risk assessments.

11. Producer Price Index (*PPI*) - The PPI measures changes in the selling prices received by domestic producers for their output. It reflects inflation at the wholesale level and serves as an early indicator of future changes in consumer prices. A rising PPI can signal higher input costs for businesses, potentially squeezing profit margins and passing the increase on to the CPI.

12. Housing Starts - This indicator tracks the number of new residential construction projects started during a specific period. It is a key measure of the health of the housing market and broader economic activity. Strong housing starts indicate consumer confidence and economic growth, while declines may signal weakened demand.

13. Consumer Confidence Index (*University of Michigan Consumer Sentiment*) - This indicator measures consumer optimism about the state of the economy and their financial situations. A high value indicates strong consumption potential, while a low value may suggest reduced spending and economic pessimism, impacting the retail and consumer sectors.

14. Trade Balance: *Trade* Deficit/Surplus - This indicator measures the difference between a country's exports and imports. A trade surplus signals strong global demand for domestic goods, while a deficit indicates greater dependence on foreign goods. It affects currency values, corporate profits, and trade policies.

15. Chicago Fed National Activity Index (*CFNAI*) - The CFNAI is a composite of 85 economic indicators that provide a broad measure of national economic activity. A reading close to zero indicates that the economy is expanding at its historical trend, while positive or negative values suggest above- or below-average growth, respectively. It offers a holistic view of economic momentum.

Monitoring these indicators helps investors anticipate market movements, understand economic conditions, and make informed decisions across different asset classes. Each indicator provides a piece of the larger economic puzzle, helping investors navigate opportunities and risks.

Chapter 5. Risk Management

Introduction to Risk Management in Stock Investing

Investing involves risk. Anyone who buys stocks, bonds, ETFs, or any other financial asset is, in a sense, taking on uncertainty. However, the difference between a successful investor and one who suffers severe losses is not only in the choice of assets, but in how they manage risk.

Risk management is the process of identifying, measuring, and mitigating the risks associated with investments. The main objective is not to eliminate risk, as this would be impossible, but rather to control it intelligently so that returns are optimized and the impact of losses is minimized.

Why is Risk Management Essential?

- Avoiding catastrophic losses: The biggest mistake many investors make is taking risks without planning. Major market crises, such as those in 2008 and 2020, have shown that those who do not protect their capital can suffer severe losses that are difficult to recover from and can take years to recover.
- Maximize risk-adjusted returns: A good investor does not only seek high returns, but rather good returns in relation to the risk taken. Strategies such as efficient asset allocation and diversification help to achieve better results with less volatility. SMIGRM takes this process to a higher level.
- Reducing emotional impacts on decisions: Fear and greed cause investors to make bad decisions. When there is a clear risk management strategy, investors are able to act rationally and disciplined.
- Avoid severe declines and accelerate recovery: A 50% loss in equity requires a 100% gain just to break even. Good risk

management protects against large declines and speeds up recovery time.

Asymmetry between Gains and Losses: The Main Reason Why You Need to Avoid Losses

When it comes to investments, we use percentages all the time. We use percentages to express both gains and losses, but we often get confused by the asymmetry of meaning between gains and losses in percentage terms. This is because, naturally, the calculation basis in a gain situation (from bottom to top) is lower than the calculation basis in a loss situation (from top to bottom). Therefore, if the price of a stock falls 50% and then rises 50%, it does not return to the same starting point. Visually, imagine starting at $100 and losing 50%, the price becomes $50. If it then rises 50%, the price reaches $75, not $100. So in percentage terms, there is this **asymmetry between gains and losses** that hurts investors. And it is exacerbated as the percentage value rises. See table below:

Loss Percentage (Drawdown)	Subsequent return required to break-even
-20%	+25%
-30%	+43%
-40%	+67%
-50%	+100%
-60%	+150%

This means that small losses are acceptable because they are normal and part of investing. A 10% loss requires a subsequent return of only 10.1%. But a 20% loss requires a subsequent return of 25%, which is more difficult and may take longer to achieve. A 40% drop will require a 67% recovery... and so on. But... ah, that's rare, you may argue. It certainly doesn't happen every day or every month, but it can happen at any time. Historically, a 10% or greater decline tends to happen every 30 months. A 20% or greater decline has occurred every 6 years. The problem is that no one has a crystal ball to know when the next one will come. So it's smart to be vigilant and prevent it from happening to you.

Let's look at two real examples:

In the first chart, we have the stock market crash of 2000, also known as the bursting of the Internet bubble of 2000. The S&P 500 fell 48.9%, and to reverse this, it had to climb 95.8% just to break even! How long did it take for this to happen, just to recover what was lost? Almost 7 years!

In the second graph, we have the crash of the 2008 subprime crisis, whose epicenter was in the US itself. The S&P 500 fell 56.8%, and to reverse this, it needed to climb 131.3% just to break even! How long did it take for this to happen, just to recover what was lost? Almost 6 years!

The moral of the story: **Instead of falling into a hole and then trying to get out of it, it is better to avoid falling into it in the first place**. The big cost is not even the money, because there is always the possibility of recovering it. **But what is the greatest loss that is irrecoverable?**

TIME! Wasting time trying to get out of the hole is not smart. Anyone who has been through these situations knows what I'm talking about. How many times have you seen your stock plummet before you had a chance to sell it, and then you were faced with the dilemma: should I sell at a loss or wait for it to recover, at least to the price I paid for it? Now imagine this happening in a crash like the ones illustrated above. When there is a market crash, you don't know in advance what type it is—there are three types of crashes:

- ***Pullbacks***: declines of 5% to 10%
- ***Correction***: declines of 10% to 20%
- ***Crashes***: declines above 20%

Generally, getting out of a *pullback* is not usually a big problem. A relatively small drop is usually recoverable in a few days or weeks. A correction can take much longer to reverse, taking weeks or even a few months. *Crashes* are much more severe drops and can take years to recover from. Depending on the severity or magnitude of *the crash*, it can take up to decades.

Below are the main risk management tools in general, which fall into the following categories:

- ***Risk Avoidance***: Avoid taking risks – In finance, avoiding risk altogether will prevent losses but also good returns. Investment always carries some risk.
- ***Risk Reduction***: Minimizing the harmful effects of risk – In finance, risks can be mitigated in asset allocation by choosing lower-risk assets or by optimizing risk (read more in Chapter 12 on Modern Portfolio Theory and Chapter 8 on the SMIGRM Method).
- ***Risk Transferring***: Transferring risk to others – In finance, this is known as *hedging*: risk can be transferred to others through derivative transactions. For example, stock investors can buy Put Options, thereby transferring the risk of a fall in the price of their stock to the seller of the Options.
- ***Risk Acceptance***: Taking acceptable risks – In finance, this means limiting risks to levels below those considered acceptable. Each person has their own risk tolerance.

Let's now examine the main risk management tools used in the financial industry:

Key Risk Management Tools

Financial market professionals use a variety of quantitative and qualitative tools to manage risk. Below are some of the most important ones:

1. Diversification

- The most basic principle of risk management.

- Don't put all your eggs in one basket; allocate investments across different sectors, asset classes, and geographies.
- This prevents a single negative event from causing a devastating loss in the portfolio.

2. Asset Allocation

- Defines how much of the portfolio will be invested in different asset classes, such as stocks, fixed income, commodities, real estate, etc.
- It is adjusted according to the investor's risk profile.
- Example: more conservative investors may have 70% in fixed income and 30% in stocks, while aggressive investors may have 70% in stocks and 30% in fixed income.

3. Stop Loss and Take Profit

- Automatic orders that limit losses or realize profits.
- **Stop Loss:** Automatically sells an asset when it reaches a certain loss price.
- **Take Profit:** Guarantees a profit by selling the asset when it reaches a certain appreciation price.
- **Trailing Stop:** Automatically adjusts the stop as the asset rises, locking in gains already realized.

4. Statistical Risk Analysis

- **Standard Deviation:** Measures the volatility of an asset (the higher it is, the more unstable the investment).
- **Beta:** Measures the risk of an asset relative to the market (Beta > 1 means that the asset is more volatile than the benchmark index, such as the S&P 500, for example).

- **Correlation Coefficient:** Measures the relationship between two assets (if close to **1**, it means that the assets move together).

5. Value at Risk (VaR)

- Measures the **maximum potential loss** of a portfolio within a given confidence level.
- We will detail this topic below as it is one of the most important and used in professional environments by risk managers.

6. *Hedging* (Portfolio Protection through Risk Transfer)

- Techniques to **reduce risk without completely exiting the market**.
- Use of **derivatives** such as **put options** to protect stocks against declines.
- Use of negatively or very low correlated assets, such as **gold or government bonds**.

7. Liquidity Risk

- Assessment of the ease of selling an asset without impacting the market price.
- **Low-liquidity** stocks can be difficult to sell quickly without incurring a loss.
- It is important to ensure that the portfolio has **highly liquid assets** for emergencies.

8. Defensive Sectors

- Some sectors of the economy are less susceptible to volatility than others and can help mitigate losses during periods of high market uncertainty and volatility.

9. Contextual Dynamic Allocation (SMIGRM Method)

- Instead of maintaining diversified asset allocations to address all types of contexts and markets, a brilliant solution is to tactically allocate assets according to the context.
- Implement an optimal allocation for each context, exploiting it in order to minimize risk.
- SMIGRM uses risk to define context. In high-risk situations, the allocation is conservative (defensive) with low-risk assets in the portfolio. In a low-risk context, the allocation is aggressive with higher-risk assets to obtain the highest possible return.
- Contextual Dynamic Allocation and SMIGRM will be discussed in greater detail in Chapters 7 and 8, respectively.

Risk management is critical to protecting portfolios and achieving consistent returns. Tools such as VaR, stress testing, and diversification offer insights into potential risks, while techniques such as hedging and position sizing provide actionable strategies to mitigate them.

Next, we will detail some of the risk management tools, starting with Value at Risk, Stop Loss, and Defensive Sectors.

Value at Risk (VaR)

Value at Risk (VaR) is one of the most widely used metrics for measuring how much an investor can lose in a given period, within a statistical confidence level. It answers the following question:

What is the maximum expected loss of my portfolio over a given time horizon, considering a confidence level?

For example, if an investor calculates that their portfolio has a VaR of $10,000 at a 95% confidence level on a given day, this means that there is a 95% chance that the daily loss will not exceed $10,000, but there is a 5% chance that the loss will be greater.

VaR is widely used by portfolio managers, investment funds, and institutional traders to monitor risk and make decisions about asset allocation.

Methods for Calculating VaR

There are three main ways to calculate Value at Risk:

- **Parametric Method (Delta-Normal)** – Assumes that returns follow a normal distribution and uses standard deviation and mean to calculate risk.
- **Historical Simulation Method** – Uses actual past data to estimate future losses.
- **Monte Carlo Simulation Method** – Simulates thousands of random scenarios to predict possible losses.

Below, we will detail the calculation using the Parametric Method, which is the simplest and most frequently used by non-professional investors.

How to Calculate the VaR of a Stock Portfolio (Parametric Method)

Step 1: Define the Time Horizon and Confidence Level

Before calculating VaR, investors need to define:

- Time horizon: This can be daily, weekly, or monthly.
- Confidence level: The most common are 95% or 99%.
- Example: An investor wants to calculate the daily VaR of their portfolio with 95% confidence.

Step 2: Collect Portfolio Return Data

The portfolio return can be calculated as the weighted average of the returns on individual stocks:

$$RC = w_1R_1 + w_2R_2 + ... + w_nR_n$$

Where:

- RC = Portfolio return
- w_i = Weight of stock i in the portfolio
- R_i = Return of stock i

Example: Suppose the portfolio has 50% invested in Stock A and 50% in Stock B, with average returns of 0.8% and 0.5%, respectively:

R_C = (0.5 x 0.008) + (0.5 x 0.005) = 0.0065 (i.e., 0.65% average daily return)

Step 3: Calculate Portfolio Volatility (Standard Deviation)

Portfolio volatility can be obtained by:

$$\sigma C^2 = w_1^2\sigma_1^2 + w_2^2\sigma_2^2 + 2w_1w_2\sigma_1\sigma_2\rho_{1,2}$$

Where:

- σC = Portfolio volatility
- σ_1, σ_2 = Volatility of each stock
- $\rho_{1,2}$ = Correlation between the stocks

◆ **Example:** If Stock A has a standard deviation of 1.5%, Stock B has a standard deviation of 2.0%, and the correlation between them is 0.6:

$$\sigma C^2 = (0.5^2 \times 0.015^2) + (0.5^2 \times 0.02^2) + (2 \times 0.5 \times 0.5 \times 0.015 \times 0.02 \times 0.6)$$

$$\sigma C^2 = 0.00005625 + 0.0001 + 0.00009 = 0.00024625$$

$$\sigma C = \sqrt{0.00024625} \approx 1.57\% \text{ (daily volatility)}$$

Step 4: Calculate VaR

Now we apply the VaR formula for 95% confidence, where the Z-score (quantile of the normal distribution) is 1.65:

$$VaR = Z \times \sigma C \times \text{Portfolio Value}$$

If the investor's portfolio is worth $100,000:

$$VaR = 1.65 \times 0.0157 \times 100{,}000$$
$$VaR = 2{,}590$$

✅ **Conclusion:** There is a 95% probability that the maximum daily loss will not exceed $2,590.

If the investor wants to estimate monthly VaR (20 trading days), we scale it by √20:

$$VaR\_monthly = 2{,}590 \times \sqrt{20} \approx 11{,}572$$

In other words, there is a 95% probability that the monthly loss will not exceed $11,572.

Conclusion: How to Use VaR in Practice?

- Set acceptable loss limits – If an investor does not want to risk losing more than 5% of their equity in a month, VaR can help them adjust their exposure.

- Compare different portfolios – If one portfolio has a daily VaR of $2,000 and another has $5,000, the former may be less risky.

- Adjust allocations to reduce risk – Investors can diversify better to decrease portfolio volatility and reduce VaR.

VaR is a powerful tool, but it has limitations. It only measures risk within a confidence interval and does not predict extreme events (market crises). Therefore, it is essential to combine it with other risk metrics, such as Maximum Drawdown, Ulcer Index, and Sortino Ratio.

Maximum Drawdown (MDD)

Maximum Drawdown (MDD) measures the **worst loss suffered by a portfolio** from its peak to its trough before a recovery. It is expressed as a percentage of the loss relative to the previous peak.

Why is it important?

- It shows the **worst possible** loss **scenario** during a past period, but it helps to plan for the future because scenarios that have occurred in the past may repeat themselves in the future.
- It helps investors **define acceptable risk limits**.
- It is useful for **comparing different investment strategies**.

How to Calculate Maximum Drawdown

1. Identify the **historical peak** of the portfolio during the period analyzed.
2. Find the **lowest subsequent value** before a recovery.
3. Calculate the percentage loss between these two points.

Drawdown =
(Peak − Trough) / Peak × 100

◆ **Example:**

The portfolio reached a peak of $100,000.
It then dropped to $70,000 before recovering.

The Maximum Drawdown was:

(100,000 − 70,000) / 100,000 × 100 = 30%

This means that, at the worst point, the investor faced a **30% loss of capital before recovery**.

Ulcer Index (UI) – Measuring the Depth and Duration of Declines

The **Ulcer Index** goes beyond Maximum Drawdown, as it not only measures the **worst decline**, but also **the duration and frequency of losses**. The Ulcer Index evaluates all declines during the period.

Why is this important?

- If two strategies have **the same return**, but one has frequent and long declines, it will be riskier.
- The **UI penalizes investments that remain below their peak for a long time**, something that **Maximum Drawdown** does not capture.

How to Calculate the Ulcer Index

1. Identify the **daily prices** of the portfolio.
2. Find the **historical cumulative maximum** (previous peak).
3. Calculate **how much the current price is below that peak** each day.
4. Take the **square root of these values.**

$$\mathrm{UI} = \sqrt{\frac{1}{N}\sum_{i=1}^{N} \mathrm{Drawdown}_i^2}$$

Example:

If a portfolio has a sequence of small recurring declines, even if the Maximum Drawdown is not large, the Ulcer Index will be high, indicating a more "painful" investment to maintain.

Interpretation: The higher the **Ulcer Index**, the more unstable and risky the portfolio is.

Sortino Ratio – Evaluating Risk-Adjusted Return

The **Sortino Ratio** is similar to the **Sharpe Ratio**, but with one fundamental difference:

- The Sharpe Ratio penalizes any type of volatility (up and down).
- The Sortino Ratio penalizes only negative volatility (declines).

This means that it **does not penalize investments with high appreciation**, but **penalizes those that experience frequent and severe declines**.

Why is this important?

- It differentiates between "good" volatility (ups) and "bad" volatility (downs).
- It is more useful than the **Sharpe Ratio** for evaluating **strategies focused on capital preservation**.

How to Calculate the Sortino Ratio

Sortino Ratio = $(R_p - R_f) / \sigma\_D$

Where:

- R_p = Average portfolio return
- R_f = Risk-free rate (e.g., U.S. Treasury bills)
- σ_D = Standard deviation of negative returns (downside deviation)

Example:

- The portfolio had an **average return of 12% per year**.
- The risk-free return (T-Bills) is **2%**.
- The standard deviation of the portfolio's **declines** was **10%**.

$$\text{Sortino Ratio} = \frac{12 - 2}{10} = 1{,}0$$

The **higher** the Sortino Ratio, **the better** the negative risk-adjusted return.

If the Sortino Ratio is less than 1, it means that the negative risk is too high in relation to the return.

Conclusion: How to Use These Metrics in Practice?

Comparative Summary of Metrics

Indicator	What is measured?	Objective
Maximum Drawdown	Worst historical loss before recovery	Estimate maximum loss given history
Ulcer Index	Depth and duration of downturns	Identify "painful" losing investments
Sortino Ratio	Return adjusted by risk of losses	Compare investment returns given risks of losses

---

- **Define risk tolerance:** If an investor is not willing to lose more than **20% of their equity**, they should monitor the **Maximum Drawdown** of their strategy.

- **Choose less volatile investments:** If an asset has **a very high Ulcer Index**, it may be difficult to hold in the long term, even if it generates good returns.
- **Compare risk-adjusted returns:** A fund may have a **high Sharpe Ratio but a low Sortino Ratio**, which means it is **very volatile to declines**.

Stop Loss: The Importance of Limiting Losses

Trading in the stock market is inherently unpredictable. Sudden changes in the market, driven by economic data, geopolitical events, or unexpected company news, can lead to significant losses if positions are not protected. Setting stop loss levels is a crucial risk management discipline that helps investors mitigate potential losses and maintain peace of mind.

Why Use Stop Loss Levels?

- **Risk Management:** A stop loss ensures that losses are limited to a predetermined level, protecting capital from excessive risk.
- **Emotional Discipline:** Stop losses prevent impulsive decisions by automating the exit strategy, reducing the influence of fear or greed.
- **Peace of Mind:** Knowing that your portfolio has safeguards in place allows you to "sleep better at night," even during volatile markets.
- **Adaptable to All Investors:** Whether managing a small portfolio or a large fund, stop losses are essential for maintaining control over potential risks.

Types of Stop Loss Orders

Fixed Stop Loss Order:

- **Definition:** A static price level set below the entry price at which the stock will be sold.
- **Use Case:** Suitable for trades where a fixed risk tolerance is predefined.
- **Example:** Buying a stock at $50 with a stop loss at $45 limits the loss to $5 per share.

Percentage Stop Loss:

- **Definition:** Exits a trade when the stock price falls by a defined percentage below the purchase price.
- **Use Case:** Ideal for volatile stocks where fixed levels may not account for daily fluctuations.
- **Example:** A 10% stop loss on a $100 stock would be triggered at $90.

Time-Based Stop Loss:

- **Definition:** Closes a position after a specified time if the stock does not move favorably.
- **Use Case:** Suitable for short-term trading, such as day trading or swing trading.

Trailing Stop Loss (Adjusted):

- **Definition:** Dynamically adjusts the stop loss level as the stock price moves in the investor's favor.
- **Use Case:** Secures gains by following the upward movement of the stock while limiting potential losses.
- **Example:**

  - Setting a trailing stop loss of $5 on a stock purchased at $50:
  - If the price rises to $60, the stop loss moves to $55.
  - If the price then falls to $55, the position is sold, securing a gain of $5.

Advantages of Trailing Stop Loss

- **Secures Profits:** Protects gains by adjusting the stop loss upward as the stock price rises.
- **Automatic Adjustment:** No need to monitor the stock continuously; the trailing stop adjusts automatically.
- **Limits Losses:** Ensures that losses are minimized, even if the stock suddenly reverses.
- **Encourages Discipline:** Prevents emotional decisions by following a systematic exit strategy.

Practical Tips for Using Stop Loss Orders

- **Determine Risk Tolerance:** Set stop loss levels based on acceptable risk per trade, typically 1-2% of the total portfolio.
- **Use Technical Analysis:** Identify support levels or average volatility to set appropriate stop loss levels.
- **Avoid Tight Stops:** Stops set too close to the purchase price can result in premature exits during normal market fluctuations.
- **Combine with Position Sizing:** Use stop losses in conjunction with position size to effectively manage overall portfolio risk.

In summary:

Stop loss orders are indispensable tools for every investor, large or small. They provide a safety net against sudden market changes, enforce discipline, and reduce the emotional stress of managing trades. Among the various types, the Trailing Stop Loss stands out for its dual benefit of securing gains while limiting losses. By adopting stop loss strategies, investors can trade with confidence, knowing that their downside risks are under control, and focus on building long-term wealth.

Defensive Sectors: Protections Against Bear Markets and Volatility

Stocks move in packs, but not all sectors move with the same intensity. The lower the correlation with the S&P 500, the better the protective effect.

Utilities: Essential Public Services (Ticker: XLU)

- **Correlation with the S&P 500**: Approximately 0.22 over a three-year period.
- **Rationale**: Utilities provide essential services (electricity, water and sewage, gas, etc.), resulting in stable demand regardless of economic conditions. This stability results in a lower correlation with the overall market, making the sector a defensive choice during recessions.

Consumer Staples (Ticker: XLP)

- **Correlation with the S&P 500**: Moderate correlation with all other sectors, with the Consumer Discretionary sector having the highest value among them.
- **Rationale**: Companies in this sector produce essential goods, maintaining steady demand even during economic slowdowns. This consistent demand contributes to the defensive nature of the sector in bear markets.

Health Care (Ticker: XLV)

- **Correlation with the S&P 500**: Moderate correlation with most sectors; low correlation of 0.28 with Utilities.
- **Rationale**: Healthcare services and products remain necessary regardless of economic cycles, providing stability and a lower correlation with the market as a whole.

Practical Application: Incorporating these sectors into a diversified portfolio can mitigate losses during market downturns. For example, during market volatility in 2024, sectors such as Consumer Discretionary and Health Care were recommended as defensive investments.

Understanding and applying correlation in portfolio construction allows investors to strategically select sectors that act as effective hedges against market volatility. By focusing on sectors with lower correlations to the S&P 500, such as Utilities, Consumer Discretionary, and Health Care, investors can increase portfolio resilience during bear markets.

Recommended Defensive Sectors Amid Market Volatility: In addition to sector diversification, investors often turn to various asset classes to protect against bear markets in equities. These asset classes typically exhibit low or negative correlations with the S&P 500, offering potential protection during market declines.

Defensive Asset Classes: Protections Against Bear Markets and Volatility

Asset Classes Commonly Used for Protection:

Bonds

- **Correlation with the S&P 500**: Historically low; for example, the iShares Core U.S. Aggregate Bond ETF (AGG) showed a correlation of approximately 0.26 with the S&P 500 from 2008 to 2024.

- **Rationale**: Bonds, especially U.S. Treasuries, are considered safe-haven assets. During stock market declines, investors often turn to bonds, driving up their prices and providing a counterbalance to falling stock values.

Gold

- **Correlation with the S&P 500**: Generally low; the SPDR Gold Shares ETF (GLD) showed a correlation of about 0.08 with the S&P 500 over the same period.
- **Rationale**: Gold is traditionally viewed as a store of value and a hedge against economic uncertainty. Its low correlation with stocks makes it a popular choice for diversification during periods of market stress.

Commodities

- **Correlation with the S&P 500**: Varies by commodity; for example, the Invesco DB Commodity Index Tracking Fund (DBC) showed a correlation of approximately 0.50 with the S&P 500.
- **Rationale**: Commodities can act as a hedge against inflation and may perform differently than stocks, offering diversification benefits.

Real Estate Investment Trusts (REITs)

- **Correlation with the S&P 500**: Moderate; the Vanguard Real Estate ETF (VNQ) showed a correlation of about 0.76 with the S&P 500.
- **Rationale**: REITs offer exposure to real estate markets, which may not move in sync with stock markets, offering diversification potential.

Conclusion and Important Considerations

It is crucial to recognize that **correlations between assets and asset classes are not constant over time**. They can change due to various factors, including economic conditions, market sentiment, and geopolitical events. For example, during periods of extreme market stress, assets that normally have low correlations may move more in concert, reducing the effectiveness of diversification.

While incorporating asset classes such as bonds, gold, commodities, and REITs can increase portfolio diversification and potentially mitigate risk during bear markets, it is essential to understand that **diversification does not guarantee risk reduction.** The dynamic nature of correlations means that the protective benefits of diversification can vary over time. Therefore, investors should regularly evaluate their portfolios and remain alert to changes in market conditions to ensure that their investment strategies are aligned with their risk tolerance and financial goals.

Another important consideration is that despite **relatively low correlations** of defensive sectors and defensive asset classes with the S&P 500, in reality the correlations are not that low and are not negative. In other words, although theoretically these sectors and asset classes are defensive, in practice, **this protection is not that good and is still variable over time**.

Author's Opinion: The best way to implement protection against risks, volatility, uncertainty, and *bear* markets is the SMIGRM Method, which you will learn about in Chapter 8.

Introduction to Alpha and Beta in Stock Investments

Alpha and Beta are key metrics in assessing the performance and risk of investments in the stock market. These measures help investors understand how a portfolio or stock behaves relative to the broader market.

Alpha (α)

Alpha measures the excess return of an investment relative to its benchmark index. It indicates whether a stock or portfolio has outperformed or underperformed the market, given its level of risk.

Formula:

$$\alpha = \text{Portfolio Return} - [\text{Risk-Free Rate} + \beta\ (\text{Market Return} - \text{Risk-Free Rate})]$$

Interpretation:

- **Positive Alpha (>0):** Outperformed the market after accounting for risk.
- **Negative Alpha (<0):** Underperformed the market after accounting for risk.

Example: If a portfolio has a return of 10%, the risk-free rate is 2%, the market return is 8%, and the portfolio's beta is 1.2:

$$\alpha = 10\% - [2\% + 1.2\ (8\% - 2\%)] = 10\% - 9.2\% = 0.8\%$$

This portfolio outperformed the market by 0.8%.

Beta (β)

Beta measures the sensitivity of a stock or portfolio to market movements. It quantifies systematic risk, reflecting how much the price of the investment changes relative to the market.

Formula:

$$\beta = \frac{\text{Covariance of Stock and Market Returns}}{\text{Variance of Market Returns}}$$

Interpretation:

- **Beta = 1:** Corresponds to market volatility.
- **Beta > 1:** More volatile than the market (e.g., technology stocks).
- **Beta < 1:** Less volatile than the market (e.g., utility stocks).
- **Beta < 0:** Moves inversely to the market (e.g., gold ETFs).

Example: If a stock's beta is 1.5, it is expected to move 50% more than the market. If the market rises 10%, the stock may rise 15%; if the market falls 10%, the stock may fall 15%.

Capital Asset Pricing Model (CAPM)

CAPM calculates the expected return of an asset based on its risk relative to the market, linking risk (beta) with expected return.

Formula:

$$\text{Expected Return} = \text{Risk-Free Rate} + \beta\,(\text{Market Return} - \text{Risk-Free Rate})$$

Components:

- **Risk-Free Rate:** Return on a risk-free investment, typically U.S. Treasury securities.
- **Market Return:** Average market return (e.g., S&P 500).
- **Beta:** Measures the sensitivity of the asset to market movements.

Interpretation:

- If the actual return exceeds the return predicted by CAPM, the stock is undervalued and offers positive alpha.

- If the actual return is below the predicted return, the stock is overvalued and generates negative alpha.

CAPM Calculation Example:

- **Risk-Free Rate:** 2%
- **Market Return:** 8%
- **Stock Beta:** 1.2

Expected Return = 2% + 1.2 (8% − 2%) = 2% + 7.2% = 9.2%

If the actual return on the stock is 10%, it has a positive alpha:

$\alpha = 10\% - 9.2\% = 0.8\%$

Practical Use Cases

- **Alpha:** Used by fund managers to demonstrate their ability to outperform the market after adjusting for risk.
- **Beta:** Helps investors understand portfolio volatility and decide whether they want exposure to high-risk/high-return stocks or stable, low-risk investments.
- **CAPM:** Assists in assessing whether a stock is correctly priced, given its level of risk and expected return.

Conclusion

Alpha and beta provide critical insights into performance and risk, helping investors build balanced portfolios aligned with their goals and risk tolerance. CAPM adds a theoretical framework for assessing expected returns, linking risk-free rates, market premiums, and beta to guide investment decisions. However, while these metrics are valuable, they rely on assumptions (e.g., market efficiency, historical data) and should be supplemented with qualitative analysis for comprehensive decision-making.

Introduction to Correlation and Its Role in Stock Diversification

Correlation measures the degree to which two assets move in relation to each other. It is expressed as a value between -1 and 1:

- **+1:** Perfect positive correlation (assets move in the same direction).
- **0:** No correlation (assets move independently).
- **-1:** Perfect negative correlation (assets move in opposite directions).

Correlation and Diversification

Diversification reduces portfolio risk by spreading investments across multiple assets. The effectiveness of diversification depends on selecting assets with low or negative correlations.

- **Positive Correlation (+):** Adding positively correlated stocks offers limited risk reduction, as they tend to move together.
- **Negative Correlation (-):** Diversifying with negatively correlated stocks significantly reduces risk by offsetting losses in one asset with gains in another.

Example: Adding a utility stock (low correlation with technology stocks) to a predominantly technology portfolio offers better risk mitigation than adding another technology stock.

Number of Stocks and Diminishing Returns from Diversification

Research suggests that the benefits of diversification diminish beyond a certain number of stocks:

- **Key Studies:** Studies, including those by Evans and Archer (1968), indicate that most of the benefits of diversification can be achieved with 20 to 30 stocks in different sectors and industries.
- **Marginal Gains:** Adding more stocks beyond this point offers minimal risk reduction, as systematic risk (market risk) cannot be eliminated through diversification.

Practical Implication:

- Investors can achieve effective diversification with a reasonably sized portfolio by focusing on uncorrelated assets rather than excessive additions of stocks.

Markowitz Efficient Frontier

Definition:

- The Efficient Frontier, introduced by Harry Markowitz in his Modern Portfolio Theory (MPT), represents the set of optimal portfolios that offer the highest return for a given level of risk or the lowest risk for a given level of return.

Concepts:

- **Portfolio Variance:** The risk in a portfolio depends on the correlations between assets. Combining uncorrelated or negatively correlated stocks minimizes variance.
- **Efficient Portfolios:** Portfolios on the frontier are efficient because they maximize returns for a given level of risk.

How Correlation Affects the Frontier:

- Low or negative correlations between assets shift the Efficient Frontier outward, allowing for higher returns with lower risk.

- A portfolio with high correlations between assets has limited movement along the frontier, offering fewer diversification benefits.

Example of Efficient Frontier Optimization:

- A portfolio of 50% stocks and 50% bonds generally has a lower standard deviation than a 100% stock portfolio, as stocks and bonds are often negatively correlated. This combination moves the portfolio closer to the Efficient Frontier.

Read more about Markowitz's Efficient Frontier in **Chapter 12**.

Problems of Diversification, Correlation, and Non-Diversifiable Systematic Risk

Correlation is fundamental to diversification, as it determines how effectively portfolio risk can be mitigated. Although the benefits of diversification are substantial up to 20-30 stocks, adding more offers negligible additional risk reduction. The Efficient Frontier is based on this, optimizing asset allocation to achieve the best risk-return ratio through diversification. By understanding correlation and applying Markowitz's principles, investors can build portfolios that minimize risk while maximizing potential returns.

In fact, it makes no sense to have portfolios with more than 20 stocks. If your investment advisor builds a very large portfolio and makes a large number of transactions, be wary. They may be doing this deliberately, not to help you achieve better results, but to enrich themselves with commissions generated at your expense. Or, at best, they are unfamiliar with this principle or do not know what they are doing: they are simply "guessing" in the hope that they will "get it right."

In practical investing, correlation is a vital tool for building diversified portfolios that can withstand market downturns. By selecting assets with low or negative correlation to the S&P 500, investors can reduce the overall risk of the portfolio and improve the resilience of investments during bear markets. However, the first major problem is that in practice **there are** virtually **no assets that have a negative or near-zero correlation with the stock market (or the S&P 500)**.

The second problem is that **diversification only eliminates the unsystematic risk of stocks. Diversification does not change systematic risk**. Passive index investors are generally over-diversified because indices are usually composed of many stocks (such as the S&P 500, which has 500 stocks from a wide range of sectors and economic). However, even so, there is still a significant amount of systematic risk. **There are few options for countering systematic risk, among them the SMIGRM Method**. We will present and discuss the SMIGRM Method in Chapter 8.

Chapter 6. Understanding the VIX ("Panic Index") and the Stock Options Market

Introduction to the Stock Options Market in the United States

The stock options market is an essential component of the U.S. financial system, offering investors versatile tools for protection, speculation, and income generation. Options are derivative contracts that give the holder the right, but not the obligation, to buy or sell an underlying asset at a specified price within a specified time frame.

Main Types of Options: Calls and Puts

Call Options: A call option gives the holder the right to buy the underlying asset at a predetermined price (strike price) before the option expires. Use Cases:

- Bullish Speculation: Traders buy calls hoping that the stock price will rise above the strike price, generating profits.
- Income Generation: Selling covered calls allows investors to earn premiums while retaining the underlying stock.
- Leverage: Call options provide exposure to stock movements with less capital than buying the stock outright.

Put Options: A put option gives the holder the right to sell the underlying asset at the strike price before expiration. Use Cases:

- Bearish Speculation: Traders buy puts in anticipation that the stock price will fall below the strike price.
- Protection: Investors use puts to protect against potential declines in the value of their portfolio.

- Income Generation: Selling covered puts allows investors to earn premiums and potentially buy the stock at a lower price.

Volatility in the Options Market

Volatility measures the degree of variation in the price of a financial asset over time. In the context of options, it plays a crucial role in determining the premium (price) of the option. Higher volatility implies greater price swings and, consequently, higher option premiums.

Types of Volatility:

- **Historical Volatility**: Measures past price fluctuations of the asset over a specific period. Calculated using the standard deviation of historical price data.

Calculation of Historical Volatility:

$$\text{Historical Volatility} = \sqrt{\frac{\sum(R_i - \bar{R})^2}{N-1}} \times \sqrt{252}$$

Where:

- R_i = daily returns
- $\bar{R}$ = average daily return
- N = number of days in the period
- 252 = trading days in a year (to annualize)

Implied Volatility:

Calculated iteratively by inputting observed option prices into an option pricing model, adjusting volatility until the model price equals the market price.

- **Implied Volatility**: Reflects the market's expectation of future price movements, embedded in the option price. Derived from option pricing models (e.g., Black-Scholes) by solving for the volatility input that aligns the theoretical price with the market price.

Implied Volatility is one of the most important parameters for measuring the level of tension and uncertainty in the stock market and is what gives rise to the famous VIX (aka "panic index"), which we will discuss in more detail later in this chapter.

Implied Volatility is calculated iteratively by entering the observed option prices into an option pricing model, adjusting the volatility until the model price equals the market price.

Practical Implications of Volatility:

- Option Premiums: High implied volatility leads to higher premiums, making options more expensive. Traders often use strategies such as selling options during high volatility to capitalize on inflated premiums.

- Risk Assessment: Higher volatility indicates higher risk, but also higher potential reward.

- Strategic Decisions: Volatility considerations help investors choose appropriate strategies, such as buying options during low volatility or selling during high volatility.

Conclusion: The U.S. stock options market offers a variety of strategies for managing risk, speculating, or generating income through calls and puts. Understanding the dynamics of volatility, both historical and implied, is essential for effective options trading. By incorporating these tools in a thoughtful manner, investors can adjust their approaches to match their risk tolerance and market outlook.

Implied Volatility and Its Role in Market Sentiment

Implied volatility reflects market expectations regarding future price movements of an asset, derived from option contract prices. Unlike historical volatility, which is based on past price data, IV is forward-looking and helps measure investor sentiment.

Is this too abstract? To understand it, think of it this way. The seller of protection against falling stock prices (through puts) needs to charge a premium as if they were selling insurance. It is, in fact, insurance because you transfer the risk of a fall in the price of your stock or index to them. They cannot simply use historical volatility in calculating the price of this premium. They need to add a margin against the risk of future uncertainty. And they also need to add a little extra to make a profit on the transaction. The volatility value they will use in the premium pricing formulas is Implied Volatility.

But when we look at the prices of puts (premiums), how can we know the implied volatility that the seller used in pricing? We use the Black & Scholes formula in reverse. This allows us to determine the implied volatility that was used to calculate the premium.

Importance of Implied Volatility

Market Sentiment Indicator:

- High IV indicates that the market expects significant price fluctuations, often driven by uncertainty or fear (bearish sentiment).
- Low IV suggests a stable market with less anticipated volatility (bullish sentiment).

Option Pricing:

- Higher IV results in higher option premiums, as the probability of larger price movements increases.
- Traders use VI to assess whether options are relatively expensive or cheap.

Market Interpretation:

- Increased VI often accompanies bearish trends or high uncertainty.
- Declining VI generally aligns with bullish trends or stable conditions.

Understanding the VIX (Volatility Index)

Volatility is always associated with risk because a variable (e.g., the price of a stock) is volatile if it is uncertain. Uncertainty often leads to negative outcomes because investors dislike uncertainty and, more often than not, sell their stocks en masse (risk aversion).

What is the VIX?

The VIX, often called the "Fear Index," measures market expectations of volatility over the next 30 days. It is based on the implied volatility of options on the S&P 500 (SPX) index.

How is the VIX determined?

The VIX is calculated using a wide range of S&P 500 option prices, focusing on short-term options with different strike prices. The formula incorporates the weighted average of the implied volatilities of calls and puts to estimate expected volatility.

VIX Formula (Simplified)

The VIX involves the sum of variances derived from option prices, adjusting for time and price sensitivities. Although the exact formula is complex, the main variable is the implied volatility of a wide range of SPX options.

The VIX is a calculated index that measures the expected volatility of the S&P500® index over the next 30 days, but annualized. In other words, the VIX is the expected variation within 1 standard deviation over the next 30 days expressed in annual terms. To convert the VIX to an expected 1-day change in the S&P$^{500®}$, all you need to do is multiply it by the square root of 252, which is the number of trading days in a year (remember that the VIX number is annualized). For example, if the VIX is 10, the expected 1-day change by the VIX is 10% x √252 = ± 0.63% per day.

VIX	Daily S&P 500 +/- Change %
10	0.63%
20	1.26%
30	1.89%
40	2.52%
50	3.15%
60	3.78%
70	4.41%
80	5.04%
90	5.67%
100	6.30%

A widely used rule of thumb is to consider a VIX of 30 as the threshold between a volatile market and a calm market. A VIX of 30 implies an expectation of 30% x √252 = ± 1.89% per day.

What the VIX Means for Investors

Risk Assessment:

- A rising VIX signals increased market anxiety or expectations of future price fluctuations.
- A falling VIX suggests improved investor confidence and stability.

Trading Implications:

- **Hedge:** Investors use VIX-linked products (e.g., VIX futures or ETFs) to protect against volatility.

- **Timing:** Extreme VIX levels can signal market bottoms (high VIX) or complacency (low VIX), aiding contrarian strategies. Studies show that the VIX alone is **not** a reliable measure for determining *timing*, but it is a very important variable in *timing* systems.

Key VIX Levels and Their Interpretation

- **Below 12:** Extremely low volatility; market complacency. Often precedes a correction, as investors may underestimate risks.
- **12–20:** Normal range, indicating a stable market. Reflects moderate investor confidence.
- **20–30:** High volatility; increased uncertainty. Often coincides with market downturns or high geopolitical/economic risks.
- **Above 30:** High volatility; extreme fear or uncertainty. Typically observed during financial crises, significant sell-offs, or major geopolitical events.

Conclusion: Implied Volatility and the VIX provide critical insights into market sentiment and expectations for future price movements. High levels of implied volatility or VIX signal caution, often aligning with bearish or uncertain market conditions, while low levels suggest stability and confidence.

Chapter 7. Market Timing for Maximum Performance: Contextual Dynamic Allocation

Ask yourself this question: **Do your current investments depend on the stock market always being up**? In other words, if the market goes down (for example, in 2022) or stagnates for long periods, what will happen to your investments? Will they suffer as a result?

We have learned from history that *bear markets* can last for weeks, months, and even years—what will you do during these periods if you have a **strategy that only works in bull markets?** Investors need **strategies that make money even when the stock market is down or stagnant**. Having a strategy that is highly dependent on an always-positive stock market is a **recipe for poor long-term performance**. This explains why many mutual funds and *hedge funds* do not have impressive performance numbers, especially when the market is not cooperating. In *bull* markets, everyone looks like a genius. Many blame industry fees for poor performance, but we believe the problem lies much deeper.

Static Allocation vs. Contextual Dynamic Allocation

This is the first fundamental pillar of SMIGRM, which we will now introduce.

How does the financial world today protect investments from storms (crashes, sharp declines, and losses) that are sure to come (we just don't know when or how much)?

Static Allocation: The Solution Adopted by Industry and Academia

The most common solution adopted by the investment management industry to deal with market declines is **asset allocation**. When the situation worsens, it is natural for them to carry out operations to protect portfolios or implement risk reduction measures. However, the central element remains asset allocation, which is kept as fixed and balanced as possible. This is because a well-planned portfolio (carefully selected stocks usually need a good time horizon to yield results) means that portfolio managers do not like to change the allocation, but when a sharp decline comes, it comes without warning. I call this type of asset allocation **Static** or **Fixed Allocation**, which is what the financial industry adopts, because the allocation does not usually vary in response to what happens in the market. In other words, the market may crash, but the same allocation remains fixed, unchanged. If it is a 60/40 allocation (the most famous in the financial industry, i.e., 60% allocation in stocks and 40% in fixed income), it will remain 60/40, even if the market is up or down.

In fact, it was designed this way precisely so that it can perform well in all types of markets (up or down). If you believe that when the market is up (*bull market*), the 60% equity portion will yield excellent results. But when the market is *bearish*, the 40% fixed income portion will be able to cover at least a good part of the losses from the equity portion. In other words, the allocation was designed to cope with both scenarios and not be changed in response to the market. This is what I call **Static Allocation**.

The idea behind a static mixed portfolio of stocks and fixed income securities (bonds) is the belief that the correlation between stock and bond returns is low, or even negative, meaning that they tend to move in opposite directions. Theoretically, if this is true, gains from bonds could offset at least part of the losses from stocks during difficult times in the stock market. This belief is so strong that the financial industry has created standard recommendations for investors of all different age groups. For young people, a higher proportion of stocks relative to bonds is suggested, such as 80% in stocks and 20% in bonds. For older people, however, the recommendations indicate a higher allocation to bonds and a lower allocation to stocks. The reason is simple: young people have a longer investment horizon, which allows them to better weather market fluctuations and declines. On the other hand, older people, especially those close to retirement, do not have as much time to recover losses, so they should prioritize bonds over stocks in their portfolios.

Theoretically, it seems perfect... the industry and academia have embraced this as the definitive solution. And they sell it ready-made to customers. Even investors who do everything themselves have adopted the same solution: building diversified portfolios with stocks from various sectors, as well as bonds and other assets. It is the well-known best practice of not putting all your eggs in one basket. I myself learned this way, always believed it, and always built portfolios with this mindset. However...

The Correlation Problem

However, this **strategy is not as solid as** it **seems**. History shows that the relationship between stocks and bonds is more complex than previously thought and assumed. Studies indicate that the correlation between them depends on multiple factors that change all the time, such as inflation, interest rates, economic growth expectations, and even stock market volatility. For example, in 2002, the S&P 500® index fell 18.6%, but **bonds did not offset these losses**. On the contrary, they had one of their worst performances in 97 years, with the Vanguard Total Bond Index showing a loss of 13.7%. In other words, both stocks and fixed-income bonds fell together, resulting in losses, regardless of how the portfolio was allocated, whether 80/20 or 20/80, in the end everyone lost.

Exhibit 3: Bonds don't hedge equities in an inflationary world
Rolling 24 month correlation between stocks and bonds

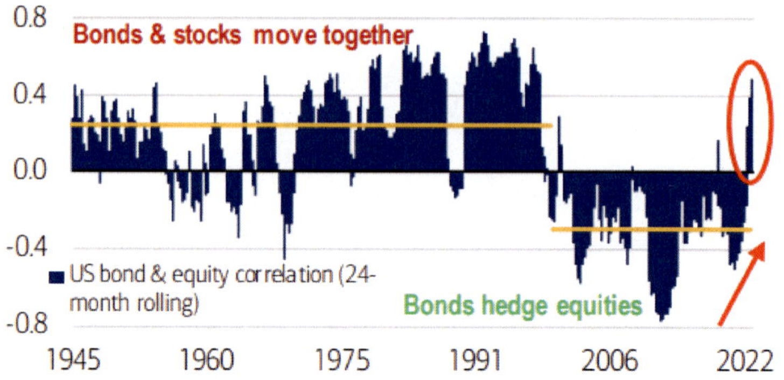

Source: BofA Research Investment Committee, Global Financial Data

BofA GLOBAL RESEARCH

See the table above prepared by Bank of America showing how the correlation between stocks and bonds has changed throughout history since the post-war period. Note that it fluctuates. There are periods when the correlation is positive and other periods when the correlation is negative. Its amplitude also varies greatly over time.

The entire theoretical basis that underpins Portfolio Theory, Portfolio Risk Minimization, and Traditional Static Allocation is based on the premise that the correlation between portfolio assets is low or preferably negative. As can be seen, this premise is ultimately very weak.

It is no wonder that investors, both amateur and professional, have poor results over time that they cannot explain. There is no point in blaming the market every time you underperform on the stock market. One reason may be that the correlation has changed and you were not even aware of it. In 2022, imagine the number of investors who were caught off guard when the correlation shifted from negative to positive and the stock and bond portfolios of countless investors immediately began to lose money heavily!

But what if, instead of bonds, which have the correlation problem, we replaced them with other assets? Great idea. However, finding assets that have a negative correlation with stocks, or at least a positive but low correlation with stocks, is very difficult. They practically don't exist!

Long Term Investment Correlations. Time Period: 5/1/2009 to 4/30/2019

Investment	1	2	3	4	5	6	7	8
1 U.S. Large Blend	1.00							
2 Foreign Large Blend	0.88	1.00						
3 High Yield Bond	0.75	0.81	1.00					
4 Corporate Bond	0.30	0.45	0.69	1.00				
5 Intermediate Core Bond	0.14	0.30	0.52	0.95	1.00			
6 Intermediate Government	-0.26	-0.14	0.02	0.62	0.82	1.00		
7 Short Government	-0.15	-0.02	0.13	0.64	0.82	0.94	1.00	
8 Money Market–Taxable	-0.02	-0.03	-0.06	-0.04	-0.04	0.01	0.10	1.00

1.00 to 0.80
0.80 to 0.60
0.60 to 0.40
0.40 to 0.20
0.20 to 0.00
0.00 to -0.20
–0.20 to –0.40
–0.40 to –0.60
–0.60 to –0.80
–0.80 to –1.00

Source: Morningstar Direct.

This table is just an example. There are almost no assets that have a low correlation with stocks, maintain this correlation over time, and also have a minimally acceptable expected return (you don't want very weak assets in your portfolio, do you?). The problem is that almost all assets in an economy align in one way or another with the economy itself. Thus, they all tend to have a positive correlation with stocks...

This was the first major problem with Static Allocation: - The Correlation Problem.

But this is not the only problem with Static Allocation. There is another one that is just as problematic...

The Problem of Attenuated Returns

Even if the correlation premise were valid, the static allocation strategy would still not be ideal, as it sacrifices returns in exchange for security. This is seen as a "protection cost," but it ends up reducing the potential return, attenuating it. For example, Vanguard's VBIAX fund is a good 60/40 fund, which maintains a fixed allocation of 60% in stocks and 40% in bonds, generating an annualized return of 6.70% since its launch in 2000. Stocks in the United States represented by the S&P 500 index have an annualized return of 8% to 12%. Thus, the return on VBIAX is low in comparison because part of the stock gains earned in good times was sacrificed to cover losses in bad times.

Understand what is happening. Whenever you take assets with lower potential returns and lower risk to compose a portfolio with assets with higher returns and risk, you create a portfolio that is average in both return and risk. Lowering risk is great, but lowering potential returns along with it is not a good idea. In static allocation, you do exactly that. You are forced to sacrifice stock returns to protect yourself from potential crashes and losses that you don't even know when or how they will come—but you know they will come. Since you don't have this information about *the timing* of crashes, you are forced to take precautions by making a 60/40 or 50/50 allocation, for example. When the crash comes, at least your losses will be mitigated. The problem is the cost of this: your returns will also be mitigated. And worse, your returns will be mitigated with 100% certainty if you have made a static allocation. The crash may be slow in coming, but you have already come out with mitigated returns in anticipation.

And that is the second big problem with Static Allocation: - The Problem of Mitigated Returns.

Now, perhaps a light bulb is going off in your brain as you read this text. You may be asking yourself: "What if, instead of allocating stocks and bonds in the portfolio to face any scenario (up or down), we put 100% in stocks when the market is up (*bull market*) and 100% in bonds when the market is down (*bear market*)?

If you asked yourself this question, congratulations, you are on your way to completing the last fundamental pillar of SMIGRM.

So why not allocate 100% to stocks in good times and switch to 100% bonds in bad times, instead of rigidly allocating 60% to stocks and 40% to bonds all the time?

If you have asked this question, you are on the right track to one of the fundamental pillars of SMIGRM, which we will detail in Chapter 8, below. It is what we call **Contextual Dynamic Allocation (context-dependent)**.

Contextual Dynamic Allocation: A Game-Changing Innovation

See the table below to visualize and contrast Contextual Dynamic Allocation with Traditional Static Allocation:

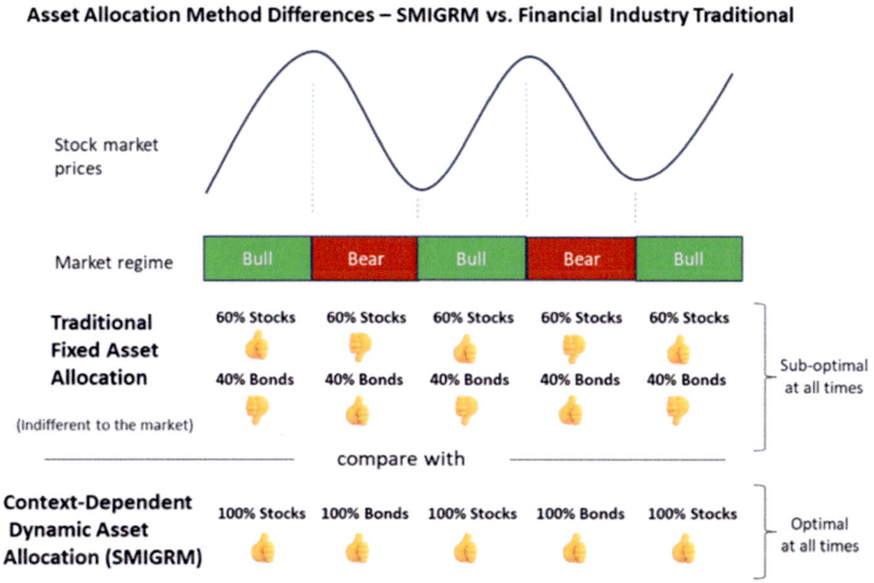

The idea is to adopt a dynamic, context-based approach rather than maintaining a fixed, static allocation. This means adjusting the assets in the portfolio according to the current scenario, maximizing returns rather than accepting a suboptimal strategy in all scenarios (high or low). While in Traditional Static Allocation, the allocation is immutable and independent of the context or risk environment around it, Contextual Dynamic Allocation will rotate the assets in the portfolio according to the context or risk environment around it at any given moment.

See the example in the table above: when the market is bullish, in Contextual Dynamic Allocation, we allocate 100% to stocks. When the market is bearish, we allocate 100% to bonds. Instead of having a suboptimal portfolio in all scenarios with Traditional Static Allocation, we will have an optimized portfolio in all scenarios with Contextual Dynamic Allocation. This is the key difference that will make a crucial difference in your results over time.

SMIGRM calls this way of allocating portfolios Contextual Dynamic Allocation, and the context is the risk environment. The solution is to apply **dynamic asset allocation, guided by the current risk context**, adjusting your exposure to risky assets (such as stocks) or safe assets (such as cash, gold, or bonds) based on the reading of the environment—something that the **RISP 500™ indicator** was designed to do with excellence. The **RISP 500™ indicator** was created precisely to consolidate risk information accurately and unequivocally, based 100% on data extracted from the market in real time, so that we can define exactly the risk environment we find ourselves in at any given moment.

In other words, **instead of maintaining a fixed and rigid allocation that is suboptimal in all scenarios, why not combine the assets that perform best in each scenario and replace them according to each scenario?**

This means **being optimized all the time instead of suboptimal all the time**. How do we define scenarios or contexts? SMIGRM defines them as the corresponding risk environment. The reason will become clear as you read the rest of this chapter, but in short, **risky assets (e.g., stocks) tend to perform better in low- and moderate-risk environments. In contrast, safe assets (e.g., T-Bills, gold, etc.) tend to**

perform better under high-risk environments. We mean relative to other assets, of course. This is due to investors' risk aversion. Everyone has a different risk tolerance, but everyone has one. As risk or uncertainty increases, investors tend to get rid of riskier assets, pushing their prices down. Therefore, SMIGRM requires continuous measurement of market risk (this is the mission of RISP 500™: Risk Index for the S&P 500®) to orchestrate the **rotation between risky assets and safe assets**. That is why we call the process **Contextual Dynamic Allocation**.

Eliminating Rigidity: The Problem with Fixed Ideas

Just as bad as allocating assets in a fixed, rigid, or static manner is having a fixed belief. You know that person who is so fixated on an idea that "no amount of persuasion" can convince them otherwise? You've surely seen experts predicting the end of the world for the stock market lately? Last year? The year before? I'm sure you even know some of them. Especially when the stock market is doing very well, these people seem to shout even louder. They assume that everything that goes up must come down. They always seem to be the same people, the *permabears* (permanent believers in *a bear market*). Do you find this kind of advice useful? The U.S. stock market has performed impressively since the end of World War II, with 80 years of a long *bull market*. There have been many sharp declines, of course, some even spectacular, but for the most part, it has been a persistent and long bull market.

Generally, these gurus never give a specific timeframe for their predictions of declines, or their timeframes are repeatedly proven wrong. Eternal prophets of doom don't really help anyone. They may scare novice investors, but most people simply ignore them after a while. On the other hand, there are also the *permabulls*. They are usually on the selling side of the financial industry. The myth that "stocks always go up in the long run" was probably also originated by them. However, neither *permabears* nor *permabulls* are useful to anyone. They do not add value to your investment methods and results, but they can destabilize them by throwing you off course for no plausible reason from time to time. Their advice would only be valuable if they could also predict the exact (or even approximate) timing of a decline. Everyone already knows that declines have occurred many times in the past and will continue to occur in the future. Without critical information about *timing*, honestly, just shouting that the big bad wolf is coming doesn't help anyone.

Investing by dynamically allocating in response to market changes does not mean you need to become a trader. There are many investors who do not want to become active traders and do not have the time for it, which is totally understandable. But sitting in a totally passive "Buy & Hold" position without caring if a crash is occurring or about to occur is not a smart solution either. We believe the best solution is somewhere in the middle: invest for the long term but keep an eye on the market—you don't have to do it every minute like traders do—but once a day or every few days and take the necessary action to protect your investments is a smart solution that most people can do without much effort.

Flexibility: Matching the Best Assets with Their Respective Risk Environments

The solution begins with understanding that each type of asset behaves differently in response to different external contextual conditions. Under the right conditions, stocks will have their best or worst days. The same is true for any other type of asset, such as bonds, real estate, gold, etc. This is obvious, but few have actually created investment decision methods or models to exploit this because the number of factors to consider is enormous and they have interdependencies, making the task very complicated. In our search for solutions, we faced the same obstacles. However, we focused on a smaller but crucial set of variables to simplify this enormous problem and concentrated our efforts solely on the stock market (since most other assets have relatively high correlations with it). This book will provide more details on how we arrived at this solution (we weren't the only ones), but I can say this much here: we chose RISK environments to define context. There are two obvious reasons for this:

Investor Risk Aversion Principle: when risks and uncertainty increase, investors seek safety by selling risky assets, which in turn reduces their prices, and vice versa. Therefore, there is more than correlation here; there is **a cause-and-effect relationship**, which is a much stronger inverse relationship than just correlation between risk and the probability of the market rising or falling.

Returns are produced by taking risks: as discussed earlier, you only had the privilege of earning a return because you took a risk. There is also a strong **cause-and-effect relationship** here: no risk, no reward; higher risk, higher chances of getting a higher return.

By categorizing various levels of risk in the stock market, the solution proposes investing only in the best-performing assets to explo t each risk level. This means combining the right assets with each contextual risk environment to maximize return potential. It also means exploiting risks to maximize investment performance, rather than being controlled by them. We believe that **risk management should be more active than reactive**. For example, when risks are high, it is time to migrate to safer assets such as Treasury bonds, money market funds, gold, or even cash. But when risks are low, invest in risky assets such as stocks, index ETFs, and even leveraged ETFs.

Now, compare this dynamic, context-dependent approach to asset allocation with the static approach to asset allocation adopted by most of the investment management industry, or even with the permanent "Buy & Hold" approach. Which one do you think should, logically, outperform? Think about it. How many carefully and skillfully planned portfolios thrived or at least survived the impacts of the sharp market declines in 2000, 2008, or 2020? It doesn't matter what percentages are allocated to stocks, bonds, commodities, real estate, etc. — it's just a question of which allocation lost more or less money, because they all lost or failed to gain what they could have gained if they had adopted a dynamic, context-dependent allocation strategy to adjust to changing market conditions in a timely manner.

Do you see the difference? In the book, you will discover why Contextual Dynamic Allocation is the first step toward a robust method of "Risk Management Guided Stock Market" (SMIGRM) investing.

Market Timing through Contextual Dynamic Allocation for Maximum Performance

With Contextual Dynamic Allocation, guided by the RISP 500 risk indicator, which we will introduce in Chapter 8 along with the SMIGRM Method, investors will be able to time the market accurately!

We will learn that when the RISP 500 risk indicator shows an increase in market risk above the risk tolerance levels predefined by each investor, they will be signaled to sell their risky positions in the market (their stocks, etc.) and seek safe assets. But when the RISP 500 indicator shows that market risk has fallen to levels within their risk tolerance, investors can return to repurchase their shares.

In this way, the investor will not only be implementing Contextual Dynamic Allocation but also executing the *timing* of their investments in the market. In Chapter 8, it will become clearer why, but compared to traditional static allocation (60/40 or *All Weather*, etc.), Contextual Dynamic Allocation will ultimately result in:

- Higher returns
- Lower risk
- Better performance (higher return/risk ratio)

Many people think that *market timing* is impossible. Traders often use technical analysis (charting) to guide them in executing *market timing*. But many people don't like technical analysis. It is based on past trends and chart patterns, but without scientific rigor or an objective formulation that everyone can agree on. Different technical analysts looking at the same charts may reach different conclusions. In other words, there is a lot of room for analyst subjectivity. On the other hand, this problem does not exist with Contextual Dynamic Allocation in the SMIGRM Method.

There is no such thing as bad weather, only inappropriate clothing

As you can see, the same is true for stock investing: **there is no such thing as a bad market; only the wrong assets invested at the wrong time, under unfavorable circumstances**.

Now, you may ask: what about so-called "***all-weather***" portfolios? Would these portfolios, specially designed to withstand all types of market conditions, solve the problem? Well, let's examine how these portfolios are constructed. If you read the fund prospectus, you will easily discover that it is still a static portfolio. It is just more diversified than most funds, with other asset classes included, such as stocks, bonds, gold, commodities, and cash. Sure, it can withstand "bad times" (market downturns) better than portfolios composed solely of stocks or stocks and bonds, but by fixing the allocation and making it largely insensitive to changes in market conditions over cycles, it seriously sacrifices gains during stock market booms.

Now consider this: wouldn't it be smarter to combine the best-performing assets specifically for each context or external scenario that arises?

You see, there is no way around this problem resulting from fixed and static portfolio allocations. You may argue that since everyone in the investment management industry does things a certain way, it must be the right way or what is called best practice, right? Yes, but only until someone comes along who has found better ways to do the same things: that's called progress. That's called evolution. It's time for the investment management industry to rethink the old, traditional ways (which only serve the interests of the industry itself and not its clients) and start evolving again.

If you're still not convinced, let me offer a simple analogy to show the absurdity of the situation. Suppose you are building or investing in a professionally managed "***all*** *weather*" portfolio with the following (very typical) allocation:

- 40% Stocks
- 40% Bonds
- 10% Commodities
- 10% Gold

... and you maintain this allocation to weather bull markets, bear markets, economic booms, recessions, inflation, and high and low interest rates, etc. What will happen? Simple: at any given moment, with a different external context (or "weather"), part of your portfolio will perform excellently, while the rest will perform poorly. Overall, you will do "so-so," with a return below potential. After all, the portfolio was designed to work exactly like this. As an obvious result, it will probably never perform very well, on average or as a whole, in the long run.

Now, let me present the analogy: you are about to go on a long *outdoor* trip full of adventures. Let's say you are hiking and exploring a trail through fields and forests with lots of nature and *outdoor activities*. Since you know you will likely encounter different types of weather (heat, cold, rain, snow, wind, etc.), you must be prepared. So, before leaving home, you will wear:

- 40% T-shirts
- 40% Raincoat
- 10% Winter jacket

- 10% Long-sleeved clothing

Would you really wear all these different layers of clothing **at the same time** (and **keep** them **on throughout the trip**), as prescribed? Or would you prefer to simply wear what is appropriate for the moment and carry the rest in your backpack? If you answered "yes," why would you do the same with your investment portfolio? It becomes so obvious when we stop to think logically.

Therefore, in our view, portfolios should be actively managed, dynamically changing the allocation in response to changing market conditions. This means rotating assets immediately as the situation unfolds in different "weather conditions." But then, the next question is: how can this be done?

We believe that the common denominator that consolidates the information from each contextual scenario is RISK. This is because, in addition to the two main reasons presented above, risk consolidates all market concerns, uncertainties, and fears into a single measurable number at any given time. By measuring risk in the system at every moment, we can gain a good understanding of changes in the market "climate" and respond appropriately.

This is precisely why the SMIGRM Method stands for *Stock Market Investment Guided by Risk Management*. Risk Management can and should be used proactively (rather than reactively) and take on the central role of guiding investment decisions. As we will show in Chapter 8, risk is directly related to the probabilities of the stock market rising or falling (remember that this is due to the principle of risk aversion). **After all, since investing in the stock market is a risky business and you can only expect to earn a return if you take risks, wouldn't it be natural to use risk information to guide investment decisions?**

Often, it is in the simple things in life that we can find the greatest wisdom. Filter out all the noise, confusion, and complexities of modern life. Go back to basics and reflect. Sometimes the answer can be found in the unpredictability of life or in common sense things, as simple as wearing the right clothes for the different weather conditions we encounter.

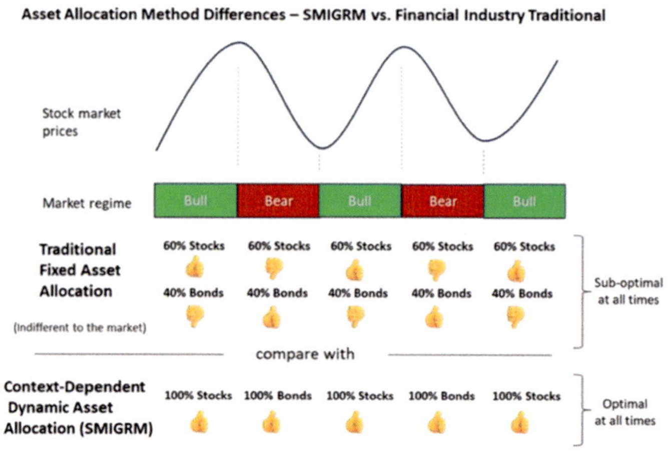

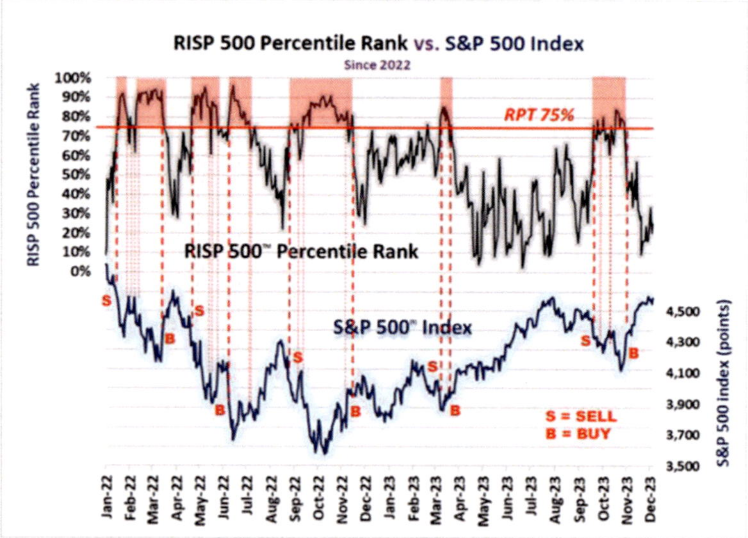

Chapter 8. SMIGRM Method: "Stock Market Investing Guided by Risk Management"

In this chapter, we will present something exceptional that you will not find in any other book or course by another author. It is the SMIGRM Method, which has proven day after day, month after month, and year after year to be extremely useful, if not crucial, in achieving exceptional results, including:

- Avoided all crashes in the US stock market since its creation and implementation, including serious corrections that occur more frequently.
- Reduced *drawdowns* across the entire investment horizon, including the average and maximum *drawdown* experienced during the period.
- Functioned as an excellent *market timing* tool, signaling optimal market entry and exit points in the vast majority of cases, especially at the most critical moments, when evaluating the post-investment past.
- Resulted in superior performance from the point of view of performance indicators such as RoMaD (*Return Over Maximum Drawdown*). In other words, SMIGRM enabled investors to maximize returns for each unit of risk assumed.
- It beat the S&P 500, which is an extremely difficult task for the vast majority of investors and professional portfolio and fund managers.

This chapter is the heart of this book—the most important one. It is what sets it apart from all other books on investing in the US stock market. SMIGRM has worked for us for over a decade (it has undergone continuous adjustments and improvements over time) and for many who follow it today. I am sure it will also work for you and many others who want to and know how to implement it.

Best Alternative to a Crystal Ball?

Imagine for a moment a world where it was possible to know in advance—especially before everyone else—where the market is headed or what the next price of a stock will be on your computer screen. That would solve all our challenges as investors and traders, wouldn't it? We would have a huge, enormous advantage. We would avoid all the downturns and make the most of all the upturns. We would be able to time the market perfectly!

Now, back to reality: there is no crystal ball. But then, what would be the best alternative to guide us in such an unpredictable world? After all, a single wrong trade or decision or a sudden market crash is enough to wipe out all the performance we have taken months or even years to build.

Stop now and think: are you using the BEST tools to manage your investments? Are these tools really protecting your profits during market downturns and helping you take advantage of them during rallies? And most importantly: are you being fairly rewarded for the risk you are taking?

When you hear "risk management," what comes to mind? Perhaps terms such as VAR, stop loss, hedge, diversification, beta, Sharpe ratio, simulations, volatility, and correlation. All of these are very useful and have their analytical value. But these tools are designed only to manage risk—not to avoid it before the worst happens. They control your exposure by adjusting or protecting positions, but they don't warn you when it's time to get out of the risk altogether. In other , they are designed to be triggered when you have already lost a lot of money in response to an unfavorable situation that is already underway.

If you had a crystal ball, you wouldn't need any of this. You would be out of the market well before the most violent declines. But since it doesn't exist, what can you do?

A Solution Emerges: SMIGRM and RISP 500™

The SMIGRM (Stock Market Investment Guided by Risk Management) method presents an approach in which risk is no longer just something to be managed but is used, or even exploited, strategically. Think about it. Let's take a few steps back to the basics. How do you make money in the stock market? By taking risks! Profits in the markets are generated precisely because we accept to take risks. But... when you decide to make investment decisions, such as building a stock portfolio, is risk at the center of your decisions? Probably not — and it's not your fault. The right tools for this have never existed... until now.

With SMIGRM, which we will explain in detail below, risk management takes on a central and proactive role. This chapter will show how SMIGRM and the RISP 500™ indicator are revolutionizing the way risk management is used — becoming the best alternative to a crystal ball. Does that sound like an exaggeration? Perhaps. But we believe you will be pleasantly surprised. Keep reading and draw your own conclusions.

Creating a Roadmap for Success in a Risk Environment

The SMIGRM method is rapidly gaining popularity in the US, but if it's new to you, don't worry, because it's easy to understand. In this book, we'll guide you step by step, always with logic and clarity.

To begin with, it is essential that you understand the **four fundamental pillars** of the SMIGRM method. They are:

- **The Risk vs. Return Duality**
- **Deterministic vs. Probabilistic World**
- **The Formula for Success: Statistical Advantage + Asymmetric Return + Law of Large Numbers**
- **Static Allocation vs. Contextual Dynamic Allocation**

These concepts are the foundation that underpins the SMIGRM philosophy, so they will be presented before we even get into the practical core of the chapter. Our goal is to prepare you—both conceptually and practically—for a new way of thinking about investments, and to invest in a much smarter and safer way.

We hope that this journey will be not only educational, but also transformative. And that it will open your eyes to a new universe of possibilities, with real potential to substantially improve your results as an individual investor or asset manager.

Investor Preferences Are Evolving

Before we dive into the core concepts of the SMIGRM method, it is worth taking a step back and looking at two major trends that are shaping investor behavior at the beginning of the 21st century.

The first major trend is the accelerated adoption of **index funds.** Since emerging in the 1990s as an alternative to traditional mutual funds, ETFs that track major stock indexes—such as the S&P 500® and Nasdaq 100®—have gained enormous popularity. That's because they offer a simple, accessible, and inexpensive way to invest in the stock market, which appeals to everyone from beginners to more experienced investors.

The second major trend is the steady growth of **the** so-called **DIY (Do It Yourself) investor**. More and more people are taking control of their own investments, making decisions on their own, without relying entirely on financial advisors. This change is largely driven by the democratization of information and technology. Today, all you need is a cell phone or computer with internet access for anyone to learn, operate, and monitor their investments on their own.

This DIY movement is not restricted to the field of finance. It is repeated in other areas of life: health, education, technology, entrepreneurship, etc. People are less dependent on traditional authorities such as doctors, lawyers, accountants, or consultants. The internet and now artificial intelligence have become primary sources of information. This has radically changed the way we deal with knowledge and important decisions.

For professionals—such as financial advisors and wealth managers—this represents a major challenge: **they need to deliver more value than ever before**. Offering basic guidance is no longer enough. Modern investors want results, protection against losses, transparency, and control. And above all, they want to know that they are being well rewarded for the risk they are taking.

Given this scenario, we need to rethink the tools and methods we use to invest. And that is exactly what this chapter proposes to do: **present a new approach, more suited to the current times and the new expectations of investors.**

The Secret to Investment Performance in an Environment of Uncertainty

Over time, I have become increasingly convinced of a simple but profound truth: **the secret to this success is hidden in plain sight—everywhere in the universe**.

As human beings, we have a natural tendency to want to relate cause and effect in a direct and predictable way. We learn that if we study, we get good grades. If we work hard, we are rewarded. If we take medicine, we are cured. If we pray hard enough, our wishes will be granted. If we invest based on what we have learned in finance, we will get good returns. This deterministic view of the world gives us comfort and a sense of control. It works very well in areas such as classical physics—for example, with Newton's Law of Gravity, we know exactly how an object will behave when it falls.

But the problem is that **the real world—especially the world of investing—doesn't work that way**. It is uncertain, unpredictable, and constantly changing. And in this type of environment, deterministic formulas and static models rarely deliver predictable and consistent results.

Despite this, many widely taught and used investment methods still operate as if we lived in a predictable world. Investors analyze companies diligently, build a balanced portfolio, wait patiently for the fruits, and review it periodically. It seems logical, doesn't it? So why do so many investors (professionals and amateurs, experienced and beginners) fail to achieve consistent returns over time? Why do those who win today lose tomorrow, and why does the life of an investor seem like a yo-yo? The answer lies precisely in **the probabilistic nature of the market**.

We live in a world of probabilities, not certainties. And this applies even more strongly to the financial market. Risk—a concept so prevalent in investors' vocabulary—exists because **we don't know what will happen tomorrow**. Prices change. The context changes. What is an opportunity today may be a trap tomorrow. Everything is in constant motion.

In this scenario, **using investment methods that ignore this variability is like driving a race car with your eyes closed and hoping the track never curves**.

That is why this chapter proposes a new approach. Instead of fighting uncertainty, **let's learn to use it to our advantage**. Do you know who can do this masterfully?

Casinos, insurance companies, and *venture* capital funds.

Casinos are the most notorious example of those who operate games in an environment of risk and uncertainty. Insurance companies price insurance policies based on actuarial science, which involves serious statistical studies of claims and the factors that affect the probability of their occurrence. Like casinos and insurance companies, venture *capital* funds that invest in start-ups that have not yet proven themselves in the market can only survive and still make a lot of money operating in highly uncertain environments because they know how to deal with probabilities very well. These funds typically invest small amounts in a large number of *start-ups*. The vast majority of these investments will not even return the capital invested, and the funds know this. And there is no point in doing fundamental analysis on these companies because it is not the right tool.

The secret to success in these ventures, as in stock market investing, lies in applying three fundamental concepts widely used by some of the most successful industries in high-risk environments, such as casinos, insurance companies, and *venture* capital funds:

- **A Small Statistical Advantage**
- **An Asymmetric Return**
- **The Law of Large Numbers**

This is the formula for investing wisely in an uncertain or probabilistic world. Let's dive into each of these pillars below — and show, with practical examples, how they can be applied to your own investment process. When used correctly, these principles allow individual investors **to play the game with the odds in their favor — just like casinos do.**

And that changes everything.

The Formula for Success: Statistical Advantage + Asymmetric Return + Law of Large Numbers

If we live in a world where the future is uncertain and outcomes are unpredictable, then it makes no sense to use tools that treat everything as if it were deterministic or guaranteed. Unfortunately, this is still very common in the world of investing. *Valuation* models, price projections, technical or fundamental analyses... many of them work as if we were dealing with the laws of physics, where everything is predictable. Of course, those who use these tools know that there is uncertainty in the stock market. But the tools, methods, and models do not include probability and statistics within them. So in practice, even though the user knows that there is a lot of uncertainty in their calculations, these do not treat uncertainty mathematically in their results and therefore lead to conclusions that implicitly assume a high degree of determinism.

The truth is that these investment methods, which have been established over decades, accepted and used throughout the financial industry, and also taught in business schools, assume that the world is more or less deterministic and that we humans have more control over outcomes than we actually do. Unfortunately, the real world is nothing like that. Any asset that appears undervalued or overvalued today will likely not look the same tomorrow because the environment is constantly changing. It is a moving target and cannot be accurately determined because the underlying context is also always changing.

In our lives, it's great when we feel like we have the whole process of anything under control because there will be no surprises. In contrast, we don't like random processes that we can't control. We don't feel safe and in control of the situation. Even Einstein was bothered by the randomness of the quantum world — he famously once said that "God does not play dice with the universe." As humans, we really don't like non-deterministic relationships. But they are everywhere in nature. The entire universe is non-deterministic. And so is the outcome of everything we do. The universe is random. Everything that happens in life is non-deterministic. We actually live in a probabilistic world. Sorry, Professor Einstein, but God does play dice with the universe. Have you ever heard the expression "game of numbers"? In business, everything is a game of numbers. For sales and marketing, for example, there is no single advertising message or marketing method that resonates with everyone, resulting in 100% success. There will be better and worse messages, but it will still be a game of numbers. So, this is where the solution begins: Probability and Statistics.

In investing, when investors ignore probabilities by focusing solely on the projected virtues of an investment, they are making bets that are ultimately riskier than they realize or less risky than they would like. The consequences of the first situation are very frequent losses that can outweigh gains. The consequences of the second situation are unimpressive gains below potential. In both situations, failing to measure risks adequately before diving into investments invariably results in *underperformance* in the long run: either through heavy losses caused by market crashes from time to time or through poor remuneration for the risks taken.

So, how can we navigate this uncertain environment that is the world of investments? The answer lies in using a tool, method, or model that has an intrinsically **statistical** approach—more specifically, a formula that combines three powerful ingredients:

1. Create a Small Statistical Edge

The logic here is simple: **you only enter into a trade when the odds are in your favor**. That's what a casino does. It doesn't know whether it will win or lose on a specific play, but it knows that over time, if it has a small statistical advantage, that will be enough to ensure consistent profits in the long run.

You see, the casino doesn't need a big advantage to ensure that the house always wins in the long run. For example, when playing roulette, the maximum a player can win for a single number bet is 36 to 1. However, if you look closely at roulette wheels, you will see that in addition to the numbers 1 through 36, they also have 0 and sometimes a 00 as well. The actual odds are then 37 to 1 or 38 to 1, not 36 to 1 as it may appear at first glance. The house edge, with these odds in its favor, represents the average gross profit that the casino can confidently expect over many plays. The casino does not intend to break a player in a single session—it just wants to make sure that, in the long run, players leave with a little less money than they came in with, leaving the house profit in the house's coffers. In this way, **even in an environment of uncertainty such as a game of roulette, the casino is able to apply the laws of probability and statistics in its favor to virtually guarantee a positive outcome**.

In the stock market, this statistical advantage can come, for example, from a tool that tells you when the environment is more likely to rise than fall in probabilistic terms—such as the **RISP 500™ indicator**, which we present in this chapter. If you only trade when the odds are in your favor, you are "playing like the house" by emulating the strategy of casinos in uncertain environments—and that completely changes the game.

2. Create a Favorable Asymmetric Return

When you risk your money, ideally the **potential reward should be much greater than the potential loss**. If you risk losing $1, you should aim to earn $2, $3, or more, for example. This asymmetry will make all the difference in your results over time.

For inspiration, look at how venture capital funds do it. Studies show that 58% of the startups they invest in typically do not even return the capital invested. That's high risk! So they need at least a few startups to return 5x-10x the capital invested or more for every 100 startups they invest in just to stay in the game. They usually target startups with a minimum potential of 10x. For early-stage startups, in the idea or incubation phase, investors aim for up to 30x! Otherwise, it's not even worth trying, which is why they filter out the vast majority of proposals submitted to them. This is necessary to ensure that the few highly profitable "unicorns" adequately compensate for the losses incurred by the majority of losing bets made in such a risky business. You see, the lower the chances of success (or the higher the risk involved) of an endeavor—any endeavor—the stronger th e asymmetric return required must be. Of course, investing in the stock market is generally much less risky than investing in venture capital (just an extreme example to illustrate the point), but the logic is exactly the same. Just as the casino manipulates the game in its favor and a venture capital fund operates in an environment of great uncertainty, how can you implement asymmetric returns in your own stock market investment strategy? Here's a suggestion. Simply adopt a behavioral stance that ensures you cut your losses quickly and let your profits run unlimited.

Unfortunately, most investors do the opposite: when their stocks fall in price, they hold on to them in the hope that they will rise again to at least recover their invested capital. This is because, ironically, they hate to lose, but the danger lies precisely in continuing to hold on to a losing position that could get worse. And when their stocks are up, they sell quickly, realizing small profits, also ironically for fear of losing their gains. The result: **they lose a lot when they are wrong and gain little when they are right**. This needs to be reversed!

Another practical way to apply this idea is to use stop-loss orders to limit losses — and let profits grow uninterrupted. For example: if a stock is worth $10 and you estimate that it could rise to $16, you can place a stop at $8. In other words, you are risking $2 to try to earn $6 — a 3-to-1 return. This is asymmetric return. In other words, this is another way to create the basic configuration for favorable asymmetric return.

3. The Law of Large Numbers

According to Wikipedia, the Law of Large Numbers states that "the average of the results obtained from a large number of independent and identical random samples converges to the true value, if it exists ." Wikipedia offers an example: "Although a casino may lose money on a single spin of the roulette wheel, its winnings will tend toward a predictable percentage over a large number of spins."

Statistics is definitely a Numbers Game. Once you have set up a strategy with Statistical Advantage and Asymmetric Return, all you need to do is **repeat that setup multiple times over time**. Just like rolling dice or flipping a coin, after enough attempts, the results will converge to the expected values. Or, just like a casino, you should start to see net profits accumulate over time. Of course, you will experience losses along the way, but you will also experience gains, and if you have set up a Statistical Advantage and Asymmetric Return in your favor, as described above, you will tend to have more gains than losses.

This is the same logic used by insurance companies, casinos, and venture capital funds. They know they will lose many times, but they win enough on other occasions to always end up in the black. You should do the same. It's not about "getting everything right" or winning on every occasion or market movement, but rather **about building a consistent positive track record with well-structured decisions**.

You should always remember to cut your losses early (limiting them to small amounts without letting them grow) and let your profits run (without limiting them while they are growing). By doing these three things together, over time the gods of statistics should favor you and reward you for your discipline.

These three pillars—**Statistical Advantage, Asymmetric Return, and the Law of Large Numbers**—together form the basis of the SMIGRM (Risk Management-Guided Stock Market Investment) method, which we will explore in this chapter. The proposal is simple yet powerful: instead of trying to predict the future, guess, project company performance, interpret figures in past charts, or estimate fair prices or stock futures, **we will operate with the odds in our favor**, as casinos and other smart businesses do in uncertain environments.

Deterministic tools work well in deterministic environments, where predictions and estimates can be made with high reliability. A civil engineer builds bridges and viaducts using deterministic formulas. A pharmacist formulates chemical medicines, and NASA sends astronauts and satellites into space using deterministic formulas and models. And they work very well. None of them really need to use probability and statistics to calculate bridge structures, chemical formulations, and rocket trajectories.

But if you agree that the stock market is a probabilistic environment, where it is impossible to make future predictions and estimates with the same high reliability, unfortunately, the same cannot be said. Using methods and models that ignore probability and statistics to make decisions in the stock market is doomed to failure in the long run. The first symptom will be underperformance (performance below potential). Over time, poor results will only get worse as statistics will be working against you.

It's like using your everyday shoes to ice skate. You can even move around, slipping and falling from time to time. But at what cost! And you will never be able to win a race against someone wearing the right shoes for the icy surface!

There is one last concept we want to discuss because it is really important and will help you understand the ideas and principles of SMIGRM.

Roger Federer, during his commencement speech to the class of 2024 at Dartmouth College, revealed that despite winning almost 80% of all singles tennis matches in his career, his point win rate was only 54%. It's almost a 1:1 ratio between points won and points lost, but Roger had a slight 4% advantage, which was all he needed to become one of the greatest of all time.

Closing the SMIGRM Formulation: Risk Calculation to Guide Decisions

Before moving on to the next fundamental pillar of SMIGRM, let's first do a quick review of the concepts discussed so far:

1. Risk vs. Return Duality

Every investment involves risk. But instead of looking only at potential return, we must monitor and control **RoMaD — Return on Maximum Drawdown** — which measures how much you have gained in relation to the worst loss that has ever been possible in the past. Drawdown is what usually destroys investment plans. Everyone has a loss tolerance limit. When this threshold is exceeded, the investor will trigger the stop loss, much to their chagrin, but they have already exceeded their limit of intelligence and sanity.

This metric helps us **choose strategies that maximize gains with the least possible risk**, which is what every investor should ultimately strive for, the true holy grail of investing.

2. Deterministic World vs. Probabilistic World

Most traditional models treat the market as if it were deterministic (or predictable to a certain extent). But we have already seen that this **is not true**. The world of investing is highly uncertain, influenced by variables that change every day. Therefore, strategies that **accept this uncertainty and operate based on probabilities** are more likely to succeed in the long run.

3. The Triad That Makes Up the Formula for Success in a Risky Environment

Putting it all together, we have the formula:
Statistical Advantage + Asymmetric Return + Law of Large Numbers

With it, we operate with the odds in our favor, we gain more than we lose, and by repeating this over several operations, we obtain consistent profits over time.

4. Contextual Dynamic Allocation

This is the last fundamental pillar of SMIGRM that we introduced in the previous chapter.

In Chapter 7, we describe how, by dynamically allocating the most appropriate assets for each risk level according to the variation in risk over time, we can:

Avoid sharp declines in a bear market and becoming victims of unexpected crashes.

Take full advantage of bull market rallies with confidence.

Explore low-risk environments to invest in higher-risk assets (e.g., leveraged or volatility ETFs) with confidence.

Execute market timing with mastery and confidence.

Optimize the risk-return ratio in all risk environments.

Achieve much higher long-term performance than traditional static allocation.

Through Contextual Dynamic Allocation, together with the tripod of Statistical Advantage + Asymmetric Return + Law of Large Numbers, we will be able to implement the SMIGRM Method.

Risk measurement becomes essential and central to the SMIGRM Method. This lives up to its name: it is truly risk management guiding investment decisions and dynamic allocation. Thus, the crucial requirement for SMIGRM to function properly is market risk measurement. It is not enough to measure the VIX or VAR, calculate historical volatility, perform Monte Carlo simulations, etc., which everyone does. These popular risk management tools are only useful for risk management. They do not help investors make investment decisions and market timing. The challenge is much greater than that.

So how did SMIGRM come about? Are you the inventor/founder of the SMIGRM Method?

Let's take a break from the theoretical formulation of SMIGRM and tell a little of its history.

I am not the only person, nor the first, to apply the fundamental pillars of SMIGRM. Other people have undoubtedly inspired me, and most of them are brilliant and genius individuals. It is possible that I am perhaps the first to bring this knowledge together and organize it, creating a theoretical formulation around it and giving it a name: SMIGRM.

History: How the SMIGRM Method Came About

It all started with a brief informal chat among friends at a bar-café near NYU after a tiring day of work at BBVA bank in New York, where I worked as a derivatives trader, followed by an evening class in the Master's Program (MSc.) in Mathematics for Finance (or Financial

Engineering) at the Courant Institute for Mathematical Sciences at New York University (NYU).

Background: The 2008 Global Financial Crisis

It was 2008, and Lehman Brothers had already gone spectacularly bankrupt. The market was extremely difficult to navigate. SMIGRM did not exist yet, of course. At the trading desk, we used the same traditional tools that everyone else used, which included Technical Analysis (Chartist School) for market timing. However, I always felt the need for a reliable tool based on objective data that was better, more accurate, and more reliable than the existing ones. For me, technical analysis never worked more than 50% of the time, even with many tests and parameter changes, etc., over time.

That night was nothing special. It was like any other night: I was mentally exhausted after a difficult day at the trading desk facing a market in financial crisis, and I ended the day even more exhausted because of the extremely heavy subject of Stochastic Calculus, brilliantly taught by the late Professor Marco Avellaneda. What I needed was a drink, that's for sure... Well, I wasn't the only one who was exhausted; several of my classmates—who also worked at Wall Street firms, banks, and funds as quants, risk managers, etc.—were equally in need of loosening their ties and relaxing a little. So, we all met up after class at this bar-café near the university.

I believe I was the only one in the small group with trading experience who was used to taking risks worth millions with billion-dollar portfolios on the line (or maybe there was one other, but I don't remember). At the time, I had already worked for several international banks and had at least 15 years of experience in trading and risk management, as well as knowledge of quantitative models. I remember telling my colleagues that night the story of a relative of mine in the US (I will omit her identity by calling her only Mary, respecting her privacy) and how much she suffered because of the 2008 Subprime Crisis, like millions of other people in the US. Mary was only two years away from retirement, but she was forced by the huge stock market losses to continue working for many years after that date. Mary had always been extremely disciplined with her finances and her family. She and her husband had worked hard all their lives, even managing to send their three children to Ivy League universities in the US (the most expensive ones), such as Columbia University in New York. Mary did everything by the book. She diversified between stocks and bonds and invested for over 30 years with excellent professional financial advisors. But the crisis caused her to lose half of the wealth she had accumulated over a lifetime of work! During this informal chat, the idea arose to create a market crash warning system based on data that we could extract from the market itself, which could give us early clues! It needed to be a system that would warn us well in advance that something very dangerous was about to happen so that we could seek safety immediately.

Since that night, the group has met for several brainstorming sessions to design something that could lead us to a first prototype. The idea was not to seek the Holy Grail and get rich from it, but to be able to avoid another 2008! It was a rewarding mental exercise in itself. We then began to develop models capable of detecting small changes in data, with the aim of issuing early warnings for market crashes. Despite many efforts and collaborations, none of the models met the standards necessary for an efficient early warning system, and our small testing lab ended up being shut down and the group eventually disbanded.

But I never gave up. Traditional tools, such as technical, fundamental, and macroeconomic analyses, often failed to provide practical answers, especially during periods of market turmoil—precisely when they were most needed. This obvious gap reinforced my determination to find a solution. After all, I had every interest in doing so because it was something that was missing in my day-to-day work!

Decades of familiarity with financial crises

My familiarity with financial crises is nothing new. I grew up in Brazil during a period of hyperinflation, when prices rose 3% a day! My career in banking began right at the time of the Mexican crisis in the early 1990s and continued through other crises, such as the Asian Tiger Crisis, the Russian Crisis, and the Maxidevaluation of the Brazilian Real. Over the years, managing billion-dollar portfolios for my employers, I experienced events such as the bursting of the Internet bubble in 2000, the Global Financial Crisis of 2008, and the Stock Market Crash of 2020 caused by the Coronavirus pandemic. These experiences taught me valuable (and hard) lessons and made it clear that much more robust risk management tools were needed than we had at the time.

After years of research and trial and error, the turning point came with new perspectives on VIX-related products that had been launched or were gaining popularity, advances in research, and more accurate data. I also learned from the work of extremely talented people. Based on this knowledge, I developed and refined new models that integrated data from multiple markets and macroeconomic variables. Still, it took more than 10 years of testing and adjustments to create an algorithm capable of delivering consistent and solid results in live trading.

SMIGRM Was Only Born 10 Years After Much Work and Endless Testing

Several prototypes were created, tested, discarded, redesigned, adjusted, and improved over the years until reaching its most recent version published in 2022. More than a decade has passed since that night at the bar-café at NYU. This algorithm produced a number that consolidated information from more than 15 variables extracted from the market in real time, measuring the risk embedded in the market accurately, quickly, and reliably. This number was named RISP 500™.

This effort then culminated in the creation of SMIGRM (Risk Management Guided Stock Market Investment), a customizable framework designed to help investors balance risk and return that went far beyond early crash detection. SMIGRM eventually became a tool for market timing and risk-return optimization. On January 3, 2022, we launched live trading of eight strategies using our most advanced algorithm, which produced the RISP 500™, a proprietary risk indicator for the S&P 500®. More than just an early crisis detector, our goal evolved to create a tool that investors could adjust to their own risk and return goals. Today, this innovation is a powerful resource for both preserving wealth and achieving above-market returns.

The RISP 500™ Indicator: The Conductor of Contextual Dynamic Allocation

The **RISP 500™ indicator** plays the role of orchestra conductor. It will indicate when we move from one risk environment to anoth (risk has increased or decreased) and what to do in response to this change in context (bull or bear market). First, it is worth explaining why we chose risk as the key variable for defining different market contexts.

There are two main reasons for this relationship:

- **Risk Aversion Principle**: When levels of risk and uncertainty increase, investors tend to seek safety by selling riskier assets. This movement causes a drop in the prices of these assets and, conversely, when risk decreases, prices rise. In this case, it is not just a correlation between risk and market movements, but a **very strong cause-and-effect relationship**, where risk has a **direct impact on the probability** of the market rising or falling.
- **Returns come from exposure to risk**: As discussed earlier, return is the reward for risk taken. There is a clear link between the two: without taking risk, there are no gains; by taking

greater risks, the chances of obtaining higher returns also increase proportionally.

By categorizing the different levels of risk in the stock market, the proposal suggests investing only in the assets that perform best for each level of risk. It is a matter of aligning the appropriate assets with the specific risk environment, maximizing the potential return. In other words, it is about taking advantage of risks to improve investment performance, rather than simply being impacted by them. We believe that risk management should be proactive, not just reactive. For example, when risks are high, it is recommended to migrate to safer assets, such as T-Bills (Treasury bills), money market funds, gold, or even cash. On the other hand, when risks are low, the strategy should focus on stocks, index funds, and even leveraged funds.

This way, we no longer need to build suboptimal portfolios in all scenarios with Static Allocation, which is used throughout the financial industry. Contextual Dynamic Allocation has indeed revolutionized this old financial market practice. I certainly did not invent it. I may be the first to put the idea on paper and give it a name, but I am not its inventor, nor am I the first to put the idea into practice with exceptional results tested in the market for years. Human progress comes precisely from these small adjustments.

Now that we understand the three pillars—**Statistical Advantage**, **Asymmetric Return**, and **the Law of Large Numbers**—and now the last fundamental pillar of Contextual Dynamic Allocation, we have covered all the main fundamental concepts of the SMIGRM method. The goal here is to show how all these pieces fit together to create a robust, logical, and effective investment strategy—one that anyone can execute with mastery and ease.

How RISP 500™ Guides Investors (Super Easy!)

All of this translates into one central question: **how do you make decisions based on measuring the actual and current risk in the market?** The answer lies in **RISP 500™** — the "maestro" that orchestrates the entire execution of SMIGRM.

You will be surprised at how easy it is to execute SMIGRM—so much so that anyone can do it in less than 1 to 5 minutes a day! It is ideal for busy people who don't have time to do a thousand analyses or follow the market all day, every day. It's actually as easy as checking the weather forecast every morning (just one glance and you're done!):

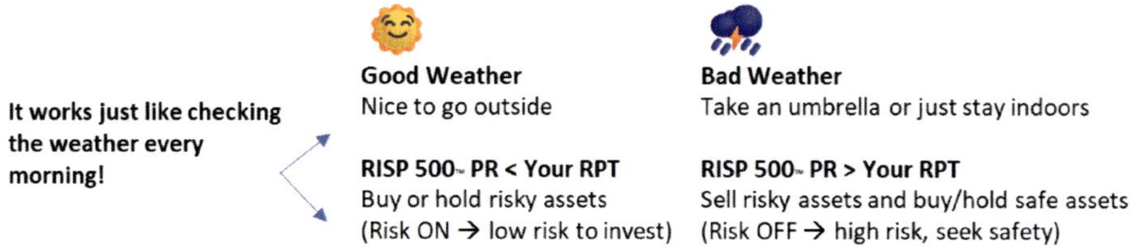

Just like checking the weather forecast for the day, just take a quick look at **the RISP 500™** for the day, usually measured around 10:30 and 11:00 a.m. New York time (at least one hour after the stock market opens at 9:30 a.m. New York time). Just look at the following:

- If today's RISP 500™ percentile is **above** your RPT (explained below), the market today is **too risky for you**, and you should stay out of the stock market. If you are already in, you should sell your stocks. If you are not in the market yet, do nothing; do not enter today. Wait on the sidelines for now. Stay invested in a safe asset, such as bonds, gold, or just stay in cash.
- If today's RISP 500™ percentile is **below** your RPT (explained below), the market today **is not too risky** for you, and you can be in the stock market. If you are already in, keep your stocks invested, just do nothing. If you are not in the market yet, you

can enter by buying stocks today. Sell your safe assets, such as bonds, gold, etc., to rotate into risky assets such as stocks.

With this routine of a few minutes a day, done every day, you will be guided by RISP 500™ and executing your own Market Timing! Who said market timing was impossible? Only people who don't know SMIGRM and those who are stubborn and mentally lazy or unwilling to try new things, stuck in the past and never evolving. We have proven through real data from real experiences in the real market battlefield that SMIGRM works very well as a Market Timing tool. We present evidence further down in this chapter.

By measuring the market risk environment daily based on more than 15 variables from different markets (stocks, bonds, derivatives, economy, volatility, etc.), RISP 500™ delivers a **consolidated risk score**, expressed as **a percentile**. This percentile shows whether the current risk is high, medium, or low compared to the history of the last 15 years and also to your own risk tolerance as an investor. In other words, **RISP 500™** is fully customizable for each investor. This is done this way because the concept of high or low risk depends entirely on each person.

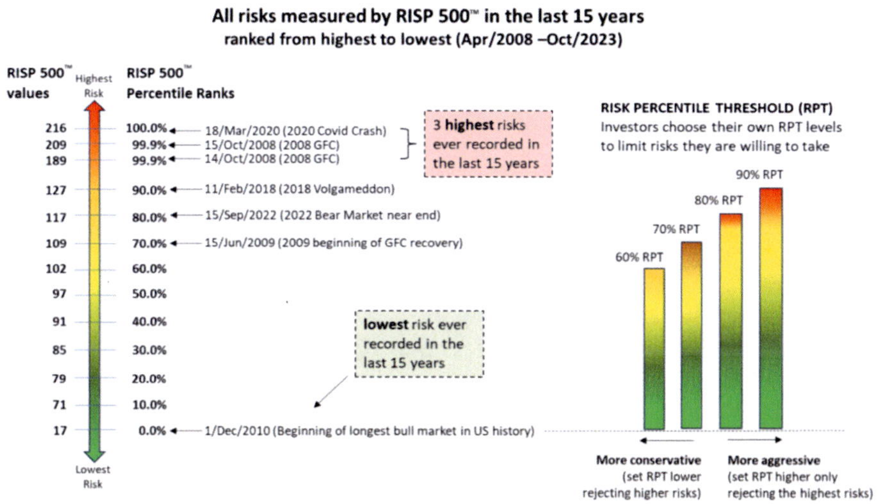

For example:

- If **RISP 500™ is at the 85th percentile**, it means that the current risk is higher than 85% of all risk values measured every day over the last 15 years.

- If you decide to sell your shares at this level, it means you are rejecting risks above the highest 15% ever measured in the last 15 years. You are probably a bold investor.

- If the **RISP 500™ is in the 60th percentile**, it means that the current risk is higher than 60% of all risk values measured every day over the past 15 years.

If you decide to sell your shares at this level, it means you are rejecting risks above the highest 40% ever measured in the last 15 years. You are probably a conservative investor.

To customize **RISP 500™** for you, set your **personal risk threshold** (called RPT — *Risk Percentile Threshold*) based on your own risk tolerance profile:

- **Conservative:** RPT of 65% to 70% — exits the market early when risk rises, avoiding exposure to increasing risks in the market.

- **Moderate:** RPT of 75% to 80% - intermediate range between conservative and aggressive.

- **Aggressive:** RPT of 85% or more - remains exposed to increasing market risks for longer, seeking higher returns.

This system gives you complete control over your risk exposure, something that passive investors and followers of the "buy and hold" strategy do not have. They remain 100% exposed at all times—even during the worst market crashes—ironically thinking that they are adopting a conservative strategy!

See how SMIGRM helped investors time the market in 2022 (a *bear market*) and 2023 (a *bull market* recovering the losses from the previous year). The chart below shows only the most relevant purchases and sales, not all of them, as that would not fit and would clutter the image too much, and illustrates the case of a moderate investor with an RPT of 75%.

Note that every time the black RISP 500™ line crosses the red horizontal RPT line from **bottom to top**, a **sell signal** is created (Risk OFF, i.e., selling risky stocks or assets in search of safety). But whenever the black line of RISP 500™ crosses the horizontal red line of RPT from **top to bottom**, a **buy signal** is created (Risk ON, i.e., buying risky stocks or assets, leaving safety).

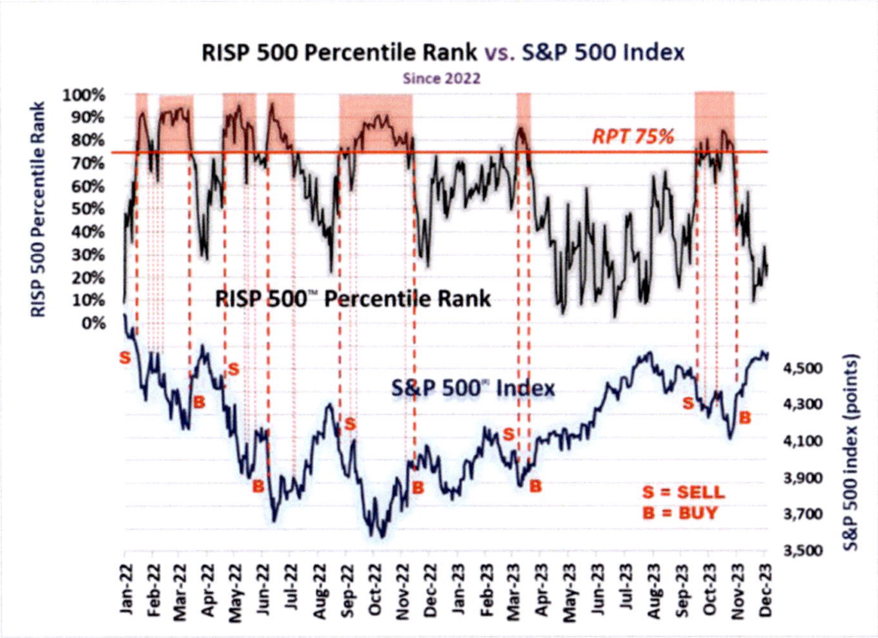

With **SMIGRM**, you are always aligned with the current risk. And with RISP 500™, you get the **best alternative to a crystal ball**: a system that guides you in advance to avoid the worst periods and capture the best moments in the market.

How RPT Impacts Your Results

The choice of RPT directly shapes the behavior and performance of your portfolio:

- A conservative investor with an RPT of 70% will exit the market as soon as risks begin to rise.
- A bold investor with an RPT of 90% will remain exposed to market risks for longer, seeking to capture profits even in turbulent times.
- When risk decreases, the aggressive investor will return to the market sooner; the conservative investor will wait longer before re-entering.

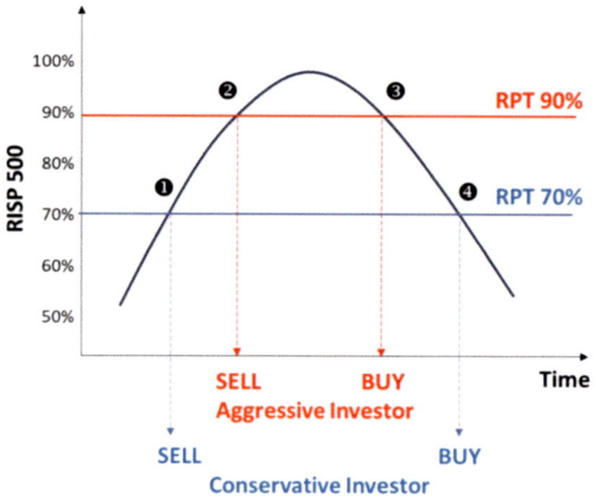

This contrasting behavior illustrates how RPT settings affect your risk exposure and return potential.

The Buy & Hold Fallacy of Passive Investors Who Ignore the Market

Now think about this if you are an investor who follows the **buy & hold** or **passive** style **via index ETFs**, such as the S&P 500. Note that by remaining unchanged in the market, your stocks and ETFs are **exposed**

to risk 100% of the time, even in the worst crises. Don't let sharp corrections and crashes cause you to lose precious time in these holes! Here are some examples to think about:

- The 2022 bear market caused passive investors in the S&P 500 index to lose almost 20%. This loss was only fully recovered at the end of 2023, meaning that passive investors threw two years (one year for the decline and one year for recovery) in the trash.
- The bursting of the Internet bubble in the early 2000s caused passive investors in the S&P 500 index to lose almost 50%. This loss was only fully recovered in 2007, meaning that passive investors threw seven years in the trash.
- The 2008 subprime crisis caused passive investors in the S&P 500 index to lose almost 60%. This loss was only fully recovered in 2013, meaning that passive investors threw 6.5 years in the trash.
- The four lost decades in Japan meant that the Nikkei 225, the Japanese stock market index, only recovered the highest level lost in the 1990s in 2024, 40 years later. Imagine, that was half the lifetime of many people.

Remember that monetary losses are not the problem: you can always recover money, but you can't recover lost time. Time that could have been used to grow your investments was thrown away by falling into a hole and then trying to get out of it. It's a huge opportunity cost. Money you didn't earn is a loss!

Conclusion: don't buy and hold. It's a terrible idea. You lose money hand over fist and convince yourself that it's the most "conservative" way to invest in stocks. The media and the mainstream press fill your head with lies and outdated ideas. Think for yourself.

With **RISP 500™**, you finally get **an objective compass** to avoid the worst moments and navigate with greater clarity and confidence.

The Science Behind the RISP 500™ Methodology

What makes **RISP 500™** so powerful and reliable? Its strength comes from the fact that it is **a multifactorial analytical model** that broadly observes the market environment. It **reads warning signs in advance**, capturing changes in behavior that precede sudden movements in asset prices.

The market is naturally zigzagging. It goes up and down all the time like waves breaking on the beach. The difficult thing is to discern which of these waves have the potential to turn into something more dangerous and which are more harmless. This is a challenge that is practically impossible for us humans, based on our memories and countless psychological biases, to discern. Only tools that process large volumes of data and work with probabilities can give us this information more accurately and at the right time. RISP 500™ was designed to perform exactly this function for us.

Instead of relying on a single indicator, RISP 500™ **synthesizes the behavior of more than 15 critical variables from different markets**—stocks, volatility, interest rates, and even macroeconomic data. This cross-analysis is what gives the model depth and makes it so sensitive to risks that its measurement becomes relevant and accurate at the right time.

Let's take a look at some of these variables and understand what they indicate:

1. Volatility Risk Premium (VRP)

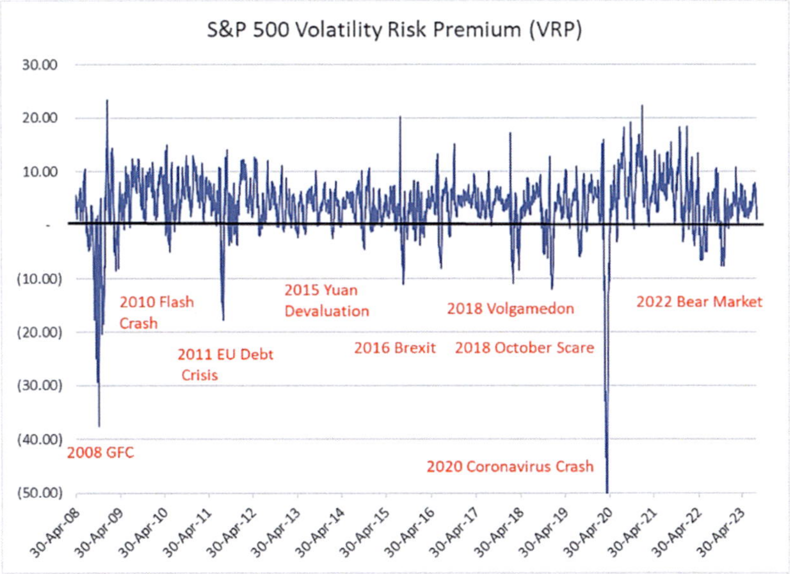

- **What it is:** The difference between implied volatility (expected by the market) and realized volatility (what actually occurred).
- **Why it matters:** When implied volatility is higher than historical volatility, it is a sign of **increased market fear**—a clear indication of stress. Those who sell volatility or hedge for other players raise the premium they charge to protect themselves or cover the increased risk.

2. VIX Index (the "panic index")

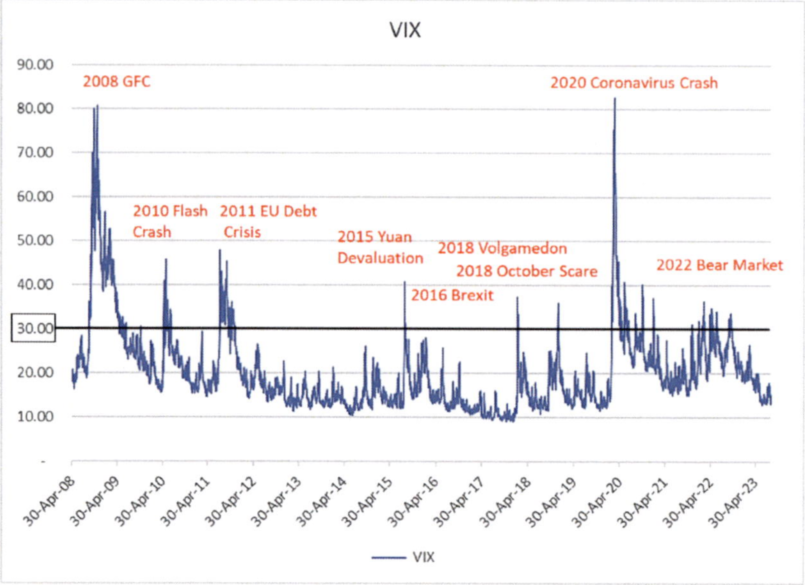

- **What it is:** Measures the expected volatility of the S&P 500 over the next 30 days.

- **Why it matters:** When the VIX rises, it is because the market is fearful. Levels above 30, for example, usually indicate **high risk aversion**. But it does not have to reach that level for the market to be bearish.

3. VIX Spot-to-Term Curve

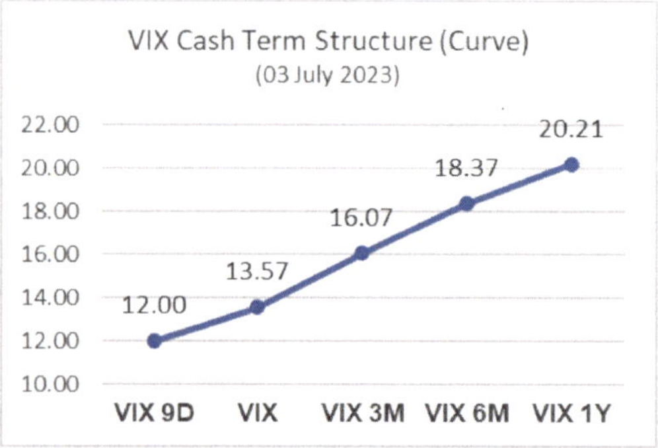

- **What it is:** Shows how expected volatility changes over short time frames (from 9 days to 1 year).
- **Why it matters:** An **inverted curve** (with short-term periods more volatile than long-term periods) indicates **fear of imminent events** — a warning sign.

4. VIX Futures Term Curve

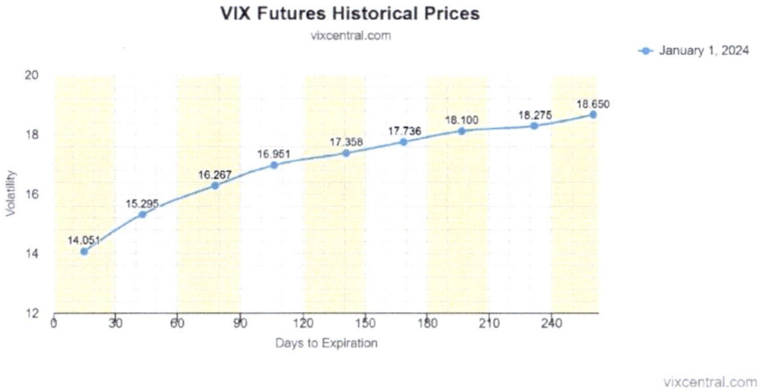

- **What it is:** Shows future prices of market volatility.
- **Why it matters:** A curve in contango (normal) indicates stability. This curve increases with time. A curve in backwardation (inverted) reveals **short-term stress** in the market. This curve decreases with time.

5. Roll Yield

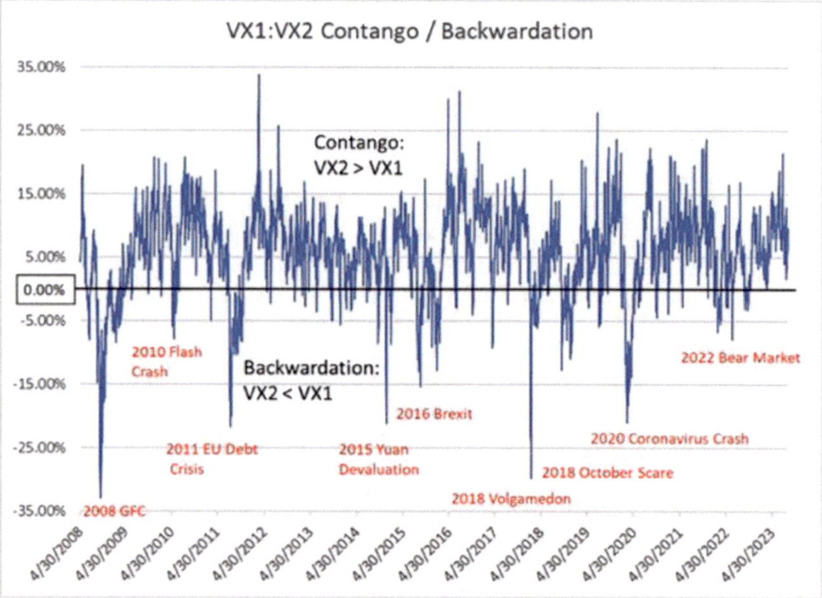

- **What it is:** Measures the cost or gain when rolling VIX futures contracts.

- **Why it matters:** Negative roll yield suggests that the market is paying more to protect itself — another **sign of growing stress**.

6. VVIX (Volatility of Volatility)

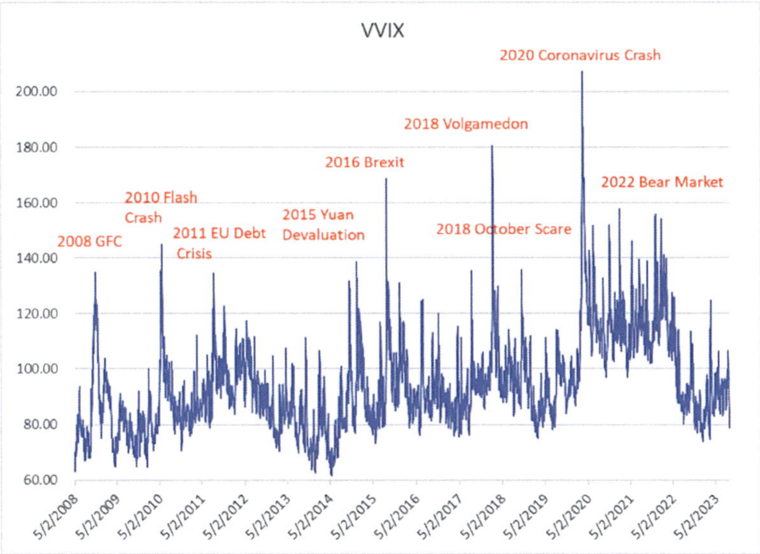

- **What it is:** The volatility of the VIX itself.
- **Why it matters:** A high VVIX shows that **uncertainty is accelerating**, anticipating sharp changes in market sentiment.

7. Equity Risk Premium (ERP)

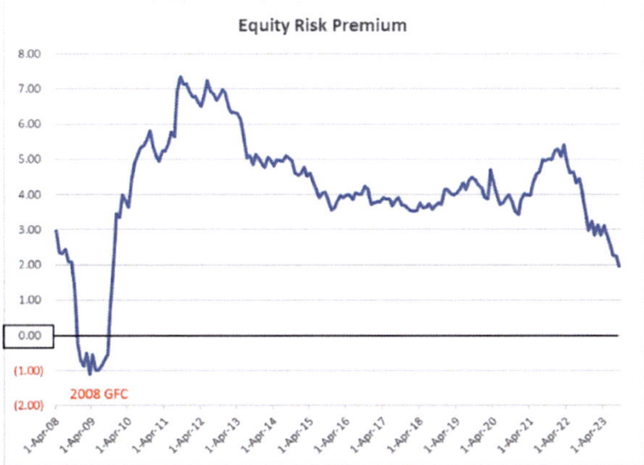

- **What it is:** The difference between the expected return on stocks and the return on bonds.

- **Why it matters:** When the ERP declines, the market is **less willing to take risk for additional return** — a sign of mistrust.

8. Yield Curve Inversions

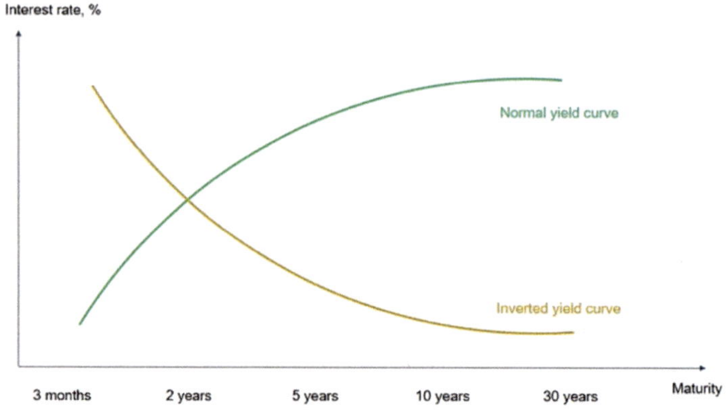

Credits: The Copenhagen Post

- **What it is:** Occurs when short-term interest rates are higher than long-term rates (e.g., 2 years > 10 years).
- **Why it matters:** A strong indicator of **recession** and that the market expects an economic slowdown.

9. MOVE Index (Bond Volatility)

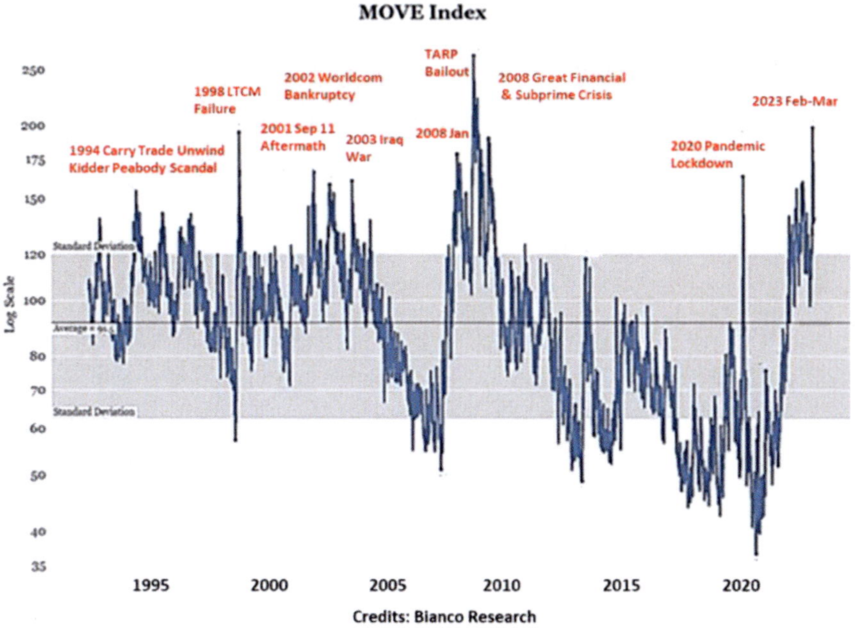

- **What it is:** Measures the expected volatility in the U.S. Treasury bond market.
- **Why it matters:** If MOVE rises, it is because investors are **fearing economic turmoil** — and this usually precedes stock market declines.

10. Leading Economic Indicators (LEI)

Source: The Conference Board

- **What it is:** A set of data such as unemployment claims, new construction, and stock prices.

- **Why it matters:** Successive declines in the LEI signal **economic weakness ahead**, impacting risk appetite.

11. Fed Monetary Policy Expectations (CME FedWatch Tool)

MEETING PROBABILITIES — Source: CME

MEETING DATE	225-250	250-275	275-300	300-325	325-350	350-375	375-400	400-425	425-450
7/27/2022	19.1%	80.9%	0.0%						
9/21/2022	0.0%	0.0%	0.0%	19.1%	80.9%	0.0%	0.0%	0.0%	
11/2/2022	0.0%	0.0%	0.0%	0.0%	13.3%	62.2%	24.5%	0.0%	0.0%
12/14/2022	0.0%	0.0%	0.0%	0.0%	6.9%	38.9%	42.5%	11.7%	0.0%
2/1/2023	0.0%	0.0%	0.0%	0.0%	6.0%	34.6%	42.0%	15.8%	1.5%
3/15/2023	0.0%	0.0%	0.0%	2.0%	15.5%	37.1%	33.3%	11.0%	1.0%
5/3/2023	0.0%	0.0%	0.7%	6.6%	22.8%	35.8%	25.8%	7.7%	0.7%
6/14/2023	0.0%	0.3%	3.4%	14.1%	28.8%	31.2%	17.4%	4.1%	0.4%
7/26/2023	0.1%	1.6%	7.8%	20.1%	29.8%	25.5%	12.1%	2.8%	0.2%

- **What it is:** Projected probabilities for interest rate cuts or increases.

- **Why it matters:** When the market prices in sudden changes in rates, it affects **capital flows, stock markets, and overall sentiment**.

Note: There are more than 15 variables that make up the RISP 500™ model. Above, we show only the most relevant ones to illustrate how it works. These variables can change over time as their relevance changes. They are also periodically calibrated to reflect regime changes in the market. There is persistent and continuous work behind the scenes conducted by my team at Risk Scientific LLC in the United States to keep the RISP 500™ relevant, agile, accurate, and powerful over time.

An Integrated View of Risk and Its Impact on Allocation for Better Performance

Each of these variables has little predictive value on its own but **provides a clue or a piece of the puzzle**. But when combined, together they form a much more complete, robust, and context-sensitive view. The RISP 500™ model gives different weight to each variable and is **continuously adjusted** based on testing, calibration, and ongoing empirical improvements.

The RISP 500™ methodology is like **a weather radar for the market**: it detects dark clouds before the worst of the storm hits us—giving investors time to protect the core of their portfolios and assets.

As a result, RISP 500™ offers an **objective, practical, and powerful reading** to guide asset allocation decisions based on actual market risk — not opinions, news, assumptions, or future projections and estimates.

Live Trading Results with RISP 500 (The Proof)

RISP 500™ has been rigorously tested in live trading since January 1, 2022, providing comprehensive proof of concept. Guided by this tool, we applied eight distinct strategies:

8 Live-Tested Strategies

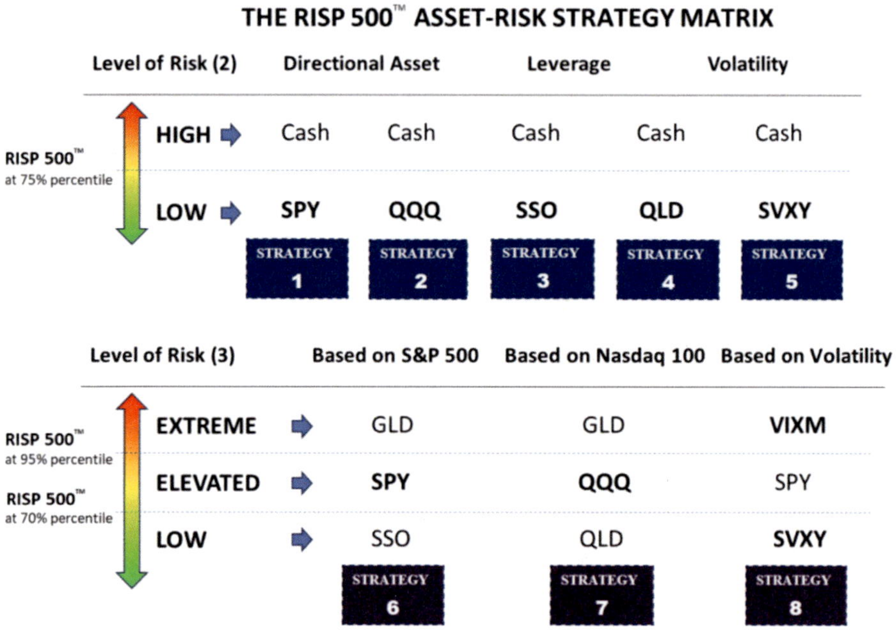

We tested 5 two-risk-level systems and 3 three-risk-level systems, totaling 8 strategies with 7 ETF and cash assets. For our testing, we selected the following assets:

Risk Assets

SPY: ETF that tracks the S&P 500® Index

SSO: ETF that tracks the S&P 500® x2 Index (2x leveraged S&P 500®)

QQQ: ETF that tracks the Nasdaq 100 Index

QLD: ETF that tracks the Nasdaq 100 x2 index (Nasdaq 100 leveraged 2x)

SVXY: ETF that tracks short VIX futures

Security Assets

GLD: ETF that tracks the price of gold

CASH: Cash

Long Volatility Asset (to exploit high risk)

VIXM: ETF that tracks long VIX futures

Strategies:

Strategy 1 (ST1-2L-SP500): Two-level risk strategy based on the S&P 500® (SPY/Cash)

Strategy 2 (ST2-2L-Nasdaq): Two-level risk strategy based on the Nasdaq 100 (QQQ/Cash)

Strategy 3 (ST3-2L-SP500x2): Two-level risk strategy based on the S&P 500® x2 (SSO/Cash)

Strategy 4 (ST4-2L-Nasdaqx2): Two-level risk strategy based on Nasdaq 100 x2 (QLD/Cash)

Strategy 5 (ST5-2L-Volatility): Two-level risk strategy based on VIX Futures (QLD/Cash)

Strategy 6 (ST6-3L-SP500): Three-level risk strategy based on the S&P 500® (SSO/SPY/GLD)

Strategy 7 (ST7-3L-Nasdaq): Three-level risk strategy based on the Nasdaq 100 (QLD/QQQ/GLD)

Strategy 8 (ST8-3L-Volatility): Three-level risk strategy based on VIX Futures (SVXY/SPY/VIXM)

We are constantly putting RISP 500™ to the test and analyzing the test results. We are also testing and backtesting new strategies all the time. We are making YTD and ITD performance results available daily on Facebook and X (formerly Twitter):www.facebook.com/risp500 and https://x.com/Risp500. As you know, each post on a social media platform has a timestamp, so you can trust the exact date and time we post our daily performance results. Here is an example of a post:

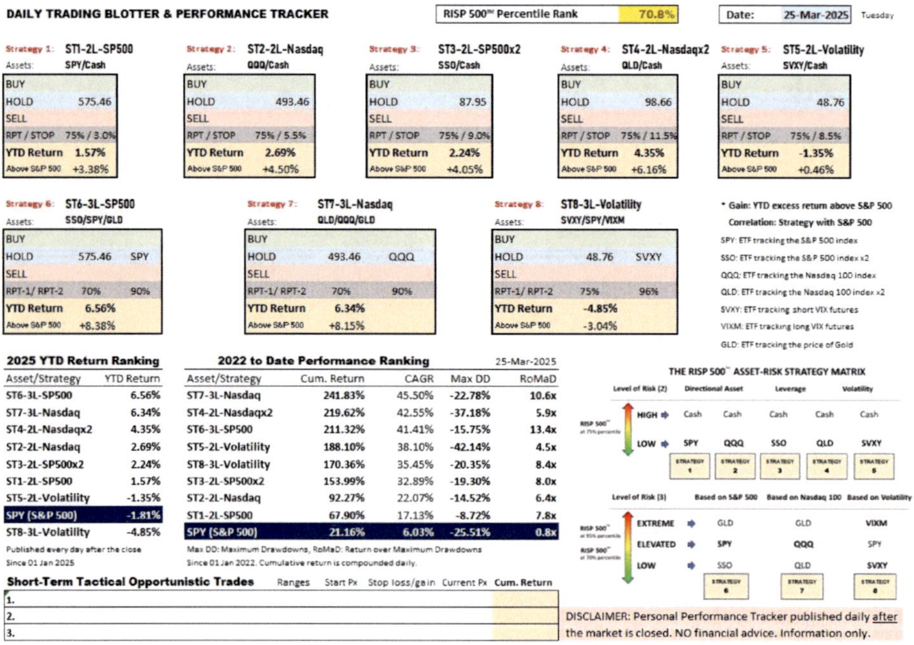

DAILY TRADING BLOTTER & PERFORMANCE TRACKER

RISP 500™ Percentile Rank 70.8%

Date: 25-Mar-2025 Tuesday

	Strategy 1: ST1-2L-SP500	Strategy 2: ST2-2L-Nasdaq	Strategy 3: ST3-2L-SP500x2	Strategy 4: ST4-2L-Nasdaqx2	Strategy 5: ST5-2L-Volatility
Assets:	SPY/Cash	QQQ/Cash	SSO/Cash	QLD/Cash	SVXY/Cash
BUY					
HOLD	575.46	493.46	87.95	98.66	48.76
SELL					
RPT / STOP	75% / 3.0%	75% / 5.5%	75% / 9.0%	75% / 11.5%	75% / 8.5%
YTD Return	1.57%	2.69%	2.24%	4.35%	-1.35%
Above S&P 500	+3.38%	+4.50%	+4.05%	+6.16%	+0.46%

	Strategy 6: ST6-3L-SP500		Strategy 7: ST7-3L-Nasdaq		Strategy 8: ST8-3L-Volatility	
Assets:	SSO/SPY/GLD		QLD/QQQ/GLD		SVXY/SPY/VIXM	
BUY						
HOLD	575.46	SPY	493.46	QQQ	48.76	SVXY
SELL						
RPT-1/ RPT-2	70%	90%	70%	90%	75%	96%
YTD Return	6.56%		6.34%		-4.85%	
Above S&P 500	+8.38%		+8.15%		-3.04%	

* Gain: YTD excess return above S&P 500
Correlation: Strategy with S&P 500
SPY: ETF tracking the S&P 500 index
SSO: ETF tracking the S&P 500 index x2
QQQ: ETF tracking the Nasdaq 100 index
QLD: ETF tracking the Nasdaq 100 index x2
SVXY: ETF tracking short VIX futures
VIXM: ETF tracking long VIX futures
GLD: ETF tracking the price of Gold

2025 YTD Return Ranking

Asset/Strategy	YTD Return
ST6-3L-SP500	6.56%
ST7-3L-Nasdaq	6.34%
ST4-2L-Nasdaqx2	4.35%
ST2-2L-Nasdaq	2.69%
ST3-2L-SP500x2	2.24%
ST1-2L-SP500	1.57%
ST5-2L-Volatility	-1.35%
SPY (S&P 500)	-1.81%
ST8-3L-Volatility	-4.85%

Published every day after the close
Since 01 Jan 2025

2022 to Date Performance Ranking 25-Mar-2025

Asset/Strategy	Cum. Return	CAGR	Max DD	RoMaD
ST7-3L-Nasdaq	241.83%	45.50%	-22.78%	10.6x
ST4-2L-Nasdaqx2	219.62%	42.55%	-37.18%	5.9x
ST6-3L-SP500	211.32%	41.41%	-15.75%	13.4x
ST5-2L-Volatility	188.10%	38.10%	-42.14%	4.5x
ST8-3L-Volatility	170.36%	35.45%	-20.35%	8.4x
ST3-2L-SP500x2	153.99%	32.89%	-19.30%	8.0x
ST2-2L-Nasdaq	92.27%	22.07%	-14.52%	6.4x
ST1-2L-SP500	67.90%	17.13%	-8.72%	7.8x
SPY (S&P 500)	21.16%	6.03%	-25.51%	0.8x

Max DD: Maximum Drawdowns, RoMaD: Return over Maximum Drawdowns
Since 01 Jan 2022. Cumulative return is compounded daily.

Short-Term Tactical Opportunistic Trades

	Ranges	Start Px	Stop loss/gain	Current Px	Cum. Return
1.					
2.					
3.					

DISCLAIMER: Personal Performance Tracker published daily after the market is closed. NO financial advice. Information only.

RISP 500™ measured once a day is sufficient for solid long-term results

In this project, we are providing the RISP 500™ reading only once a day to prove that even a single reading per day will be sufficient to deliver very solid results. We take the official RISP 500™ measurement for the day between 10:00 a.m. and 2:00 p.m. (New York/ET time). In fact, we measure the RISP 500™ all day long, even during pre-market and post-market hours, which is even more powerful as a live, real-time indicator. But the results show that long-term investors are able to achieve the above results with just one RISP 500™ reading per day.

This means there will be no more than one trade per day (made after reading the RISP 500), and on most days there will be no need to make any trades at all.

Due to the very low frequency of trades, on most days there will be no trading at all, which is perfect for most investors and wealth management professionals. The average frequency is only 2 to 3 trades per month.

Key Results of Live Trading of the 8 Strategies

2022 Return Ranking		**2023 Return Ranking**		**2024 Return Ranking**	
Asset/Strategy	YTD Return	Asset/Strategy	YTD Return	Asset/Strategy	YTD Return
ST6-3L-SP500	**33.42%**	**ST4-2L-Nasdaqx2**	**131.44%**	**ST4-2L-Nasdaqx2**	**54.46%**
ST5-2L-Volatility	**27.33%**	**ST7-3L-Nasdaq**	**131.29%**	**ST3-2L-SP500x2**	**47.87%**
ST8-3L-Volatility	**22.99%**	**ST8-3L-Volatility**	**113.02%**	**ST7-3L-Nasdaq**	**35.77%**
ST7-3L-Nasdaq	**2.37%**	**ST5-2L-Volatility**	**107.55%**	**ST6-3L-SP500**	**32.71%**
ST1-2L-SP500	**0.53%**	**ST3-2L-SP500x2**	**67.71%**	**ST2-2L-Nasdaq**	**28.21%**
ST3-2L-SP500x2	**0.18%**	**ST6-3L-SP500**	**64.99%**	**ST1-2L-SP500**	**23.51%**
ST2-2L-Nasdaq	**-7.61%**	**ST2-2L-Nasdaq**	**58.07%**	**SPY (S&P 500)**	**23.30%**
ST4-2L-Nasdaqx2	**-14.32%**	**ST1-2L-SP500**	**33.13%**	**ST5-2L-Volatility**	**10.51%**
SPY (S&P 500)	**-19.48%**	**SPY (S&P 500)**	**24.29%**	**ST8-3L-Volatility**	**8.45%**
Published every day after the close From 01 Jan 2022 to 31 Dec 2022		Published every day after the close From 01 Jan 2023 to 31 Dec 2023		Published every day after the close From 01 Jan 2024 to 31 Dec 2024	

2025 YTD Return Ranking

Asset/Strategy	YTD Return
ST6-3L-SP500	6.56%
ST7-3L-Nasdaq	6.34%
ST4-2L-Nasdaqx2	4.35%
ST2-2L-Nasdaq	2.69%
ST3-2L-SP500x2	2.24%
ST1-2L-SP500	1.57%
ST5-2L-Volatility	-1.35%
SPY (S&P 500)	-1.81%
ST8-3L-Volatility	-4.85%

Published every day after the close
Since 01 Jan 2025

2022 to Date Performance Ranking 25-Mar-2025

Asset/Strategy	Cum. Return	CAGR	Max DD	RoMaD
ST7-3L-Nasdaq	241.83%	45.50%	-22.78%	10.6x
ST4-2L-Nasdaqx2	219.62%	42.55%	-37.18%	5.9x
ST6-3L-SP500	211.32%	41.41%	-15.75%	13.4x
ST5-2L-Volatility	188.10%	38.10%	-42.14%	4.5x
ST8-3L-Volatility	170.36%	35.45%	-20.35%	8.4x
ST3-2L-SP500x2	153.99%	32.89%	-19.30%	8.0x
ST2-2L-Nasdaq	92.27%	22.07%	-14.52%	6.4x
ST1-2L-SP500	67.90%	17.13%	-8.72%	7.8x
SPY (S&P 500)	21.16%	6.03%	-25.51%	0.8x

Max DD: Maximum Drawdowns, RoMaD: Return over Maximum Drawdowns
Since 01 Jan 2022. Cumulative return is compounded daily.

- **Outperformance Across All Strategies** In over 2½ years of live trading (January 2022 to March 2025), all eight strategies outperformed the S&P 500®, even during the challenging bear market of 2022. Leverage- and volatility-based strategies performed particularly well in both bear and bull markets, demonstrating SMIGRM's adaptability to diverse market conditions.

- **Significant Reductions in Drawdowns** While the S&P 500® experienced a maximum drawdown of -25.51% during the 2022 bear market, SMIGRM strategies experienced smaller drawdowns, helping to preserve capital during volatile periods. This ability to avoid the worst market declines is a hallmark of RISP 500™'s effectiveness.

- **Enormously Increased Risk-Return Ratio** SMIGRM strategies consistently achieved higher RoMaD ratios compared to the S&P 500®, indicating superior returns for the risks taken. By avoiding periods of high risk and capitalizing on favorable conditions, RISP 500™ has proven its value as a risk management and performance enhancement tool.

- **Real Results with Transparency** All live trading results are shared daily on Facebook and X (formerly Twitter), ensuring complete transparency. This allows wealth managers and investors to monitor the performance of RISP 500™ and

validate its effectiveness on a daily basis:
www.facebook.com/risp500 or https://x.com/Risp500.

SMIGRM, powered by RISP 500™, transforms wealth management. Whether avoiding the worst losses of the 2022 bear market or outperforming during subsequent rallies, it consistently proves its ability to protect and grow wealth. By leveraging this system, you can offer clients unmatched performance and peace of mind in any market environment. At the time of this writing, all 8 strategies have exceeded expectations in live trading. We chose an RPT of 75% for all 5 two-risk-level strategies. For the three-risk-level strategies, we chose RPT-1 at 70% and RPT-2 at 95%. The following charts illustrate the growth of $1,000 from 1/1/2022 to 1/7/2024 and the drawdowns experienced during the period.

How RISP 500 Protects Portfolios (More Proof!)

Seeing is believing! Let's clarify the details of RISP 500™'s protection objective by showing how a two-risk-level strategy with Strategy 1, the most basic (SPY or Cash), would have performed during two major downturns: the Coronavirus Crash of 2020 and the Global Financial Crisis of 2008. We will illustrate three levels of RPT: 70%, 80%, and 90%.

* * * 2020 Coronavirus Crash * * *

2020 COVID CRASH: HOW RISP 500 PROTECTED S&P 500 AT 70% RPT

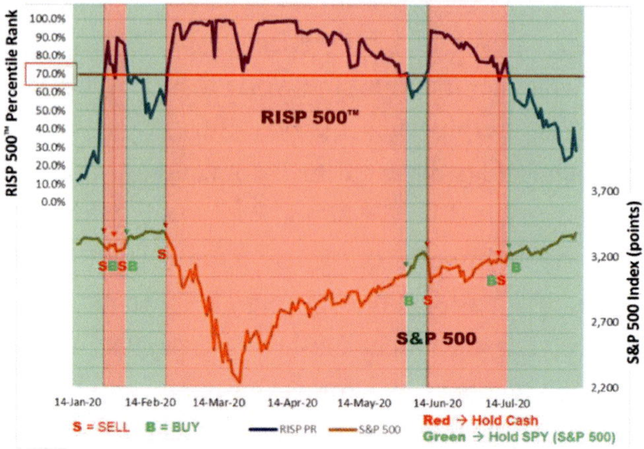

2020 COVID CRASH: HOW RISP 500 PROTECTED S&P 500 AT 80% RPT

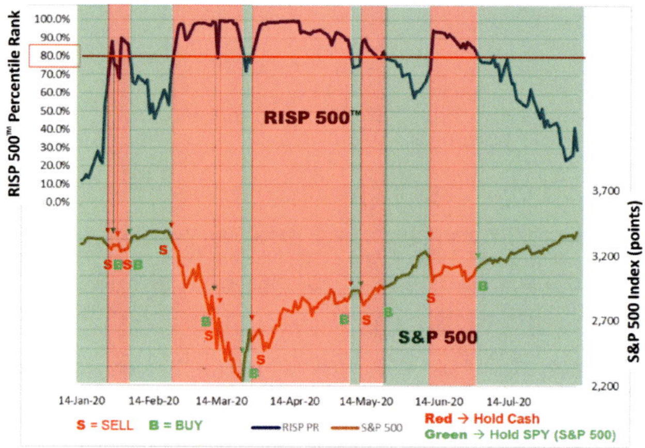

2020 COVID CRASH: HOW RISP 500 PROTECTED S&P 500 AT 90% RPT

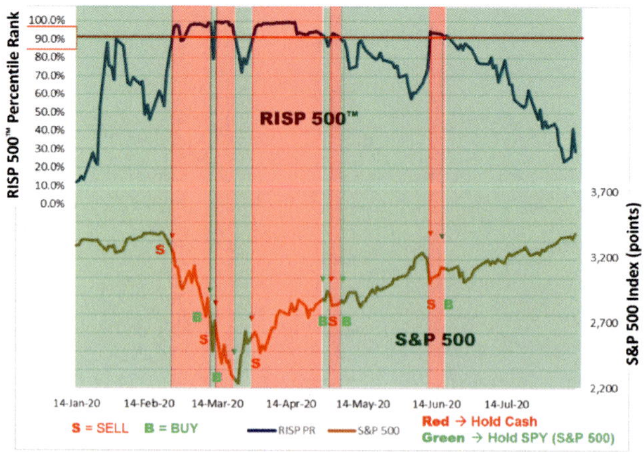

* * * 2008 Global Financial Crisis * * *

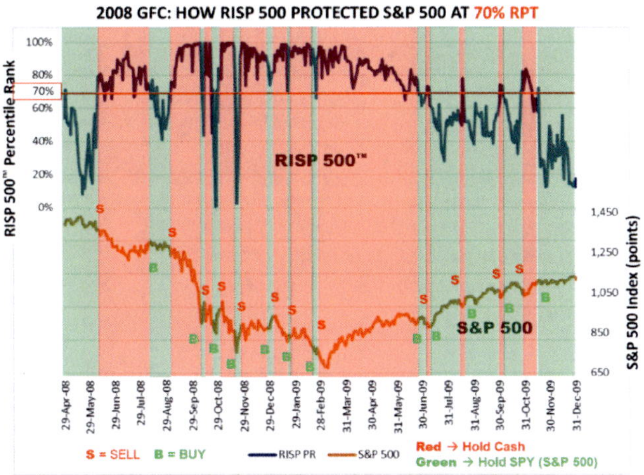

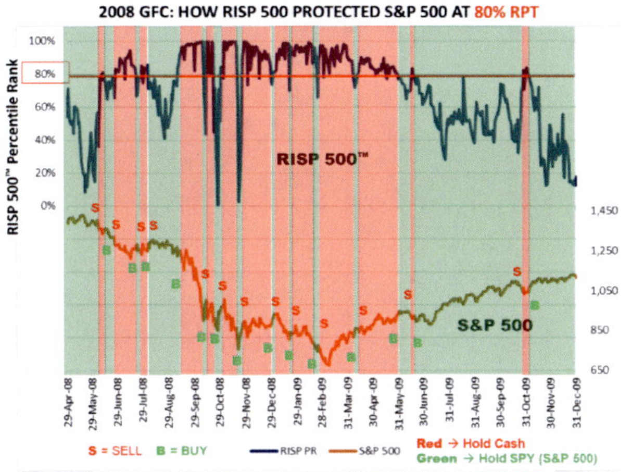

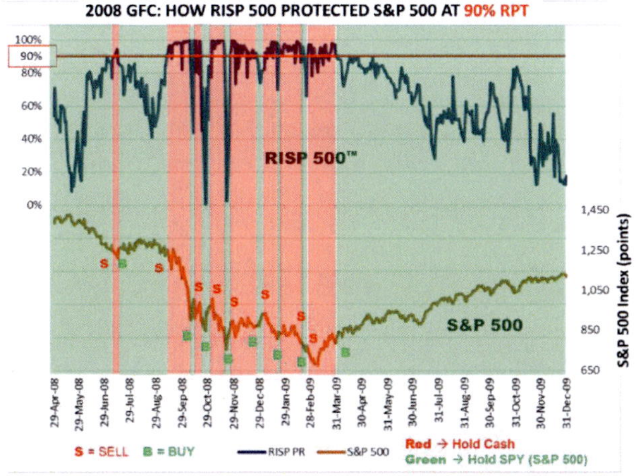

STRATEGY 1 (SPY or Cash) vs. SPY
Strategy 1 is based on RISP 500 risk-o-meter (RPT 75%) + Trailing Stop 3%
SPY is an ETF that tracks the S&P 500 index
$1,558
$1,148
STRATEGY 1
SPY (S&P 500)
$1,700
$1,600
$1,500
$1,400
$1,300
$1,200
$1,100
$1,000
$900
$800
$700
3-Jan-22
3-Feb-22
3-Mar-22
3-Apr-22
3-May-22
3-Jun-22
3-Jul-22
3-Aug-22
3-Sep-22
3-Oct-22
3-Nov-22
3-Dec-22
3-Jan-23
3-Feb-23
3-Mar-23
3-Apr-23
3-May-23
3-Jun-23
3-Jul-23
3-Aug-23
3-Sep-23
3-Oct-23
3-Nov-23
3-Dec-23
3-Jan-24
3-Feb-24
3-Mar-24
3-Apr-24
3-May-24
3-Jun-24
SPY
Strategy 1

STRATEGY 2 (QQQ or Cash) vs. QQQ
Strategy 2 is based on RISP 500 risk-o-meter (RPT 75%) + Trailing Stop 5.5%
QQQ is an ETF that tracks the Nasdaq index
$1,778
$1,211
STRATEGY 2
QQQ (NASDAQ 100)
$2,000
$1,800
$1,600
$1,400
$1,200
$1,000
$800
$600
3-Jan-22
3-Feb-22
3-Mar-22
3-Apr-22
3-May-22
3-Jun-22
3-Jul-22
3-Aug-22
3-Sep-22
3-Oct-22
3-Nov-22
3-Dec-22
3-Jan-23
3-Feb-23
3-Mar-23
3-Apr-23
3-May-23
3-Jun-23
3-Jul-23
3-Aug-23
3-Sep-23
3-Oct-23
3-Nov-23
3-Dec-23
3-Jan-24
3-Feb-24
3-Mar-24
3-Apr-24
3-May-24
3-Jun-24
QQQ
Strategy 2

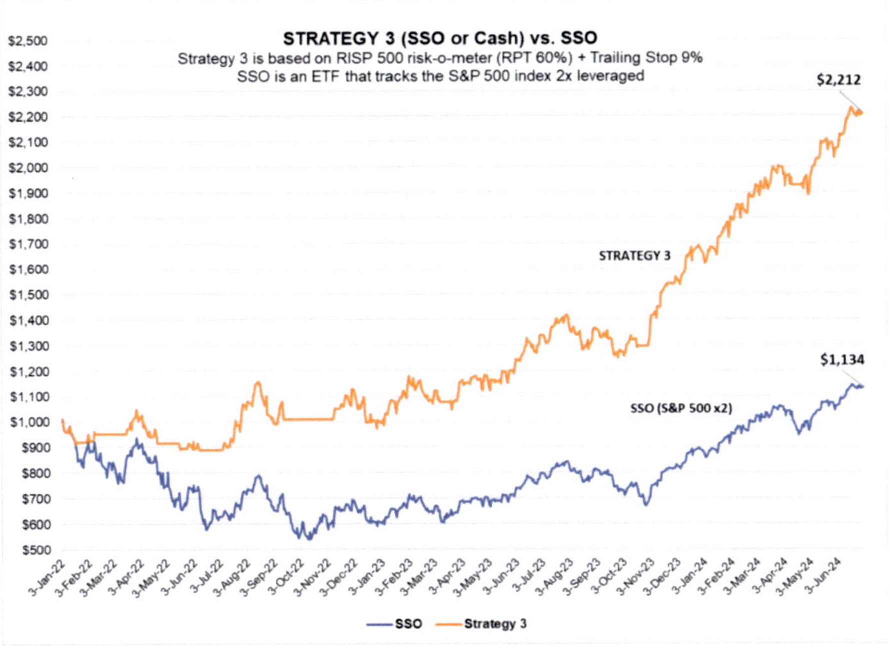
STRATEGY 3 (SSO or Cash) vs. SSO
Strategy 3 is based on RISP 500 risk-o-meter (RPT 60%) + Trailing Stop 9%
SSO is an ETF that tracks the S&P 500 index 2x leveraged
$2,212
STRATEGY 3
$1,134
SSO (S&P 500 x2)
SSO
Strategy 3

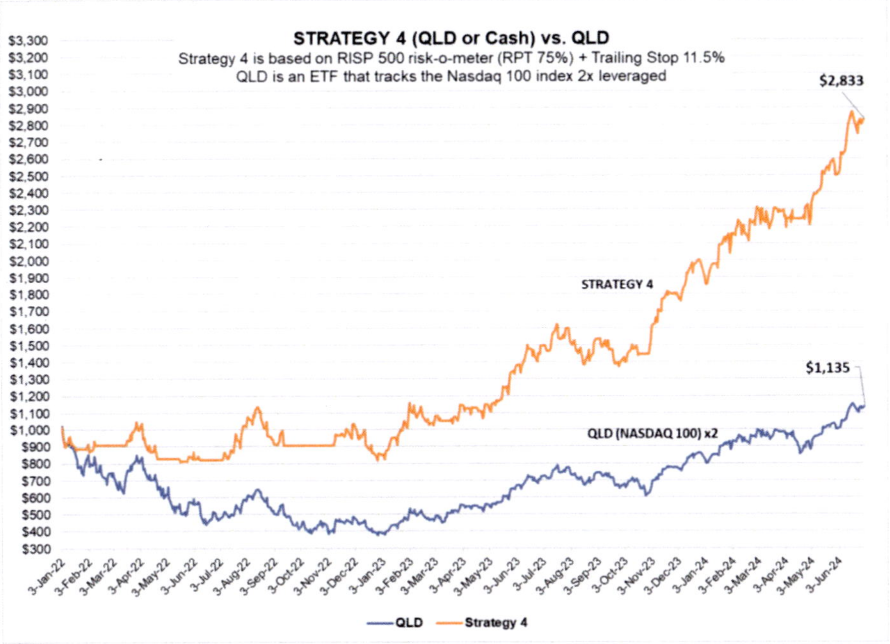
STRATEGY 4 (QLD or Cash) vs. QLD
Strategy 4 is based on RISP 500 risk-o-meter (RPT 75%) + Trailing Stop 11.5%
QLD is an ETF that tracks the Nasdaq 100 index 2x leveraged
$2,833
STRATEGY 4
$1,135
QLD (NASDAQ 100) x2
QLD
Strategy 4

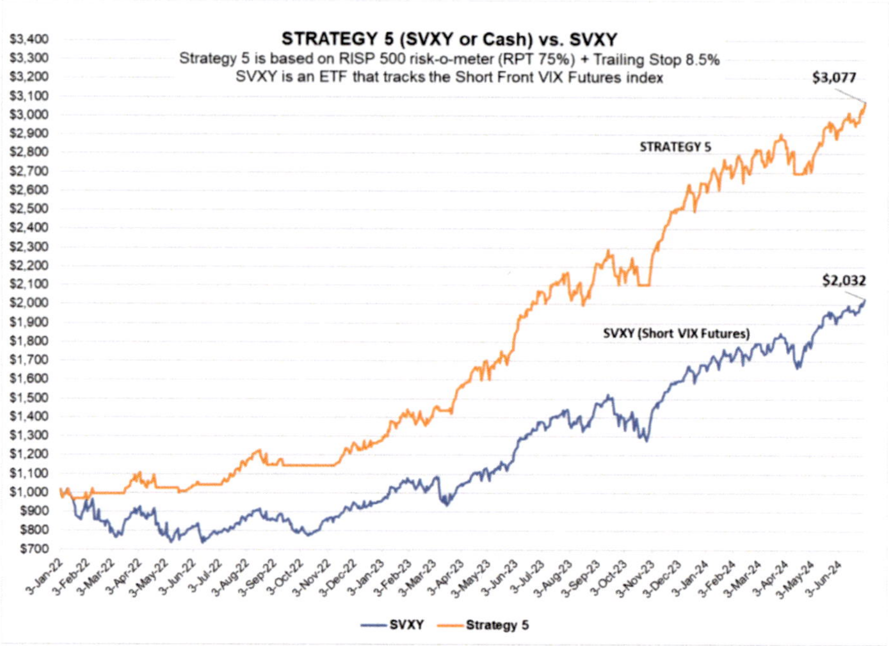
STRATEGY 5 (SVXY or Cash) vs. SVXY
Strategy 5 is based on RISP 500 risk-o-meter (RPT 75%) + Trailing Stop 8.5%
SVXY is an ETF that tracks the Short Front VIX Futures index
$3,077
STRATEGY 5
$2,032
SVXY (Short VIX Futures)
SVXY
Strategy 5

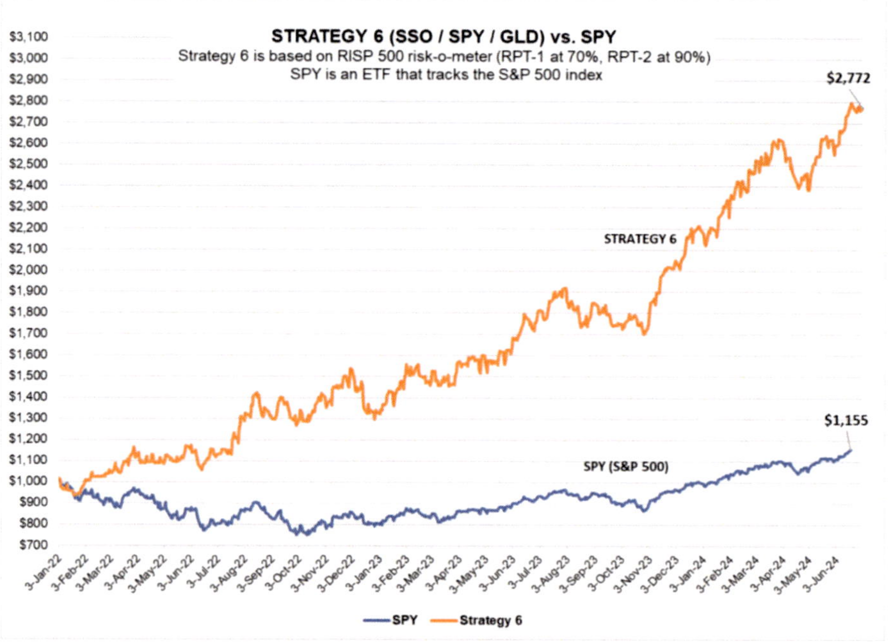
STRATEGY 6 (SSO / SPY / GLD) vs. SPY
Strategy 6 is based on RISP 500 risk-o-meter (RPT-1 at 70%, RPT-2 at 90%)
SPY is an ETF that tracks the S&P 500 index
$2,772
STRATEGY 6
$1,155
SPY (S&P 500)
SPY
Strategy 6

STRATEGY 7 (QLD / QQQ / GLD) vs. QQQ
Strategy 7 is based on RISP 500 risk-o-meter (RPT-1 at 70%, RPT-2 at 90%)
QQQ is an ETF that tracks the NASDAQ 100 index
$3,098
STRATEGY 6
$1,211
QQQ (NASDAQ 100)
$3,600
$3,100
$2,600
$2,100
$1,600
$1,100
$600
3-Jan-22
3-Feb-22
3-Mar-22
3-Apr-22
3-May-22
3-Jun-22
3-Jul-22
3-Aug-22
3-Sep-22
3-Oct-22
3-Nov-22
3-Dec-22
3-Jan-23
3-Feb-23
3-Mar-23
3-Apr-23
3-May-23
3-Jun-23
3-Jul-23
3-Aug-23
3-Sep-23
3-Oct-23
3-Nov-23
3-Dec-23
3-Jan-24
3-Feb-24
3-Mar-24
3-Apr-24
3-May-24
3-Jun-24
QQQ
Strategy 7

STRATEGY 8 (SVXY / SPY / VIXM) vs. SPY
Strategy 8 is based on RISP 500 risk-o-meter (RPT-1 at 75%, RPT-2 at 96%)
SPY is an ETF that tracks the S&P 500 index
$3,102
STRATEGY 8
$1,148
SPY (S&P 500)
$3,500
$3,400
$3,300
$3,200
$3,100
$3,000
$2,900
$2,800
$2,700
$2,600
$2,500
$2,400
$2,300
$2,200
$2,100
$2,000
$1,900
$1,800
$1,700
$1,600
$1,500
$1,400
$1,300
$1,200
$1,100
$1,000
$900
$800
$700
3-Jan-22
3-Feb-22
3-Mar-22
3-Apr-22
3-May-22
3-Jun-22
3-Jul-22
3-Aug-22
3-Sep-22
3-Oct-22
3-Nov-22
3-Dec-22
3-Jan-23
3-Feb-23
3-Mar-23
3-Apr-23
3-May-23
3-Jun-23
3-Jul-23
3-Aug-23
3-Sep-23
3-Oct-23
3-Nov-23
3-Dec-23
3-Jan-24
3-Feb-24
3-Mar-24
3-Apr-24
3-May-24
3-Jun-24
SPY
Strategy 8

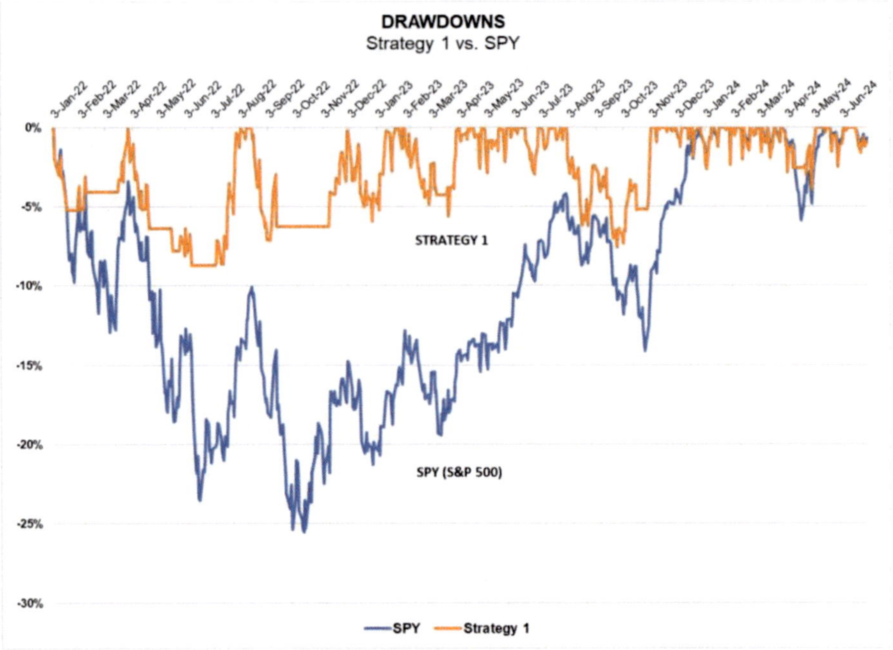
DRAWDOWNS
Strategy 1 vs. SPY
3-Jan-22
3-Feb-22
3-Mar-22
3-Apr-22
3-May-22
3-Jun-22
3-Jul-22
3-Aug-22
3-Sep-22
3-Oct-22
3-Nov-22
3-Dec-22
3-Jan-23
3-Feb-23
3-Mar-23
3-Apr-23
3-May-23
3-Jun-23
3-Jul-23
3-Aug-23
3-Sep-23
3-Oct-23
3-Nov-23
3-Dec-23
3-Jan-24
3-Feb-24
3-Mar-24
3-Apr-24
3-May-24
3-Jun-24
0%
-5%
-10%
-15%
-20%
-25%
-30%
STRATEGY 1
SPY (S&P 500)
SPY
Strategy 1

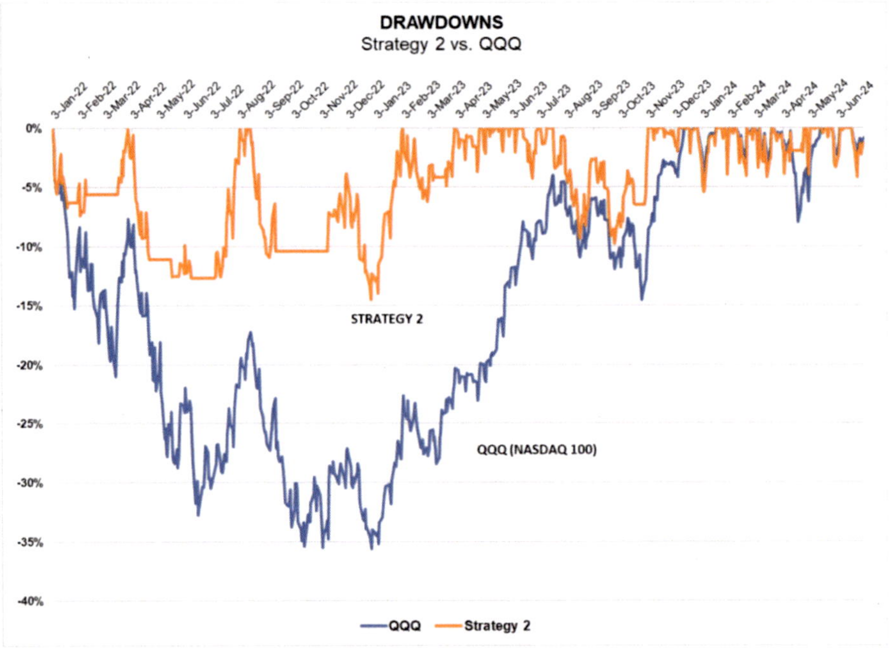
DRAWDOWNS
Strategy 2 vs. QQQ
3-Jan-22
3-Feb-22
3-Mar-22
3-Apr-22
3-May-22
3-Jun-22
3-Jul-22
3-Aug-22
3-Sep-22
3-Oct-22
3-Nov-22
3-Dec-22
3-Jan-23
3-Feb-23
3-Mar-23
3-Apr-23
3-May-23
3-Jun-23
3-Jul-23
3-Aug-23
3-Sep-23
3-Oct-23
3-Nov-23
3-Dec-23
3-Jan-24
3-Feb-24
3-Mar-24
3-Apr-24
3-May-24
3-Jun-24
0%
-5%
-10%
-15%
-20%
-25%
-30%
-35%
-40%
STRATEGY 2
QQQ (NASDAQ 100)
QQQ
Strategy 2

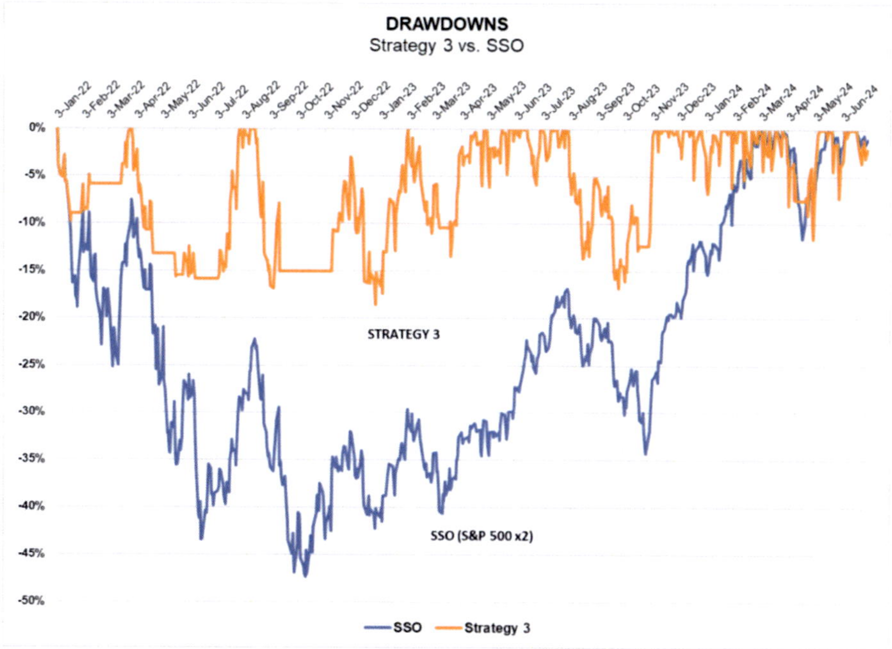
DRAWDOWNS
Strategy 3 vs. SSO
3-Jan-22
3-Feb-22
3-Mar-22
3-Apr-22
3-May-22
3-Jun-22
3-Jul-22
3-Aug-22
3-Sep-22
3-Oct-22
3-Nov-22
3-Dec-22
3-Jan-23
3-Feb-23
3-Mar-23
3-Apr-23
3-May-23
3-Jun-23
3-Jul-23
3-Aug-23
3-Sep-23
3-Oct-23
3-Nov-23
3-Dec-23
3-Jan-24
3-Feb-24
3-Mar-24
3-Apr-24
3-May-24
3-Jun-24
0%
-5%
-10%
-15%
-20%
-25%
-30%
-35%
-40%
-45%
-50%
STRATEGY 3
SSO (S&P 500 x2)
SSO
Strategy 3

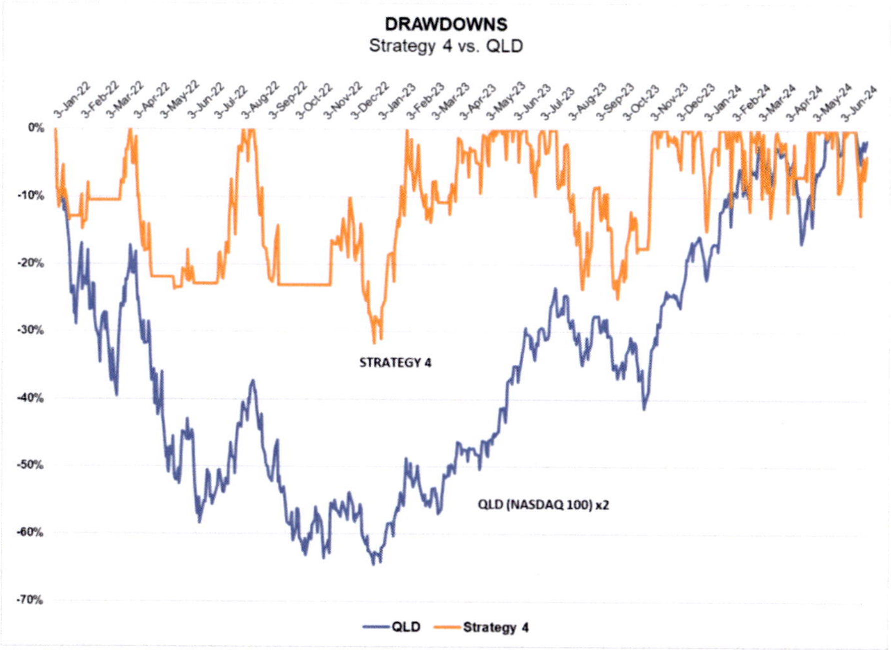
DRAWDOWNS
Strategy 4 vs. QLD
3-Jan-22
3-Feb-22
3-Mar-22
3-Apr-22
3-May-22
3-Jun-22
3-Jul-22
3-Aug-22
3-Sep-22
3-Oct-22
3-Nov-22
3-Dec-22
3-Jan-23
3-Feb-23
3-Mar-23
3-Apr-23
3-May-23
3-Jun-23
3-Jul-23
3-Aug-23
3-Sep-23
3-Oct-23
3-Nov-23
3-Dec-23
3-Jan-24
3-Feb-24
3-Mar-24
3-Apr-24
3-May-24
3-Jun-24
0%
-10%
-20%
-30%
-40%
-50%
-60%
-70%
STRATEGY 4
QLD (NASDAQ 100) x2
QLD
Strategy 4

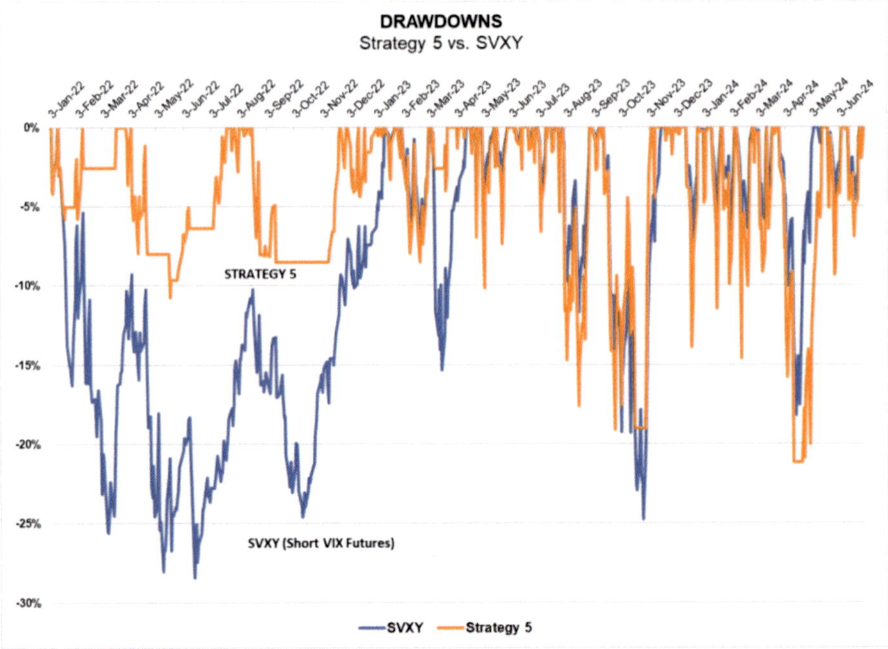
DRAWDOWNS
Strategy 5 vs. SVXY
STRATEGY 5
SVXY (Short VIX Futures)
0%
-5%
-10%
-15%
-20%
-25%
-30%
SVXY
Strategy 5

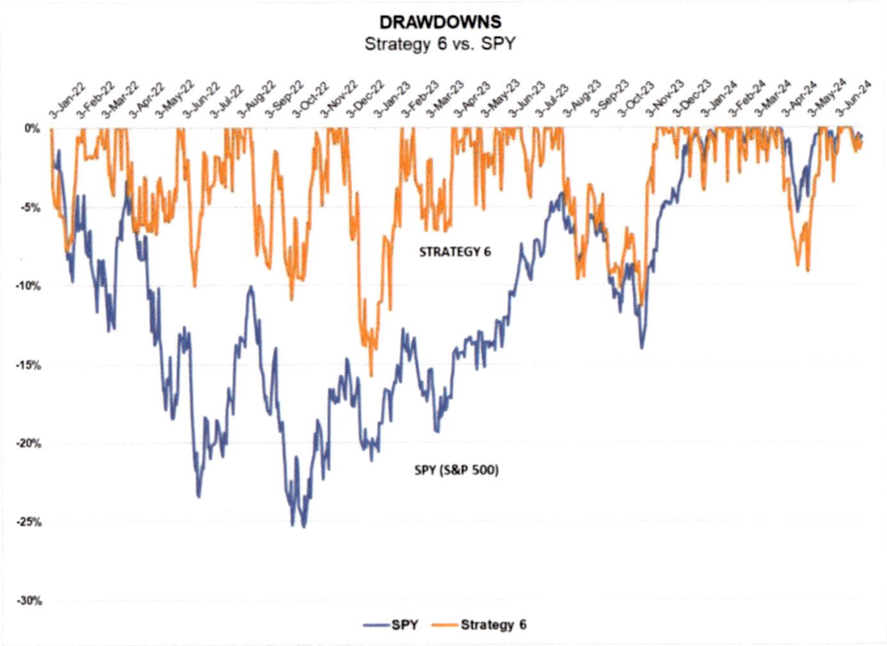
DRAWDOWNS
Strategy 6 vs. SPY
STRATEGY 6
SPY (S&P 500)
0%
-5%
-10%
-15%
-20%
-25%
-30%
SPY
Strategy 6

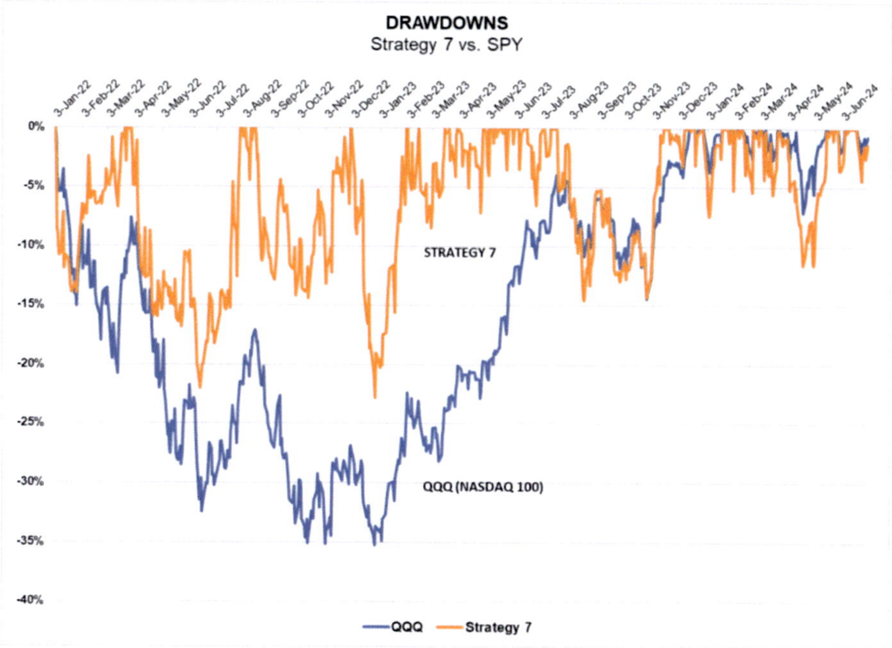
DRAWDOWNS
Strategy 7 vs. SPY
STRATEGY 7
QQQ (NASDAQ 100)
QQQ
Strategy 7

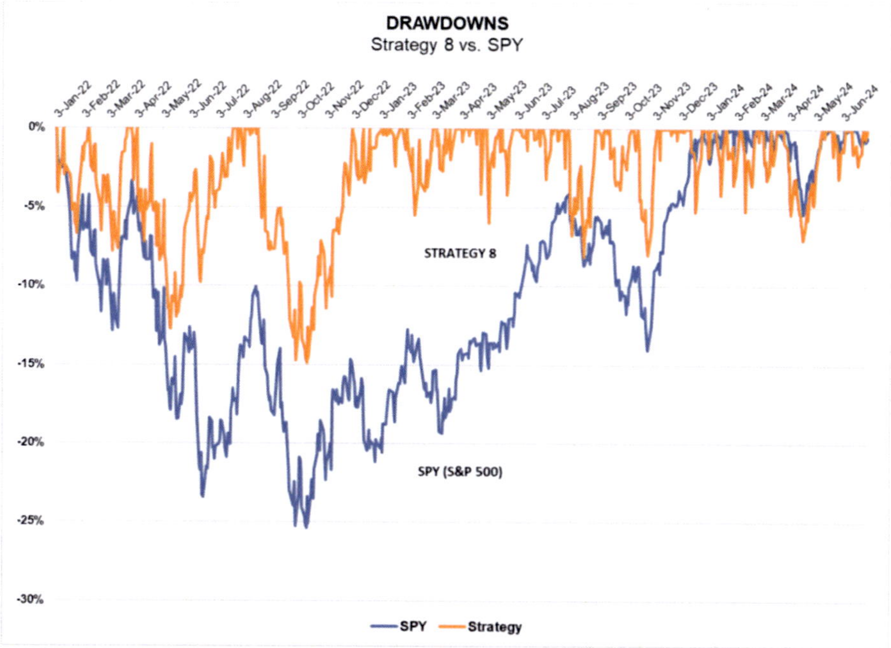
DRAWDOWNS
Strategy 8 vs. SPY
STRATEGY 8
SPY (S&P 500)
SPY
Strategy

STRATEGY 1 (SPY or Cash) vs. SPY
Strategy 1 is based on RISP 500 risk-o-meter (RPT 75%) + Trailing Stop 3%
SPY is an ETF that tracks the S&P 500 index
Strategy I avoided the major dips of the 2022 bear market
The SPY ended 2022 with -19.48%
Strategy I ended 2022 with +0.53%
Since 2023, Strategy I let profits run riding the bull market
STRATEGY 1
SPY (S&P 500)
SPY finally breaks even! It took the entire year of 2023 just recovering from 2022
$1,558
$1,148
$1,700
$1,600
$1,500
$1,400
$1,300
$1,200
$1,100
$1,000
$900
$800
$700
3-Jan-22
3-Feb-22
3-Mar-22
3-Apr-22
3-May-22
3-Jun-22
3-Jul-22
3-Aug-22
3-Sep-22
3-Oct-22
3-Nov-22
3-Dec-22
3-Jan-23
3-Feb-23
3-Mar-23
3-Apr-23
3-May-23
3-Jun-23
3-Jul-23
3-Aug-23
3-Sep-23
3-Oct-23
3-Nov-23
3-Dec-23
3-Jan-24
3-Feb-24
3-Mar-24
3-Apr-24
3-May-24
3-Jun-24
SPY
Strategy 1

Chapter 9. Active vs. Passive Investing

Investing in the stock market can be approached in two main ways: active investing and passive investing. Each way of investing has distinct characteristics that influence the potential return, the costs involved, and the level of involvement required on the part of the investor.

Which is better: active or passive investing?

Active Investing

Active investing, or "stock picking," involves carefully selecting assets (stocks) with the goal of outperforming market indices, such as the S&P 500. Managers or individual investors analyze companies, sectors, and economic trends in detail to identify the best opportunities that can offer above-average returns. This approach aims to take advantage of short-term and long-term fluctuations in asset prices.

Advantages of Active Investing:

Potential for Higher Returns: With effective analysis, it is possible to identify opportunities that outperform the average market performance.

Flexibility: Allows for portfolio adjustments in response to changes in the conditions and prospects of the companies behind the stocks.

Personalized Management: Possibility of adapting the portfolio to individual preferences, such as focusing on specific sectors or excluding certain assets or sectors.

Disadvantages of Active Investing:

High Costs: Frequent transactions and the need for in-depth analysis result in higher management fees and operating costs.

High Risk of Underperformance: Despite the goal of outperforming the market, the vast majority of active managers are unable to achieve this goal consistently.

Complexity: It requires significant knowledge and resources to make informed decisions when choosing stocks and companies.

Absurd Time Demand: Requires immense time for analysis and monitoring, which is impractical for most non-professional investors, who end up relying more on guesswork than on serious fundamental analysis of each company and stock.

Passive Investing

Passive investing seeks to replicate the performance of a market index, such as the Ibovespa or the S&P 500, by adopting a long-term "buy and hold" strategy. This is usually done through index funds or ETFs, which have a portfolio of assets corresponding to the composition of the benchmark index. For example, the S&P 500 is an index composed of a theoretical portfolio of the 500 largest American companies under certain criteria. The Nasdaq 100 is similar but includes more technology companies. Both indices are replicated by Index Funds, including ETFs such as SPY and QQQ, which replicate the S&P 500 and Nasdaq 100, respectively.

Advantages of Passive Investing:

Reduced Costs: Less intensive management results in lower management fees and operating costs.

Simplicity: It does not require any complex analysis, making it accessible even to novice investors.

Consistent Performance: Historically, many passive index funds have been able to match or even outperform active funds, especially after considering fees.

Disadvantages of Passive Investing:

Limited Returns: Returns are directly linked to the performance of the index, with no possibility of outperforming it. You are at its mercy. In weak years, returns are often low and even negative, especially if there has been a crash during the year.

Lack of Flexibility: It does not allow for adjustments to take advantage of market opportunities or avoid losses in periods of volatility.

Total Market Exposure: During market downturns, the portfolio will fully reflect the losses of the benchmark index.

Final Considerations

The choice between active and passive investing should be based on financial goals, risk tolerance, investment horizon, and the level of involvement desired by the investor. Investors seeking to maximize returns and willing to take on higher risks and costs may prefer active management. On the other hand, those who value simplicity, lower costs, and are satisfied with returns in line with the market may opt for passive management.

It is important to note that, according to studies, in the long term, passive funds tend to outperform active funds in terms of net returns, due to the lower costs involved.

In addition, it is possible to combine both strategies by adopting a hybrid approach that takes advantage of the benefits of each method, diversifying the investment portfolio in a balanced way.

Always remember to consider your personal preferences and circumstances as well. Do you have the necessary knowledge to perform investment analysis to choose stocks (we can teach you too, see an introductory summary in Chapter 10)? Another important consideration is the time available to perform analysis and monitoring. Think about that too.

Warren Buffett's Million-Dollar Bet on the Fund Industry

Everyone knows who Warren Buffett is, the most revered and admired investor in U.S. history. What many people don't know is that Warren Buffett made a $1 million bet in 2007 with the active investment fund industry. His bet was that professional managers actively choosing stocks would not be able to outperform the S&P 500 index (i.e., a passive investment in an index fund) over a 10-year period. If he lost the bet, Warren Buffett would pay $1 million to the winning fund. In the end, after the bet was announced, no one came forward for the challenge except a fund of funds manager named Ted Seides from Protégé Partners. Ted Seides handpicked five of the best active investment funds to win the challenge. The result?

It wasn't even necessary to wait 10 years for the results. Halfway through, after just a few years into the challenge, Ted threw in the towel because the difference had become so great that not even a future miracle would save the active investment funds from beating the S&P 500. Warren Buffett donated the money he won from the bet to charity, but he confirmed his point that it is indeed very difficult to beat the S&P 500 index by actively choosing stocks to invest in. We have already talked about this: fundamental analysis has many flaws due t 's numerous assumptions that need to be made. Again, the bet does not prove that passive investing is better than active investing. But it does prove how difficult it is—even for highly skilled professionals—for active investing to outperform passive investing or beat the S&P 500 index.

Now, imagine if the bettors had access to the SMIGRM Method. I will reproduce the results we obtained using the RISP 500 risk indicator based on SMIGRM to refresh your memory:

2024 Return Ranking

Asset/Strategy	YTD Return
ST4-2L-Nasdaqx2	54.46%
ST3-2L-SP500x2	47.87%
ST7-3L-Nasdaq	35.77%
ST6-3L-SP500	32.71%
ST2-2L-Nasdaq	28.21%
ST1-2L-SP500	23.51%
SPY (S&P 500)	23.30%
ST5-2L-Volatility	10.51%
ST8-3L-Volatility	8.45%

Published every day after the close
Since 01 Jan 2024

2022 - 2024 Performance Ranking 31-Dec-2024

Asset/Strategy	Cum. Return	CAGR	Max DD	RoMaD
ST7-3L-Nasdaq	221.47%	46.75%	-22.78%	9.7x
ST4-2L-Nasdaqx2	206.30%	44.44%	-37.18%	5.5x
ST6-3L-SP500	192.15%	42.21%	-15.75%	12.2x
ST5-2L-Volatility	192.04%	42.19%	-36.40%	5.3x
ST8-3L-Volatility	184.14%	40.92%	-14.88%	12.4x
ST3-2L-SP500x2	148.43%	34.84%	-18.86%	7.9x
ST2-2L-Nasdaq	87.24%	22.88%	-14.52%	6.0x
ST1-2L-SP500	65.30%	17.95%	-8.72%	7.5x
SPY (S&P 500)	23.40%	7.15%	-25.51%	0.9x

Max DD: Maximum Drawdowns, RoMaD: Return over Maximum Drawdowns
Since 01 Jan 2022. Cumulative return is compounded daily.

Note that unlike highly professional actively managed funds that manage billions of dollars for clients, we beat the S&P 500 without having to pick a single stock! As I said earlier, the secret is not in the pieces of the puzzle, but in how the pieces are handled. We explain how SMIGRM works and why it works for you in detail in Chapter 8. By following the teachings of SMIGRM and the RISP 500 indicator on a daily basis, you too can beat the S&P 500 and outperform most professional fund managers. Still have doubts? Keep reading!

Author's Final Note: Active or Passive Investing?

In my personal opinion, I believe that for the vast majority of people, anywhere in the world, passive investing makes more sense than active investing. Why?

Reason #1: Active investing requires a very keen **knowledge** of fundamental analysis, *valuation*, corporate finance, and business accounting. Most people do not have this knowledge or experience; it is simply a reality.

Reason #2: Active investing requires a huge amount of **time** to do the necessary analysis, whether you are an expert or not. Most people who are not finance or investment professionals simply do not have the time for these activities.

Reason #3: Warren Buffett has proven how **difficult it is to outperform the S&P 500 Index** (Passive Investing) through Active Investing.

Reason #4: Active investing in a managed portfolio done by professionals on your behalf (financial advisor, bank, broker, etc.) or investing in a fund that does active investing usually **costs more** than doing passive investing directly. The costs tend to accumulate over time and negatively impact your long-term results.

Note that fundamental analysis, *valuation*, and even technical analysis are tools used by Wall Street and financial professionals, which have been popularized in finance books and also taught to non-professional individual investors. This is like trying to fit a square into a circle. Investment professionals, especially on Wall Street, have much better access to information than the general public, including insider information. You see, if you learned certain relevant information through TV, newspapers, or commentators, don't you think that the information reached professionals well befor d and that the market has already changed in response to that information by the time you decide to do something with your shares?

However, passive investing loses out to active investing in one very important way: potential return. Generally, because it is less risky, less labor-intensive, and less costly, passive index investing tends to result in average returns compared to the best stocks (if you manage to pick them correctly, of course). But for that, the SMIGRM Method we teach in Chapter 8 will solve this problem—you will find that it is a solution that will tremendously improve the risk-return profile of your investment, resulting in higher returns with less risk.

I personally believe that Passive Investing combined with the SMIGRM Method is best for most people, so they:

- Do not need to know, study, or perform fundamental analysis, *valuation*, and technical analysis;
- Do not need to spend more than 5 minutes a day on investing;
- Can avoid sudden and unexpected market crashes early on, preventing greater losses;
- Can potentially obtain amplified returns, surpassing the S&P 500.

Can SMIGRM also be used with Active Investing? Absolutely! People with a financial background and investment professionals who are masters of Active Investing will be able to greatly improve their results with SMIGRM, even if they use any other method to choose stocks and build their portfolio allocation. This is because SMIGRM helps with the timing of investments and not with the analysis and choice or allocation of assets.

Chapter 10. [Active] Fundamental Analysis (with *Valuation) and Technical Analysis*

Fundamental Analysis vs. Technical Analysis in Stock Investing Stock investing has been influenced by two main schools of thought: Fundamental Analysis and Technical Analysis. These approaches differ in methodology, theoretical foundations, and the insights they offer investors.

Fundamental Analysis

- **Definition**: Fundamental analysis seeks to assess the intrinsic value of a company by examining its financial statements, competitive position, industry dynamics, and macroeconomic factors. The goal is to identify stocks trading below their intrinsic value for long-term investment.
- **Theoretical Foundations**:
    - **Efficient Market Hypothesis**: Markets reflect publicly available information, but inefficiencies may exist, allowing investors to identify undervalued stocks.
    - **Value Investing Principles**: Originating with Benjamin Graham and David Dodd, this school emphasizes buying stocks at a discount to their intrinsic value.
    - **Corporate Finance Theories**: Metrics such as discounted cash flow (DCF) and price-to-earnings (P/E) ratio are rooted in corporate valuation methodologies.
- **Key Components**:
    - **Quantitative Analysis**: Focuses on financial metrics such as revenue, profit margins, debt levels, and cash flow.

- **Qualitative Analysis**: Evaluates non-numerical factors, including management quality, brand strength, and industry position.

Pros

- Provides a holistic view of the company's health and potential.
- Encourages long-term investment strategies, reducing the impact of market noise.
- Emphasizes risk reduction through fundamental analysis.

Cons

- Requires time and in-depth financial knowledge.
- Assumes that markets will eventually recognize undervalued stocks, which may not happen in the short term.
- Less effective at predicting short-term price movements.

How an Analyst Performs Fundamental Analysis in Practice in the US

Fundamental analysis is a method of evaluating companies based on financial and economic data to determine the intrinsic value of a stock. In the United States, fundamental analysts use audited financial statements, macroeconomic information, industry trends, and qualitative factors to decide whether an asset is undervalued or overvalued.

The process generally follows four main steps:

1. Collect and Examine Financial Statements

In the US, publicly traded companies are required to disclose their audited financial statements quarterly (10-Q) and annually (10-K) to the SEC (Securities and Exchange Commission). This information is available on the SEC website and on company websites.

The main documents analyzed are:

Income Statement → Evaluates revenues, profits, margins, and growth.

Balance Sheet → Examines assets, liabilities, liquidity, and capital structure.

Cash Flow Statement → Analyzes the company's ability to generate operating cash, investments, and financing.

Explanatory Notes and MD&A (Management Discussion & Analysis) → Provide insights into management decisions, risks, and future prospects.

2. Evaluation of Financial Indicators (Quantitative Analysis)

Based on the financial statements, analysts calculate key metrics to assess the **company's financial health and performance**.

a) Profitability Indicators:

✓ **Earnings per Share (EPS)** = Net Income / Number of Shares

✓ **Gross Margin (%)** = (Revenue - Cost of Goods Sold) / Revenue

✓ **Operating Margin (%)** = Operating Profit / Revenue

✓ **Net Margin (%)** = Net Income / Revenue

b) Valuation Indicators:

✓ **P/E Ratio (Price/Earnings)** = Share Price / Earnings per Share

✓ **P/B Ratio (Price/Book Value)** = Share Price / Book Value per Share

✓ **EV/EBITDA** = Enterprise Value / EBITDA

c) Financial Health Indicators:

✓ **Debt/EBITDA** = Total Debt / EBITDA

✓ **Current Ratio** = Current Assets / Current Liabilities

✓ **ROE (Return on Equity)** = Net Income / Shareholders' Equity

Comparison with competitors: The analyst compares these multiples with **companies in the same sector** to see if the stock is **undervalued or overvalued**.

3. Qualitative and Macroeconomic Analysis

In addition to the numbers, the analyst evaluates **qualitative factors** that impact the company in the long term:

Competitive Advantages – Does the company have **high barriers to entry**, patents, or strong brand recognition?
Industry Trends – Is the industry growing or facing challenges?
Management and Strategy – Do executives have a good track record of delivery?
Macroeconomics – How do inflation, interest rates, and the economic cycle affect the company?

4. Fair Value Calculation (*Valuation*) and Buy/Sell Decision

Finally, the analyst uses **valuation** models, such as **Discounted Cash Flow (DCF)** or **market multiples**, to set **the target price of the stock** and decide whether it is a **good investment**.

✓ If the market price is below fair value → Undervalued Stock (Good to buy)
✓ If the market price is above fair value → Overvalued Stock (Good to sell or avoid)

Practical Example: Analyzing the Hypothetical Company "TechNova Inc."

Scenario:

TechNova Inc. (TNV) is a Nasdaq-listed technology company specializing in artificial intelligence for financial companies. Its rapid growth attracts investors, but there are risks associated with high competition and regulation in the industry.

1. TechNova Inc. Financial Statements

- **Annual Revenue:** $5 billion (20% YoY growth)
- **Net Income:** $750 million
- **Operating Cash Flow:** $800 million
- **Total Debt:** $2 billion
- **Total Assets:** $10 billion

2. Financial Indicators

Indicator	TechNova (TNV)	Competitor A	Competitor B
P/E Ratio	30x	35x	28x
EV/EBITDA	18x	20x	16x
ROE (%)	18%	16%	14%
Net Margin (%)	15%	12%	10%
Debt/EBITDA	2.5x	3.0x	2.2x

Conclusion: TNV is well positioned, with better margins and less debt than its competitors. Its valuation is not excessively high, but its P/E ratio suggests that expected growth is already partially priced in.

3. Qualitative and Sector Analysis

Competitive Advantage:

✓ Patents and proprietary technology

✓ Large contracts with banks and fintechs

✓ Strong investment in R&D

Industry Trends:

✓ Expansion of AI in the financial sector

✓ Stricter regulation in the US and EU (compliance risk)

Management:

✓ CEO has a track record of growth in technology startups

✓ Institutional investors hold 60% of shares

Macroeconomic Factors:

✓ Higher interest rates may affect the technology sector

✓ Growing demand for financial automation

4. *Valuation* and Decision

Fair Value Calculation by DCF:

- Current Free Cash Flow: $600 million
- Projected Growth: 15% over the next 5 years
- Discount Rate (WACC): 9%
- Fair Value per Share: **$120**
- Current Market Price: **$110**

Analyst Conclusion:

- **TechNova is undervalued by 9%** relative to its fair value.
- **Risk:** Regulation may impact future growth.
- **Recommendation: Buy** with a target price of **$120**.

In Summary: How to Apply Fundamental Analysis?

Fundamental analysis is not based solely on numbers, but combines financial data, market strategies, industry trends, and macroeconomic factors.

Essential Steps:

✓ Examine **financial statements**

✓ Compare **financial indicators with competitors**

✓ Assess **competitive advantages and sector risks**

✓ Calculate ***valuation*** **and determine fair value**

Final Tip: A successful fundamental investor **thinks long term** and seeks out **quality companies with attractive** ***valuations*** **and solid fundamentals**.

Below, we will discuss some ways to perform *valuation*, which in itself could be a separate chapter.

Stock *Valuation*

Stock *valuation* is a fundamental practice in finance, allowing investors and analysts to estimate the fair value of a stock. Several methods are commonly used, each with different methodologies, advantages, and limitations. Below is an exploration of the main valuation techniques:

1. Discounted Cash Flow (DCF) Analysis

- **Overview**: DCF analysis estimates the intrinsic value of a company by projecting its future cash flows and discounting them to their present value using an appropriate discount rate, typically the Weighted Average Cost of Capital (WACC).

- **Pros**:

  - **Focus on Intrinsic Value**: Provides a valuation based on the company's fundamentals, independent of market conditions.
  - **Comprehensive Analysis**: Incorporates detailed financial projections, offering insights into the company's future performance.
  - **Flexibility**: Applicable to companies with predictable and stable cash flows.
- **Cons**:
  - **Sensitivity to Assumptions**: Highly dependent on the accuracy of projected cash flows and the discount rate chosen; small changes can significantly impact the valuation.
  - **Complexity**: Requires detailed financial data and sophisticated modeling, which can be time-consuming.
  - **Limited Applicability**: Less effective for companies with volatile or unpredictable cash flows, such as startups or companies in emerging industries.
- **Example**: Consider a company that is expected to generate $10 million in free cash flow next year, growing at 5% annually. If the WACC is 8%, the DCF valuation would involve projecting these cash flows into the future, discounting them to their present value, and summing them to determine the intrinsic value of the company.

2. Comparable Company Analysis (CCA)

- **Overview**: CCA, or "comps," involves valuing a company by comparing it to similar public companies using valuation multiples such as Price/Earnings (P/E), Enterprise Value/EBITDA (EV/EBITDA), and Price/Book Value (P/B).

- **Pros**:
  - **Market-driven**: Reflects current market sentiment and valuations.
  - **Relative Simplicity**: Easier and faster to perform compared to DCF, given the availability of market data.
  - **Benchmarking**: Allows comparisons with industry peers, highlighting relative performance.
- Cons
  - **Lack of Unique Consideration**: Does not take into account company-specific factors that may justify a premium or discount.
  - **Influence of Market Volatility**: Subject to market fluctuations, which can lead to overvaluation or undervaluation during market extremes.
  - **Difficulty Finding True Comparables**: Identifying truly comparable companies can be challenging, especially for niche or diversified companies.
- **Example**: If the average P/E ratio of comparable companies is 15x and the target company's earnings are $2 million, the implied valuation would be $30 million ($2 million * 15).

3. Precedent Transaction Analysis

- **Overview**: This method involves analyzing the valuations paid for similar companies in past merger and acquisition transactions to estimate the value of a company.
- **Pros**:
  - **Real-World Data**: Based on actual transaction prices, reflecting what buyers were willing to pay.

  - **Incorporates Control Premiums**: Takes into account premiums paid for control in acquisitions.
  - **Market Sentiment Indicator**: Provides insights into market trends and appetite for deals within an industry.
- **Cons**:
  - **Variability of Market Conditions**: Past transactions may have occurred under different market conditions, limiting comparability.
  - **Data Availability**: Detailed information on private transactions may be scarce or undisclosed.
  - **Non-Standardization**: Each deal has unique terms, making direct comparisons challenging.
- **Example**: If similar companies were acquired at an average EV/EBITDA multiple of 10x, and the EBITDA of the target company is $5 million, the implied enterprise value would be $50 million.

4. Asset-Based Valuation

- **Overview**: This approach calculates the value of a company based on the sum of the market values of its individual assets minus any liabilities, essentially determining the net asset value (NAV).
- **Pros**:
  - **Simplicity**: Direct calculation based on balance sheet figures.
  - **Useful for Asset-Intensive Businesses**: Particularly relevant for companies with significant tangible assets, such as real estate companies.

    - **Liquidation Scenarios**: Provides a baseline value in cases of liquidation or crisis.

- **Cons**:
    - **Ignores Intangibles**: May overlook valuable intangible assets, such as brand equity or intellectual property.
    - **Does Not Reflect Future Profit Potential**: Focuses on current asset values without considering future profitability.
    - **Potential for Obsolescence**: Asset values may be outdated or may not reflect current market conditions.
- **Example**: A manufacturing company with total assets valued at $100 million and liabilities of $40 million would have a NAV of $60 million.

Conclusion: Each stock valuation method offers unique insights and is suitable for different scenarios:

- **DCF Analysis**: Ideal for companies with predictable cash flows, but sensitive to assumptions.
- **Comparable Company Analysis**: Useful for market-based valuations, but may overlook company-specific factors.
- **Precedent Transaction Analysis**: Based on actual transaction data, but dependent on the availability and relevance of past deals.
- **Asset-Based Valuation**: Applicable for companies with many assets, but may ignore future growth prospects.

It is crucial to recognize that all valuation methods rely on numerous assumptions, from projections of future cash flows to appropriate discount rates and comparable selections. These assumptions introduce a degree of subjectivity and potential for error. Therefore, it is common practice to use multiple valuation methods together to calculate a more accurate estimate of a company's fair value.

Let's see how to *value* a US stock using the four methods described above.

How Analysts Perform Valuation in Practice in the US (4 methods)

Let's look at a simple hypothetical numerical example of ***valuation*** for an American stock using the four different methods presented above:

- **DCF (Discounted Cash Flow)**
- **CCA (Comparable Company Analysis)**
- **Precedent Transaction Analysis**
- **Asset-Based Valuation (Net Asset Value - NAV)**

Hypothetical Scenario: TechNova Inc. (TNV)

TechNova Inc. (TNV) is a Nasdaq-listed technology company specializing in artificial intelligence for the financial sector.

◆ **Hypothetical Financial Data for TNV:**

- Annual revenue: **$5 billion**
- EBITDA: **$1 billion**
- Current Free Cash Flow: **$600 million**
- Estimated Growth Rate (Next 5 Years): **15% per year**
- Discount Rate (WACC): **9%**
- Number of Shares Outstanding: **100 million**

Now, let's calculate the fair value of the stock using the four methods.

1. Valuation Using the Discounted Cash Flow (DCF) Method

The DCF method projects the company's future cash flows and discounts them to the present using the **WACC** as the discount rate.

Step 1: Free Cash Flow (FCF) Projection

We use a growth rate of **15% per year** for 5 years:

Year	Free Cash Flow ($ Million)
1	690
2	794
3	913
4	1,050
5	1,208

Step 2: Present Value of Cash Flows

We apply a discount rate **of 9% WACC**:

$$\text{PV} = \frac{\text{FCF}}{(1 + WACC)^t}$$

$$PV_1 = \frac{690}{(1.09)^1} = 633.03$$

$$PV_2 = \frac{794}{(1.09)^2} = 669.16$$

$$PV_3 = \frac{913}{(1.09)^3} = 706.27$$

$$PV_4 = \frac{1050}{(1.09)^4} = 744.31$$

$$PV_5 = \frac{1208}{(1.09)^5} = 783.26$$

Total Present Value of FCFs (sum): **$3.54 billion**

Step 3: Terminal Value Calculation

We use the **Gordon Growth Model**, assuming perpetual growth of **4%**:

Terminal Value =
FCF_6 / (WACC − g)

Terminal Value =
1.208 × 1.04 / (0.09 − 0.04)
= 1.256 / 0.05
= 25.12 billion

Bringing this value to present value:

PV of Terminal Value =
25.12 / $(1.09)^5$ = 16.33 billion

Step 4: Total Enterprise Value (EV)

EV = Sum of the PVs of the FCFs + PV of the Terminal Value

EV = 3.54 + 16.33 = 19.87 billion

Subtracting net debt of **$2 billion**:

Equity Value = 19.87 − 2.0 = $17.87 billion

Dividing by the number of shares **(100 million)**:

Fair Value per Share (DCF) = 17.87 / 100 = $178.7

---

2. Valuation by Comparable Company Analysis (CCA)

We compare TechNova with companies in the same industry.

Company	EV/EBITDA	P/L
Company A	20x	35x
Company B	18x	30x
Company C	22x	32x
Average	**20x**	**32.3x**

We use the average to estimate TechNova's value:

EV = EBITDA × EV/EBITDA

EV = 1 × 20 = 20 billion

Equity Value =
EV − Net Debt = 20 − 2 = 18 billion

Fair Value per Share (CCA) =
18 / 100 = $180

3. Valuation by Precedent Transactions

Here, we use multiples from recent acquisitions in the sector.

Transaction	EV/EBITDA	P/L
Acquisition 1	21x	34x
Acquisition 2	19x	31x
Acquisition 3	20x	33x
Average	**20x**	**32.7x**

Again, we apply the average:

EV = 1 × 20 = 20 billion

Equity Value =
20 − 2 = 18 billion

Fair Value per Share (Precedent Transactions) =
18 / 100 = $180

4. Asset-Based Valuation (NAV - Net Asset Value)

NAV is based on the company's net assets.

- **Total Assets:** $10 billion
- **Total Liabilities:** $5 billion

NAV =
Total Assets − Total Liabilities = 10 − 5 = 5 billion

Fair Value per Share (NAV) =
5 / 100 = $50

Conclusion: Comparison of Methods

Method	Fair Price per Share
DCF	$178.7
CCA	$180
Precedent transactions	$180
NAV	$50

Conclusion:

- The **DCF, CCA, and Precedent Transactions** methods indicate a fair value close to **$180**.
- The NAV (**$50**) suggests that the company is being priced above the value of its net assets, which is common for technology companies.
- If the stock is trading at **$150**, it may be a buying opportunity.
- If the stock is above **$180**, it may be overvalued.

Recommendation: Buy if the price is **below $180**.

Understanding the Price/Earnings Ratio (P/E Ratio)

The Price/Earnings Ratio (P/E) is a widely used metric for assessing the relative value of a stock, sector, or market index. It measures the relationship between a company's stock price and its earnings per share (EPS), providing insights into investor expectations and stock valuation.

Formula and How It Works

- **P/E Ratio Formula**:
  - P/E = Price per Share / Earnings per Share (EPS)
- **Stock Level**:
  - The P/E ratio compares the price investors are willing to pay for $1 of a company's earnings. For example, a P/E ratio of 20 indicates that investors are paying $20 for every $1 of earnings.
- **Sector Level**:
  - Aggregating P/E ratios of companies within a sector helps identify whether the sector is overvalued or undervalued compared to historical norms or other sectors.
- **Market Index Level**:
  - P/E ratios for indices such as the S&P 500 provide an overview of market valuation, reflecting macroeconomic trends and investor sentiment.

P/E Ratio in Historical Terms

- **Bull Markets**: During bull markets, P/E ratios often expand as investors anticipate future growth and are willing to pay premiums for earnings.

  - **Example**: The tech boom of the 1990s saw the S&P 500 P/E ratio rise above 30, driven by optimism about technology stocks.

- **Bear Markets**: In bear markets, P/E ratios contract as earnings decline or investor confidence weakens.

  - **Example**: During the 2008 financial crisis, the S&P 500's P/E ratio fell below 15, dominated by fears of economic collapse.

Historical Averages and Deviations:

- Historically, the average P/E ratio for the S&P 500 has ranged between 15 and 20.

Extreme Deviations:

- During the dot-com bubble (1999-2000), the P/E ratio skyrocketed to over 40, far exceeding historical norms.
- On the other hand, during the 1982 recession, it fell below 7, reflecting severe pessimism.
- Deviations of more than 2-3 standard deviations often signal extreme overvaluation or undervaluation, serving as warning signs for investors.

Types of P/E Ratios

- **Forward P/E (P/E for the Next 12 Months)**:

  - **Definition**: Uses analysts' projections of a company's earnings for the next 12 months.

  - **Advantages**: Reflects investors' expectations for future performance, offering forward-looking insights.

  - **Limitations**: Highly dependent on analysts' accuracy and prone to over-optimism.

- **Historical P/E (P/E for the Last 12 Months)**:
  - **Definition**: Based on actual earnings for the last 12 months.
  - **Advantages**: Based on historical data, making it less speculative.
  - **Limitations**: Retrospective, potentially outdated in rapidly changing environments.

- **CAPE (Cyclically Adjusted P/E or Shiller P/E)**:
  - **Definition**: Uses the average inflation-adjusted earnings over the last 10 years to smooth out short-term fluctuations.
  - **Advantages**: Takes economic cycles into account, offering a long-term perspective.
  - **Limitations**: May lag during periods of rapid economic or structural market changes.

Application and Warnings P/E ratios are powerful tools, but they should be interpreted with caution:

- **Sector Differences**: A high P/E ratio for a growth sector (e.g., technology) may be justified, while the same for a mature industry (e.g., utilities) may signal overvaluation.
- **Earnings Quality**: Companies with volatile or declining earnings may have misleading P/E ratios.
- **Contextual Analysis**: Comparing P/E ratios across different time periods, industries, or geographies requires consideration of macroeconomic factors such as interest rates and inflation.

- Investors should use P/E ratios as part of a broader valuation framework, combining them with other metrics and qualitative insights to make well-informed investment decisions.

Technical Analysis (Charting)

- **Definition**: Technical analysis focuses on price charts, volume data, and historical trends to predict future stock movements. It assumes that market patterns and investor behavior repeat themselves over time.
- **Theoretical Foundations**:
  - **Efficient Market Hypothesis**: Past price data contains useful information about future price movements, contradicting the idea that prices are purely random.
  - **Behavioral Finance**: Stock prices are influenced by psychological factors such as fear, greed, and herd mentality, leading to predictable patterns.
- **Key Tools and Indicators**:
  - **Price Patterns**: Head and shoulders, triangles, and support/resistance levels.
  - **Technical Indicators**: Moving averages, relative strength index (RSI), Bollinger Bands, and MACD (moving average convergence/divergence).
  - **Volume Analysis**: Examines buying and selling pressure to confirm price trends.

Pros:

Ideal for short-term trading due to its focus on entry and exit timing.

Simple tools make it accessible to novice traders.

Works in all markets, including stocks, forex, and commodities.

Cons:

Ignores the fundamental value of a company, making it unsuitable for long-term investments.

Over-reliance on patterns that may not always repeat.

Requires continuous monitoring, making it resource-intensive for active traders.

Key Differences Between Fundamental Analysis and Technical Analysis

Perspective	Fundamental Analysis	Technical Analysis
Focus	Company's intrinsic value	Market price and volume trends
Time Horizon	Long-term investing	Short to medium term trading
Approach	Based on data, using financial reports and qualitative factors	Based on patterns, depending on charts and indicators
Objective	Identify undervalued stocks for sustained growth	Predict price movements and identify entry/exit points

---

Which to Use?

- **Fundamental Analysis**: More suitable for long-term investors seeking to build wealth through value- or growth-based investments. Helps identify stable companies with strong financial fundamentals.

- **Technical Analysis**: Ideal for active traders, such as day traders or swing traders, who aim to profit from short-term price fluctuations.

Conclusion Fundamental analysis and technical analysis cater to different investment styles and objectives. Fundamental analysis builds its foundation on the intrinsic value of companies, making it a staple for long-term investors. On the other hand, technical analysis thrives on price patterns and momentum, appealing to traders focused on timing the market.

While each approach has its merits, combining the two can often provide a more comprehensive investment strategy. For example, investors can use fundamental analysis to select undervalued stocks and technical analysis to identify the best entry or exit points, blending the strengths of both methodologies.

Principles of Technical Analysis (TA)

Technical Analysis (TA) involves evaluating stocks and other financial instruments using price charts, volume, and statistical indicators. The goal is to predict future price movements by identifying patterns, trends, and support and resistance levels.

Below are the 15 most commonly observed technical indicators and how they are used:

1. Moving Averages (MA)

- **What It Is**: A smoothed line that calculates the average of past prices over a specific period (e.g., 50 days, 200 days).
- **How It Is Used**:
    - **Key Levels**: The price crossing above a moving average signals a bullish trend; crossing below indicates a bearish trend.

- **Example**: The 200-day MA is a critical long-term trend indicator.

2. Relative Strength Index (RSI)

- **What it is**: A momentum oscillator that measures the speed and change of price movements on a scale from 0 to 100.
- **How It Is Used**:
  - **Key Levels**: Overbought (>70) or oversold (<30) conditions often signal reversals.
  - **Example**: RSI at 25 suggests potential for a price recovery.

3. Bollinger Bands

- **What it is**: Bands plotted two standard deviations above and below a moving average.
- **How It Is Used**:
  - **Key Levels**: Price approaching the upper band signals overbought; approaching the lower band signals oversold.
  - **Example**: A breakout beyond the bands indicates high volatility.

4. Moving Average Convergence/Divergence (MACD)

- **What It Is**: A trend-following momentum indicator showing the relationship between two moving averages.
- **How It Is Used**:
  - **Key Levels**: A bullish crossover occurs when the MACD line crosses above the signal line; a bearish crossover occurs when it crosses below.

  - **Example**: MACD divergence from price suggests potential reversals.

5. Fibonacci Retracement

- **What it is**: Horizontal lines indicating potential support/resistance levels based on Fibonacci ratios (23.6%, 38.2%, 50%, 61.8%).
- **How It Is Used**:
  - **Key Levels**: Price often returns to these levels before resuming its trend.
  - **Example**: A retracement to 61.8% is seen as a strong level for action.

6. Support and Resistance Levels

- **What It Is**: Horizontal lines marking price levels where buying (support) or selling (resistance) pressure is high.
- **How It Is Used**:
  - **Key Levels**: Price breaking through resistance often signals a bullish trend; breaking through support signals a bearish trend.

7. Volume

- **What it is**: The number of shares traded during a specific period.
- **How It Is Used**:
  - **Key Levels**: High volume during price movements confirms strength; low volume suggests weak trends.

8. Stochastic Oscillator

- **What It Is**: A momentum indicator comparing a stock's closing price to its price range over a specific period.
- **How It Is Used**:
    - **Key Levels**: Overbought (>80) and oversold (<20) levels signal reversals.

9. Exponential Moving Average (EMA)

- **What it is**: A moving average that gives more weight to recent prices.
- **How It Is Used**:
    - **Key Levels**: EMA crossovers are used for trend signals, such as a 10-day bullish crossover above a 50-day EMA.

10. Average True Range (ATR)

- **What it is**: Measures market volatility by showing the average price range over a specified period.
- **How It Is Used**:
    - **Key Levels**: High ATR indicates high volatility; low ATR indicates consolidation.

11. Candlestick Patterns

- **What it is**: Visual patterns on candlestick charts indicating potential reversals or continuations.
- **How It Is Used**:
    - **Key Patterns**: Hammer (bullish), Shooting Star (bearish), Doji (indecision).

12. Parabolic SAR (Stop and Reverse)

- **What it is**: Points plotted on a chart indicating potential reversals.
- **How It Is Used**:
    - **Key Levels**: Points below the price signal a bullish trend; points above the price signal a bearish trend.

13. Ichimoku Cloud

- **What it is**: A comprehensive indicator that shows support/resistance, trend direction, and momentum.
- **How It Is Used**:
    - **Key Levels**: Price above the cloud signals a bullish trend; below the cloud signals a bearish trend.

14. On-Balance Volume (OBV)

- **What it is**: Tracks cumulative volume flow to confirm trends.
- **How It Is Used**:
    - **Key Levels**: Rising OBV confirms upward price trends; falling OBV confirms downward trends.

15. Chart Patterns

- **What it is**: Recognizable shapes in price charts, such as triangles, head and shoulders, and flags.
- **How It Is Used**:
    - **Key Levels**: Pattern breakouts often signal strong movements in the direction of the breakout.

Conclusion Each of these indicators provides valuable insights, but they should not be used in isolation. Combining multiple indicators and considering broader market conditions can help investors make more informed decisions. In addition, investors should understand that technical analysis reflects probabilities, not certainties, and should always incorporate risk management strategies.

Momentum Indicators and Market Breadth/Depth Indicators In addition to the 15 key indicators discussed above, momentum indicators and market breadth/depth indicators provide deeper insights into market trends and investor sentiment.

Momentum Indicators Momentum indicators measure the strength or speed of price movements, helping investors identify trends and potential reversals.

16. Rate of Change (ROC)

- **What It Is**: Measures the percentage change in price over a specific period.
- **How It Is Used**:
    - **Key Levels**: Positive ROC indicates upward momentum; negative ROC signals downward momentum. Extreme values suggest overbought or oversold conditions.
    - **Example**: ROC above 10% may indicate strong upward momentum.

17. Commodity Channel Index (CCI)

- **What it is**: A momentum-based oscillator that compares the current price to its average over a defined period.
- **How It Is Used**:
    - **Key Levels**: Values above +100 indicate overbought conditions; below -100 indicate oversold conditions.

  - **Example**: A CCI moving from -120 to +110 may signal a bullish reversal.

18. Momentum Indicator

- **What It Is**: Measures the speed of price changes over a fixed period, showing whether the trend is strengthening or weakening.
- **How It Is Used**:
  - **Key Levels**: Increasing momentum confirms the direction of the trend; decreasing momentum may signal a reversal.

19. Williams %R

- **What it is**: A momentum oscillator that measures overbought and oversold levels on a scale from 0 to -100.
- **How It Is Used**:
  - **Key Levels**: Above -20 is overbought; below -80 is oversold.
  - **Example**: A reading of -85 may signal a potential buying opportunity.

20. Acceleration/Deceleration Oscillator (AC)

- **What it is**: Measures change in momentum, identifying early changes in trend direction.
- **How It Is Used**:
  - **Key Levels**: Positive AC indicates acceleration; negative AC suggests deceleration.

Market Amplitude Indicators Market amplitude indicators assess the overall direction of the market by analyzing the number of rising versus falling stocks ( ). They help measure the strength behind price movements.

21. Advance-Decline Line (A/D Line)

- **What It Is**: Tracks the cumulative difference between the number of stocks rising and falling.
- **How It Is Used**:
    - **Key Levels**: A rising A/D line confirms an uptrend in the market; a falling line indicates weakening market strength.
    - **Example**: A divergence between the A/D line (declining) and market indices (rising) may signal an impending market reversal.

22. McClellan Oscillator

- **What It Is**: An amplitude indicator calculated using the difference between the number of advancing and declining stocks.
- **How It Is Used**:
    - **Key Levels**: Positive readings indicate bullish amplitude; negative readings indicate bearish amplitude.

23. New Highs/New Lows Index

- **What it is**: Tracks the number of stocks reaching new 52-week highs versus new 52-week lows.
- **How It Is Used**:
    - **Key Levels**: A market with more new highs than lows indicates strength; the opposite signals weakness.

24. Turnover Ratio (TRIN)

- **What it is**: Measures the ratio of advancing/declining stocks and their volume.
- **How It Is Used**:
  - **Key Levels**: A TRIN below 1 signals bullish sentiment; above 1 signals bearish sentiment.

25. Percentage of Stocks Above Moving Average

- **What it is**: Tracks the percentage of stocks trading above a specific moving average (e.g., 50 days or 200 days).
- **How It Is Used**:
  - **Key Levels**: High percentages indicate overbought conditions; low percentages indicate oversold conditions.
  - **Example**: If 90% of stocks are above their 50-day moving average, the market may be overvalued.

Market Depth Indicators Market depth indicators provide insights into the volume and dynamics of the order book, revealing the strength of buy and sell orders at various price levels.

26. Volume Profile

- **What It Is**: Plots the volume traded at each price level, showing where significant buying and selling activity occurs.
- **How It Is Used**:
  - **Key Levels**: High-volume areas indicate strong support/resistance levels; low-volume areas suggest weak interest.

27. Order Book Data

- **What It Is**: Displays pending buy and sell orders at different price levels.
- **How It Is Used**:
  - **Key Levels**: Concentrations of buy orders suggest support; concentrations of sell orders suggest resistance.

28. Market Depth Chart

- **What it is**: A visual representation of the order book, highlighting liquidity and potential price barriers.
- **How It Is Used**:
  - **Key Levels**: Steep curves indicate imbalances, signaling potential volatility.

Conclusion Momentum indicators help measure the strength and direction of trends, while breadth and depth indicators provide a broader perspective on the market. By combining these tools with other technical analysis techniques, investors can better understand price movements, identify actionable opportunities, and assess market health. However, like all TA tools, these indicators should be used as part of a comprehensive strategy that incorporates risk management and macroeconomic context.

Trading Styles: Trend Following and Contrarian

Investors and traders adopt different styles depending on their goals, market outlook, and risk tolerance. Among the most prominent approaches are trend following and contrarian trading, each offering unique strategies for profiting from market movements.

1. *Trend Following*

Definition: *Trend following* involves identifying and following the direction of a prevailing trend (upward or downward). Traders seek to capitalize on sustained price movements over time. Key Characteristics:

- Focus: Momentum and technical indicators (e.g., moving averages, MACD).
- Entry/Exit Points: Enter positions when trends are confirmed and exit when they weaken or reverse.

Advantages:

- Simplicity: Trend-following strategies are straightforward, relying on clear signals from price trends.
- Potential for Large Gains: Captures significant movements in trending markets.
- Widely Applicable: Works across multiple time frames and asset classes.

Disadvantages:

- Lagging Indicators: Signals often appear after a trend has already begun, leading to delayed entries and exits.
- Sideways Markets: Erratic movements in sideways or volatile markets can result in frequent losses.
- Over-Reliance on Momentum: Ignores fundamentals, which can lead to overexposure to overvalued assets. Example: A trader buys a stock when it breaks above its 200-day moving average, expecting the upward momentum to continue.

2. *Contrarian* Trading

Definition: Contrarian traders take positions opposite to the prevailing market sentiment, buying undervalued assets during pessimistic phases and selling overvalued assets during optimism. Key Characteristics:

- Focus: Market sentiment, valuation metrics, and extreme price deviations.
- Entry/Exit Points: Enter positions when markets are overbought/oversold or significantly diverge from intrinsic value.

Advantages:

- Opportunistic: Profits from market inefficiencies and mispricing.
- Low Competition: Fewer participants take opposing positions, potentially leading to greater rewards.
- Potential for High Returns: Capitalizes on market turning points, often before others.

Disadvantages:

- High Risk: Going against trends can lead to losses if markets continue in the same direction longer than expected.
- Requires Patience: Contrarian trades can take a long time to become profitable.
- Difficulty in Timing Reversals: Identifying the exact moment of reversal is challenging. Example: A contrarian trader buys stocks amid a market sell-off, believing that pessimism is exaggerated and that prices will rebound.

Comparison Between *Trend Following* and *Contrarian*

Perspective	Trend Following	Contrarian
Market Direction	Follow the main trend	Position against the market's main sentiment or trend
Main Tools	Technical indicators (e.g., moving averages, etc.)	Valuation metrics, sentiment indicators, etc.
Risk	Lower in trending markets, greater in non-trending markets	Greater risk due to timing uncertainty and during long-lasting trends
Return Potential	Moderate returns during sustained trends	High returns during major reversions
Tenor	Works in short, medium, and long-term strategies	Generally best for medium and long-term strategies

---

Conclusion Neither approach, *Trend Following* or Contrarian, is inherently superior; both have strengths and weaknesses that make them suitable for different scenarios:

- ***Trend Following*:** Less risky in stable markets with strong directional movements. Benefits from momentum and requires less precision in timing.
- ***Contrarian*:** Offers opportunities during extreme conditions when markets deviate significantly from intrinsic value . May be the safer bet during bubbles or crashes, as long as traders exercise patience and discipline.

Investors should align their strategy with their risk tolerance, market conditions, and objectives. Combining elements of both styles, such as following trends in normal markets and adopting contrarian approaches in extremes, can lead to a balanced and adaptive investment strategy.

How to Read Reports from Professional Wall Street Analysts

Stock research analyst reports are valuable tools that provide in-depth analysis of publicly traded companies, offering insights into their financial health, industry position, and growth prospects. However, investors should approach these reports critically, looking beyond the analyst's recommendation to make informed decisions.

Key Components of a Stock Research Report:

- **Analyst Recommendation**: Typically labeled as "buy," "hold," or "sell," indicating the analyst's position on the stock.
- **Target Price**: The price level the analyst expects the stock to reach, based on their analysis.
- **Investment Thesis**: The rationale behind the recommendation, detailing the company's strengths, opportunities, and strategic position.
- **Valuation**: Assessment of the company's value using metrics such as Price/Earnings (P/E) ratio, Discounted Cash Flow (DCF) analysis, and comparisons with industry peers.
- **Risks**: Potential challenges or threats that could impact the company's performance and stock price.
- **Financial Analysis**: Detailed examination of financial statements, including revenue, earnings, margins, and cash flow projections.

Tips for Investors Using Analyst Reports

- **Read Beyond the Recommendation**: While "buy," "hold," or "sell" labels provide a quick overview, detailed analysis offers the context needed to understand the reasoning behind the recommendation. This deeper insight can help you assess whether the analyst's perspective aligns with your investment goals and risk tolerance.

- **Evaluate the Investment Thesis**: Assess the strengths and opportunities highlighted by the analyst. Do they align with your own research and understanding of the company and industry? This alignment is crucial for making investment decisions that fit your strategy.

- **Critically Examine Valuation Metrics**: Understand the valuation methods used and compare them to industry standards. Are the assumptions realistic? This examination helps determine whether the stock is fairly valued, overvalued, or undervalued.

Practical Example: How to Read Analyst Reports Beyond Recommendations

Imagine that you are interested in investing in **TechNova Inc. (TNV)**, a technology company listed on Nasdaq. You find an analysis report from a reputable brokerage firm, which gives the following recommendation:

Recommendation: "BUY"
Target price: $200
Current price: $150

The report justifies this recommendation by highlighting:

- **Accelerated** revenue **growth** of 20% per year.

- **Leadership in the artificial intelligence sector** for fintechs.

- **Improvement in operating margins**, indicating increasing efficiency.

- **Attractive valuation**, with a P/E multiple of 30x, below the industry average of 35x.

Now, let's apply the **tips for investors when using analyst reports**:

1. Read Beyond the Recommendation

Common mistake: Blindly trusting the "Buy" recommendation without understanding the fundamentals.

What to do:

- Read the **entire** report to understand the **risks and challenges** mentioned.
- Ask yourself: **Why does the analyst believe the stock will rise?**

When reviewing the report, you notice that the analyst mentions two risks:

1. **Dependence on large customers:** If a key contract is terminated, the company's growth may slow down.
2. **Increasing competition:** New startups are entering the market.

Conclusion: Even if the analyst recommends "Buy," **you should assess whether these risks are acceptable for your profile**.

2. Evaluate the Investment Thesis

Common mistake: Buying a stock just because an analyst recommended it, without checking whether it fits your strategy.

What to do:

- Are you investing for **accelerated growth or stable dividends?**
- **Does** TechNova **fit your investment time horizon?**

If you are looking **for long-term growth**, TechNova may be interesting. But if you prefer defensive, dividend-paying stocks, it may not be the best option.

Conclusion: Does the analyst's thesis **align with your goal of investing in growth companies**? If so, continue your analysis. If not, it may be better to look for another stock.

3. Critically Examine Valuation Metrics

Common mistake: Assuming that the analyst's target price is correct without checking the calculations.

What to do:

- **Did the analyst use DCF, multiples, or precedent transactions to estimate the target price?**
- **Are the assumptions realistic?**

In the report, the analyst says that **the $200 target price is based on a P/E multiple of 35x, equal to the industry average**. However, you discover that:

- TechNova's historical P/E has always been **30x or less**, so **35x may be overly optimistic.**
- The industry is facing **possible tighter regulation**, which could limit growth.

Conclusion: The target price may be **overestimated**. You decide to be more conservative and consider a target price of **$180** instead of $200.

Final Decision: Buy or Not?

Positive points:

- Strong growth and industry leadership.
- Valuation seems reasonable compared to the sector.
- Potential for appreciation if the company continues to expand.

Points of concern:

- The target price may be optimistic.
- The company is highly dependent on large customers.
- The sector faces new regulations.

Your choice: You decide **to buy**, but instead of investing all your capital at once, you buy **50% now at $150** and wait for new information before investing more.

Conclusion: Always Do Your Own Analysis

Analyst reports are **a great starting point**, but **they should never be the sole basis for investment decisions**. Use them as **additional input in your analysis**, always checking:

✓ **Does the investment thesis make sense to me?**
✓ **Are the analyst's assumptions realistic?**
✓ **Are the risks acceptable for my profile?**

Final tip: If an analyst recommends "Buy" but you identify flaws in the analysis, it may be more prudent to wait and monitor the stock before investing.

Chapter 11. [Active] Asset Allocation and Stock Portfolio Construction

Investing in the stock market involves more than just buying stocks at random. Decisions based on guesswork, or because your cousin or someone mentioned it on an internet forum, or simply because you are familiar with brands and company names have no place in this book. Here we treat investing almost like a profession, with great seriousness, and we want to avoid emotional involvement as much as possible.

To maximize returns and minimize risks, investors need to adopt structured strategies to **select stocks, allocate resources efficiently, and manage their portfolio over time**. Active stock allocation is based on the idea that, through rigorous analysis, it is possible to identify opportunities that consistently outperform the market.

Active stock allocation contrasts with the passive approach, which simply replicates market indices, such as the S&P 500. While the passive approach seeks to track the market, the active approach is based on **the careful selection of stocks** that have the potential to generate above-average returns. This selection requires a deep understanding of several factors, such as:

- **Fundamental analysis**: Evaluation of companies' financial fundamentals, including profitability, balance sheet, and cash flow.
- **Quantitative analysis**: Use of metrics and models to filter companies with the best financial indicators.
- **Macroeconomic analysis**: Monitoring of key economic indicators and understanding of how the macroeconomic context affects companies' profitability.
- **Technical analysis**: Observation of chart patterns and trading volume to identify trends.

- **Risk management**: Diversifying the portfolio to balance risk and return.

In addition, active investors often employ different stock selection strategies, the two main approaches being:

1. **Growth Investing** – Focus on companies with high future growth potential, even if they are highly valued in the short term.
2. **Value Investing** – Search for stocks that are undervalued by the market, based on their financial fundamentals.

Below, we will explore these two approaches in detail, explaining how investors can use **quantitative criteria** to filter and select the best investment opportunities.

Growth Stocks vs. Value Stocks

In the world of stock investing, active investors who choose stocks in the United States highlight two main approaches: *growth stocks* and *value stocks*. Each represents a distinct strategy, aligned with different investor profiles and financial objectives.

Growth Stocks

Growth stocks are stocks of companies that are expected to grow significantly faster than the average company in the market. These companies often reinvest their profits to fuel this growth rather than pay dividends.

Key Characteristics of Growth Stocks:

- **High Earnings Growth:** These companies show high and consistent revenue and earnings growth.

- **Innovative and Expansive:** Often involved in innovative industries such as technology or biotechnology and expanding into new markets.
- **Reinvestment:** Profits are often reinvested in the business to maintain or accelerate growth.
- **Higher Valuations:** They typically have higher P/E (price/earnings) ratios, reflecting high investor expectations.

Growth Stock Investment Strategy:

1. **Identify Potential:** Look for companies with strong growth potential due to new products, technologies, or market expansion.
2. **Long-Term Investment:** Be prepared for a long-term commitment, as growth can take time to materialize.
3. **Accept Higher Volatility:** Understand that growth stocks can be more volatile, but with the potential for higher returns.
4. **Diversify:** Spread investments across different sectors to mitigate risk.

Growth Stocks

Growth stocks represent companies that are considered undervalued in the market. These stocks are typically traded at lower prices than their intrinsic values, often offering dividends to shareholders.

Key Characteristics of Value Stocks:

- **Underpriced:** Traded at a lower price relative to their fundamentals, such as earnings, dividends, or book value.
- **Stable Companies:** Often established companies with solid and reliable performance.

- **Dividends:** Many value stocks pay dividends, providing regular income to investors.
- **Lower Valuations:** They typically have lower P/E (price/earnings) ratios compared to growth stocks.

Value Stock Investment Strategy:

1. **Find Undervalued Stocks:** Look for stocks trading below their intrinsic value due to market overreactions or temporary problems.
2. **Perform Financial Analysis:** Use fundamental analysis to assess intrinsic value, focusing on financial ratios such as P/E, P/B (Price/Book Value), and dividend yield.
3. **Consider a Margin of Safety:** Ensure there is a significant discount to intrinsic value to protect against potential risks.
4. **Long-Term Perspective:** Be patient and wait for the market to recognize and correct the undervaluation of the stock.

Understanding these strategies helps investors make more informed decisions and build a diversified portfolio that balances growth and value opportunities.

As you can see, the game is different: you buy growth stocks for their growth potential because the company likely has a competitive advantage, such as a patent on a new and disruptive technology, or the potential to dominate the market, for example. And you buy value stocks because you believe they should be worth more because the market is underestimating them and you expect that value to be corrected in the future. Certainly, growth stocks involve more risk, but value stocks can also cause losses. In this respect, growth stocks generally have higher potential returns but also higher risk than value stocks. Institutional players such as funds, etc., typically have a preference for growth stocks.

You may have heard of the Magnificent 7 (or Mag 7). These are the seven high-performance and influential companies in the S&P 500 index:

- Alphabet (GOOGL)
- Amazon (AMZN)
- Apple (AAPL)
- Meta Platforms (META)
- Microsoft (MSFT)
- NVIDIA (NVDA)
- Tesla (TSLA).

These are examples of growth stocks. And these are some examples of famous value stocks:

- General Motors (GM)
- Target (TGT)
- Bank of America (BAC)
- Walgreens Boots Alliance (WBA)
- Procter & Gamble (PG)
- Berkshire Hathaway (BRK-A, BRK-B)

Active Stock Allocation through Rapid Screening – "Stock Screening"

There are around 6,000 stocks traded on the stock exchange in the United States. That's a lot of stocks on the menu, enough to make anyone dizzy just thinking about where to start. The best way to quickly list a subset of viable stocks that are worth further analysis is to start by doing a good screening. There are several tools on the internet—some paid and some free—that help ordinary investors do stock screening. We have listed a few for the reader to consider, noting that we have no preference for any of them in particular:

- Yahoo Finance
- FinViz

- StockFetcher
- ChartMill
- Stock Analysis
- Seeking Alpha
- Quicken
- Morningstar

Below are the screening parameters and guidelines I use. They work for me with my personal risk-return profile, which is moderate (neither too conservative nor too aggressive). You can use them as a reference if you are a beginner and have no idea how to get started. This will give you a starting point. With time and experience, you can adjust both the parameters you choose (choice of parameters) and the guidelines (parameter values) to better reflect your own investment style, risk appetite, and individual preferences.

Investors use various screening parameters to identify value and growth stocks, each with distinct financial metrics and characteristics. Below is an organized overview of common screening criteria for both categories:

Quick Screening of Growth Stocks

Growth stocks are associated with companies that are expected to grow earnings at an above-average rate compared to other companies. Investors focus on metrics that indicate strong future growth potential.

Common Screening Parameters for Growth Stocks:

1. Market Capitalization

- **Description:** Measures the total market value of a company, calculated by multiplying the stock price by the total number of shares outstanding. Smaller-cap companies tend to be riskier.

- **Guideline:** Set a minimum market capitalization of **$150 million**. More risk-averse investors should increase this threshold to **$500 million** to avoid excessively small companies.

2. Price/Sales Ratio (P/S Ratio)

- **Description:** Indicates how many times a company's revenue is reflected in its share price. A low P/S suggests undervalued shares, while a high P/S may indicate rapid growth or overvaluation.

- **Guideline:** Specify a minimum P/S of **2** and a maximum of **9**. Companies with a P/S below 2 are generally classified as value stocks, and this is a filter for growth stocks.

3. Revenue Growth

- **Description:** Measures a company's revenue growth over time, indicating its ability to expand and gain market share.

- **Guideline:** Set a minimum of **15% growth over the last 5 years, 20% over the last 3 years,** and **20% over the last year**.

4. Analyst Ratings (Consensus Ratings)

- **Description:** Average of buy, hold, and sell recommendations from market analysts. The lower the value, the better the recommendation.

- **Guideline:** Set a maximum value of **2**, which is equivalent to a **weak buy** recommendation.

5. Last Quarter Earnings Surprise

- **Description:** Measures whether reported earnings exceeded or fell short of analysts' expectations.

- **Guideline:** Require a minimum of **0%**, ensuring that companies have at least met analysts' expectations.

6. Estimated Earnings Growth for the Next 5 Years

- **Description:** Projection of average annual earnings growth for the next five years, based on analysts' estimates.
- **Guideline:** Set a minimum of **18%**, which may be reduced to **14%** to include companies with more moderate growth.

7. Current Ratio

- **Description:** Measures the company's ability to pay its short-term obligations with its short-term assets.
- **Guideline:** Set a minimum of **1.5**, as a value below **1** suggests financial difficulties.

8. Long-Term Debt/Equity Ratio (D/E Ratio)

- **Description:** Compares long-term debt to shareholders' equity. Highly indebted companies are at greater financial risk.
- **Guideline:** Set a maximum of **0.5**, which may be raised to **1.5** if a more detailed financial analysis is performed.

9. Minimum Annual Revenue

- **Description:** Measures the company's gross annual revenue, ensuring that it is large enough to compete in the market.
- **Guideline:** Set a minimum of **$50 million** in annual revenue.

10. Return on Assets (ROA)

- **Description:** Measures the company's efficiency in generating profits from its assets.
- **Guideline:** Set a minimum of **8%**, avoiding companies with low profitability. It is not recommended to lower this limit to less than **5**%.

11. Minimum Share Price

- **Description:** The share price may reflect the market's perception of the company. Shares below certain values may indicate high risks.
- **Guideline:** Set a minimum of **$5** per share, avoiding companies with higher risk.

12. Institutional Ownership Percentage

- **Description:** Measures the percentage of shares held by institutional investors, such as investment funds and insurance companies.
- **Guideline:** Set a minimum of **30%**. Low institutional ownership may indicate a lack of confidence in the company among large investors.

13. Revenue Growth:

- **Description**: Measures a company's sales growth over a specific period.
- **Guideline**: A revenue growth rate of more than 10% per year is typical for growth stocks.

14. Earnings Per Share (EPS) Growth:

- **Description**: Indicates the annual growth rate of earnings per share.
- **Guideline**: Consistent EPS growth above 10% per year is desirable.

15. Return on Invested Capital (ROIC):

- **Description**: Assesses a company's efficiency in allocating capital to profitable investments.
- **Guideline**: An ROIC above 10% suggests effective use of capital.

16. Profit Margins:

- **Description:** Reflects the percentage of revenue that turns into profit after all expenses.
- **Guideline**: Improvement in profit margins over time indicates operational efficiency.

17. Price/Earnings to Growth (PEG) Ratio:

- **Description**: Evaluates the P/E ratio in relation to the company's earnings growth rate.
- **Guideline**: A PEG ratio below 1 may indicate undervaluation relative to growth.

18. Relative Strength:

- **Description**: Compares a stock's performance to the overall market or a specific index.
- **Guideline**: A relative strength above 70 indicates that the stock is outperforming the market.

19. Market Capitalization:

- **Description**: Represents the total market value of a company's outstanding shares.
- **Guideline**: Growth stocks typically have a market capitalization above $1 billion, indicating established companies with growth potential.

By applying these screening parameters, investors can systematically identify potential value and growth stocks that align with their investment strategies.

Quick Screening of Value Stocks

Value stocks are typically undervalued by the market, trading at prices below their intrinsic value. Investors seek out these stocks based on specific financial metrics that indicate potential undervaluation.

Common Parameters for Screening Value Stocks:

1. Market Capitalization

- **Description:** Measures the total market value of a company, calculated by multiplying the stock price by the total number of shares outstanding. Very small companies tend to be riskier and may not meet value criteria.
- **Guideline:** Set a minimum of **$250 million** in market capitalization, as value strategies typically lead to mid- and large-cap stocks.

2. Price/Sales Ratio (P/S Ratio)

- **Description:** Indicates how many times a company's revenue is reflected in its share price. A low P/S ratio indicates potentially undervalued shares.
- **Guideline:** Set a maximum P/S of **3.0**, with most viable candidates having a P/S below **2.0**.

3. Analyst Ratings (Consensus Ratings)

- **Description:** Average of analysts' buy, hold, and sell recommendations. The higher the value, the worse the recommendation.

- **Guideline:** Set a **minimum of 2.2**, filtering out stocks that are poorly rated by analysts (between "weak buy" and "hold/sell").

4. Current Ratio

- **Description:** Measures the company's ability to pay its short-term obligations with its short-term assets.
- **Guideline:** Set a minimum of **1.5**, ensuring that the selected companies are financially sound.

5. Long-Term Debt/Equity Ratio (D/E Ratio)

- **Description:** Compares long-term debt to shareholders' equity. Companies with low financial leverage are preferred in value strategies.
- **Guideline:** Set a maximum of **0.4**, excluding excessively indebted companies.

6. Minimum Annual Revenue

- **Description:** Measures the company's annual gross revenue, ensuring that it has legitimate business operations.
- **Guideline:** Set a minimum of **$50 million** in revenue over the last 12 months (**TTM – Trailing Twelve Months**).

7. Minimum Share Price

- **Description:** Very low-priced stocks may indicate problematic or excessively risky companies.
- **Guideline:** Set a minimum of **$5** per share, in line with the practice of many institutional funds that avoid stocks below this value.

8. Relative Strength Index

- **Description:** Measures stock price performance relative to all stocks in the market over the last 12 months. A lower value indicates an un r stock with potential for future appreciation.
- **Guideline:** Set a maximum of **60**, excluding stocks that already show strong performance.

9. Institutional Ownership Percentage

- **Description:** Measures the percentage of shares held by institutional investors, such as investment funds. Stocks that are very out of favor may have little or no institutional ownership, which can be a negative warning sign.
- **Guideline:** Set a **minimum of 5% and a maximum of 60%**, ensuring that companies have some institutional participation but are not too popular among large investors.

10. Price-to-Earnings Ratio (P/E):

- **Description**: Measures a company's current stock price relative to its earnings per share.
- **Guideline**: A P/E ratio below 15 is often considered indicative of a value stock.

11. Price/Book Ratio (P/B):

- **Description**: Compares a company's market value to its book value.
- **Guideline**: A P/B ratio below 1 suggests that the stock may be undervalued.

12. Debt-to-Equity Ratio (D/E):

- **Description**: Assesses a company's financial leverage by comparing total liabilities to shareholders' equity.

- **Guideline**: A D/E ratio below 0.5 indicates lower financial risk.

13. Current Liquidity Ratio:

- **Description**: Assesses a company's ability to cover short-term obligations with short-term assets.
- **Guideline**: A current liquidity ratio above 1.5 is preferable, indicating good liquidity.

14. Dividend Yield:

- **Description**: Shows the annual dividend payment as a percentage of the stock price.
- **Guideline**: A dividend yield above 1% is often attractive to value investors.

15. Return on Equity (ROE):

- **Description**: Measures profitability by revealing how much profit a company generates from shareholders' equity.
- **Guideline**: An ROE above 10% indicates efficient use of equity.

16. Earnings Growth:

- **Description**: Tracks the annual growth rate of earnings per share over a specified period.
- **Guideline**: Positive earnings growth over the last five years is a favorable indicator.

Building a Stock Portfolio: The Art of Selecting and Balancing Investments

Investing in stocks is not just about selecting good individual stocks; true success comes from building a balanced and efficient portfolio. A well-structured portfolio seeks to maximize risk-adjusted returns, diversify intelligently, and align with the investor's goals and risk tolerance.

After conducting rigorous screening and carefully analyzing growth and value stocks, it is time to select the best candidates and build a solid portfolio. This process involves several strategic decisions, including asset allocation, diversification, risk optimization, and periodic rebalancing.

Key Factors in Building a Stock Portfolio

To build an efficient portfolio, investors should consider the following elements:

1. Smart Diversification: Balancing Risk and Return

- A well-constructed portfolio does not depend on a single stock or sector to generate returns.
- Diversification reduces the specific risk of individual companies.
- Combining different sectors (technology, healthcare, energy, consumer goods, etc.) can smooth out volatility.

Example: An investor may choose a mix of **growth** and **value** stocks, combining defensive sectors (healthcare, consumer staples) with cyclical sectors (technology, industrials, financials).

2. Size and Number of Stocks in the Portfolio

- What is the ideal number of stocks in a portfolio?
- **Less than 10 stocks:** Excessive exposure to specific risk.
- **Between 15 and 25 stocks:** Effective diversification without excessively diluting returns.
- **More than 30 stocks:** Greater protection against specific risks, but may hinder active management.

Studies show that marginal diversification becomes insignificant after **20 to 30** well-chosen **assets**.

3. Weight of Each Stock in the Portfolio

- **Equal weights**: Each stock receives the same proportion within the portfolio (example: 5% each in a portfolio of 20 stocks).
- **Weights proportional to return potential**: More capital is allocated to stocks with greater conviction.
- **Risk-based weights**: More volatile stocks receive a lower allocation, while more stable stocks receive a higher weight.

Practical example: An investor may allocate 40% of the portfolio to growth stocks, 40% to value stocks, and 20% to defensive assets (such as REITs or dividend stocks).

4. Risk Reduction Strategies

In addition to diversification, other techniques help control risk:

- **Stop Loss and Take Profit Parameters:** Set loss and profit limits to protect capital.
- **Correlation Tracking:** Monitor the relationship between assets to avoid excessive concentration in the same market behavior.

- **Hedging:** Use uncorrelated assets, such as gold, fixed-income ETFs, or options, to mitigate risk.

Portfolio Optimization Techniques

To build a more efficient portfolio, there are quantitative methods that help maximize risk-adjusted returns:

1. Modern Portfolio Theory (MPT)

- Created by Harry Markowitz, it suggests that **combining assets with different risks and correlations** can reduce overall portfolio volatility without compromising return.
- The **efficient frontier** shows which combinations of assets offer **the best return for a given level of risk**.

Example: By including **value** stocks that are more defensive, an investor can balance **growth** stocks, which have higher volatility.

2. CAPM (Capital Asset Pricing Model)

- Helps define the expected return on each stock based on market risk (Beta).
- Investors can calculate whether a stock is offering sufficient return for the risk involved.

3. Volatility-Based Allocation

- Instead of dividing the portfolio equally among stocks, the weight is distributed according to the volatility of each asset.
- **Higher-risk stocks** receive a lower allocation, while **stable stocks** receive a higher proportion.

4. Periodic Rebalancing

- A portfolio needs to be adjusted periodically to maintain the original strategy.
- **When to rebalance?**
    - If a stock grows too much and exceeds its ideal weight.
    - If a stock falls more than expected and your investment thesis is still valid.
    - On a scheduled basis (every 6 months or annually).

Conclusion: Building a Solid and Efficient Portfolio

Building a stock portfolio is a **strategic process** that goes beyond simply buying good stocks. It is necessary to balance growth, risk, and diversification to create a **resilient** portfolio **that is aligned with the investor's objectives**.

After learning about **stock screening**, investors now have all the tools they need to select the **best assets** and organize them in a way that **maximizes returns and reduces risk**. The next step is **to monitor the portfolio and adjust** it **as necessary**, ensuring effective long-term investment.

Chapter 12. [Asset] Modern Portfolio Theory (MPT)

Modern Portfolio Theory (MPT) is a financial framework that aims to help investors build portfolios that maximize expected returns for a given level of risk. Developed by economist Harry Markowitz in the 1950s, MPT emphasizes the importance of diversification and the relationships between different assets to achieve an optimal balance between risk and return.

Purpose and Functioning of MPT

At the heart of MPT is the suggestion that the risk and return of an individual investment should not be analyzed in isolation, but rather in the context of how that investment contributes to the risk and return of the portfolio as a whole. By combining assets with different degrees of correlation, investors can build a portfolio that offers the highest possible expected return for a given level of risk. This is achieved through diversification, which reduces the impact of a single asset's performance on the overall portfolio.

Historical Context

Harry Markowitz introduced MPT in his 1952 article entitled "Portfolio Selection," published in *the Journal of Finance*. His groundbreaking work laid the foundation for modern investment strategies by formalizing the benefits of diversification and providing a quantitative method for balancing risk and return. For his contributions, Markowitz was awarded the Nobel Memorial Prize in Economic Sciences in 1990.

How Portfolio Optimization Works in MPT

Portfolio optimization is based on mathematical principles to determine the best combination of assets. It uses expected return, risk (standard deviation), and correlations between assets to create a portfolio that is on the Efficient Frontier—the set of portfolios that offers the highest expected return for a given level of risk.

To optimize a portfolio, it is necessary to:

1. **Define Expected Returns** — Estimate the returns of each asset.
2. **Measure Risk (Standard Deviation)** – Assess the volatility of each asset.
3. **Determine Correlations** – Understand how assets move in relation to each other.
4. **Build the Efficient Frontier** – Identify optimal combinations of assets.
5. **Select the Best Portfolio Based on Risk Tolerance** – Choose a portfolio that is aligned with the investor's objectives.

Let's take a closer look at how optimization works.

Numerical Example

Consider a simple portfolio with two assets: **Stock A** and **Bond B**.

- **Expected Returns:**
    - Stock A: 8%
    - Bond B: 4%
- **Standard Deviations (Risk):**
    - Stock A: 10%
    - Bond B: 5%
- **Correlation Coefficient:**

  - Stock A and Bond B: 0.2

Our goal is to find the optimal weights (**w_1** for Stock A and **w_2** for Bond B) that **minimize the variance of the portfolio** for a given expected return.

Mathematical Formulation for Portfolio Optimization

To calculate the optimal allocation, we use the following main formulas:

Expected Portfolio Return

The expected return of a portfolio *E*[Rp] is the weighted sum of the expected returns of its assets:

$$E[R_p] = w_1 E[R_1] + w_2 E[R_2] + \ldots + w_n E[R_n]$$

Where:

- w_i = Weight of asset i in the portfolio
- $E[R_i]$ = Expected return of asset i

Portfolio Risk (Variance and Standard Deviation)

The variance σ_p^2 of the portfolio, which measures the total risk, is given by:

$$\sigma_p^2 = \sum w_i^2 \sigma_i^2 + \sum\sum w_i w_j \sigma_i \sigma_j \rho_{i,j}$$

Where:

- σ_i^2 = Variance of asset i
- $\rho_{i,j}$ = Correlation between asset i and asset j
- $\sigma_i \sigma_j \rho_{i,j}$ = Contribution to total portfolio risk based on how assets move together

The formula shows that combining assets with low or negative correlation reduces the overall risk of the portfolio. But don't be alarmed by the formula, the concept is simple and we can give a numerical example with two assets.

Formulas:

- **Expected Portfolio Return ($E[R_p]$):**

$$E[R_p] = w_1 \times E[R_1] + w_2 \times E[R_2]$$

- **Portfolio Variance (σ_p^2):**

$$\sigma_p^2 = (w_1 \times \sigma_1)^2 + (w_2 \times \sigma_2)^2 + 2 \times w_1 \times w_2 \times \sigma_1 \times \sigma_2 \times \rho_{12}$$

Where:

- $E[R_1]$ and $E[R_2]$ are the expected returns of Stock A and Bond B, respectively.
- σ_1 and σ_2 are the standard deviations of Stock A and Bond B, respectively.
- ρ_{12} is the correlation coefficient between Stock A and Bond B.

Calculation Steps

1. Define the Expected Return of the Portfolio:

We want an expected return of 6%.

$$0.06 = w_1 \times 0.08 + (1 - w_1) \times 0.04$$

$$0.06 = 0.08w_1 + 0.04 - 0.04w_1$$

$$0.02 = 0.04w_1 \Rightarrow w_1 = 0.5$$

$$w_2 = 1 - w_1 = 0.5$$

2. Calculate the Portfolio Variance:

$$\sigma_p^2 = (0.5 \times 0.10)^2 + (0.5 \times 0.05)^2 + 2 \times 0.5 \times 0.5 \times 0.10 \times 0.05 \times 0.2$$

$$\sigma_p^2 = 0.0025 + 0.000625 + 0.00025 = 0.003375$$

3. Calculate the Portfolio Standard Deviation:

$$\sigma_p = \sqrt{0.003375} \approx 5.81\%$$

Conclusion of the Example

By allocating 50% to Stock A and 50% to Bond B, the portfolio achieves an expected return of 6% with a standard deviation of approximately 5.81%.

This example shows how MPT helps investors choose the ideal asset weights to optimize the balance between risk and return.

Modern Portfolio Theory provides a structured approach to portfolio construction, focusing on:

- Efficient diversification
- Reduction of unsystematic risk
- Risk-return optimization

This theory remains the basis for many professional and institutional investment decisions to this day.

Step-by-Step Example of Optimization with Numbers

Consider a portfolio with three assets:

Asset	Expected Return	Standard Deviation (Risk)	Correlation with Other Assets
Stock A	8%	12%	-
Stock B	6%	10%	0.3 with Stock A
Bond C	4%	5%	0.1 with A, 0.2 with B

We want to determine the optimal allocation among these assets.

Step 1: Define the Risk-Return Objective

Suppose the investor wants a moderate-risk portfolio with an expected return of around 6%.

Step 2: Assign Initial Weights and Calculate the Portfolio Return

Let's start with the following allocation:

- 50% in Stock A
- 30% in Stock B
- 20% in Bond C

Using the expected return formula:

$$E[R_p] = (0.50 \times 0.08) + (0.30 \times 0.06) + (0.20 \times 0.04)$$

$$E[R_p] = 0.04 + 0.018 + 0.008 = 0.066 = 6{,}6\%$$

The expected return is **6.6%**, which is close to our target of 6%.

Step 3: Calculate Portfolio Risk (Standard Deviation)

We use the portfolio variance formula with the correlations provided:

$$\sigma_p^2 = (0.50^2 \times 0.12^2) + (0.30^2 \times 0.10^2) + (0.20^2 \times 0.05^2) + 2(0.50 \times 0.30 \times 0.12 \times 0.10 \times 0.3)$$

Solving step by step:

$$\sigma_p^2 = (0.25 \times 0.0144) + (0.09 \times 0.01) + (0.04 \times 0.0025) + 2(0.50 \times 0.30 \times 0.12 \times 0.10 \times 0.3)$$

$$\sigma_p^2 = 0.0036 + 0.0009 + 0.0001 + 0.00432 + 0.00024 + 0.00012$$

$$\sigma_p^2 = 0.00928$$

$$\sigma_p = \sqrt{0.00928} \approx 9.63\%$$

The total portfolio risk is approximately **9.63**%.

Step 4: Adjust Weights to Improve Risk-Return Ratio

Now we can adjust the weights to **reduce risk** while keeping the return close to 6%.

Suppose we increase the allocation in Security C to **30%** and reduce Stock A to **40%**.

New expected return: 6.2%
New standard deviation: 8.9%

This new allocation presents **lower risk with similar return**, moving the portfolio closer to the **Efficient Frontier**, i.e., delivering a **better risk-adjusted return**.

Markowitz Efficient Frontier – Portfolio with 3 Assets

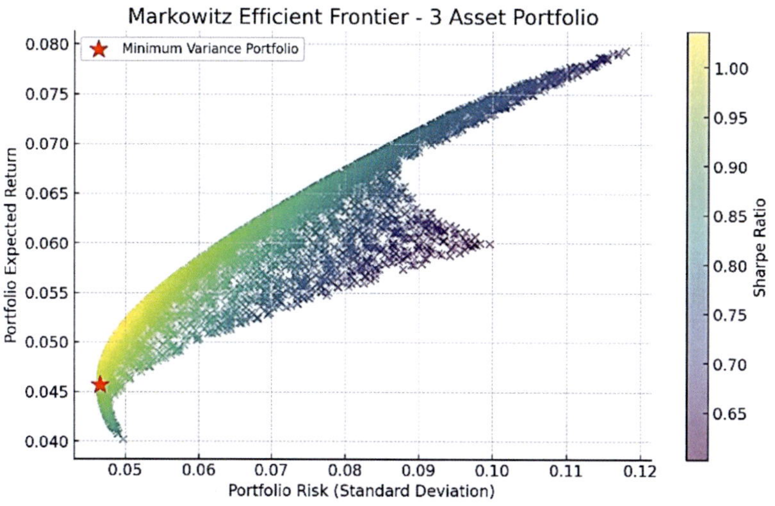

Here is the Markowitz Efficient Frontier for the portfolio with 3 assets (Stock A, Stock B, and Bond C). The chart illustrates different portfolio combinations, with the Minimum Variance Portfolio (MVP) highlighted in red. This MVP represents the portfolio with the lowest possible risk for a given return, demonstrating how diversification can help investors optimize the relationship between risk and return.

Why MPT Optimization Works

Diversification Reduces Risk:

Adding bonds to the portfolio reduces volatility without significantly compromising return.

Correlations Are Crucial:

Assets with low or negative correlation offer the best diversification benefits.

The Efficient Frontier Guides Decisions:

Investors should seek to be on the Efficient Frontier, where it is possible to maximize returns for a given level of risk.

Optimization Tools Exist:

Although manual calculations aid understanding, tools such as Excel Solver, Python, or online optimizers facilitate the process of finding the ideal combination of assets.

Conclusion

Portfolio optimization with MPT is about **adjusting asset weights** to achieve the best combination of risk and return.

By selecting a **mix of stocks, bonds, and other assets**, investors can **reduce risk while maintaining solid returns**.

The **Efficient Frontier** represents the **best possible portfolios**, and by adjusting allocations, investors can get **closer to the best risk-adjusted return**.

This process leads to **smarter investment decisions**, balancing risk and reward in a scientific way!

Post-Modern Portfolio Theory (PMPT)

Post-Modern Portfolio Theory (PMPT) emerged as an improvement on traditional Modern Portfolio Theory (MPT), addressing some of its limitations by offering a more detailed approach to risk assessment and portfolio optimization. PMPT was introduced in 1991 by software designers Brian M. Rom and Kathleen Ferguson, who identified limitations in MPT-based software and sought to develop a more comprehensive framework for portfolio optimization.

Key Differences Between MPT and PMPT:

Risk Measurement:

- **MPT:** Uses the standard deviation of returns as the primary risk metric, treating all volatility—both gains and losses—as equal.
- **PMPT:** Focuses on downside risk, emphasizing the potential for losses below a certain threshold, aligning more closely with investor concerns.

Assumptions About Return Distribution:

- **MPT:** Assumes that returns follow a normal distribution, implying symmetry between potential gains and losses.
- **PMPT:** Recognizes that returns can be asymmetric and exhibit fat tails, leading to a more accurate representation of real-world return patterns.

Advantages of PMPT:

- **Improved Risk Assessment:** By focusing on downside risk, PMPT provides a clearer view of potential losses, which is often more relevant to investors.
- **Improved Performance Metrics:** It incorporates measures such as the Sortino Ratio, which refines performance evaluation

by considering only negative volatility, offering a more accurate analysis than the traditional Sharpe Ratio.

By addressing the limitations of MPT, Postmodern Portfolio Theory offers investors a more refined set of tools for portfolio construction, emphasizing downside risk and accommodating the complexities of real-world return distributions.

Capital Asset Pricing Model (CAPM)

The Capital Asset Pricing Model (CAPM) is an extension of **Modern Portfolio Theory (MPT)**, introduced by **Harry Markowitz** in 1952. While MPT emphasizes **diversification** to build efficient portfolios that optimize return for a given level of risk, CAPM expands on this framework by offering a method for evaluating the **expected return of an individual asset based on its systematic risk** relative to the market as a whole.

Developed in the early 1960s by economists such as **William Sharpe**, **John Lintner**, and **Jan Mossin**, CAPM establishes a **linear relationship between the expected return of an asset and its beta** (a measure of market-related risk).

Objective of CAPM

The objective of CAPM is to determine the **required rate of return** for an asset, considering its risk relative to the market. The model helps investors **make more informed decisions about which assets to include in their portfolio** by assessing whether the asset offers a fair expected return for the level of systematic risk it carries.

CAPM formula

The expected return on an asset according to CAPM is calculated as:

$$E(R_i) = R_f + \beta_i \times (E(R_m) - R_f)$$

Where:

- $E(R_i)$: Expected return of asset i
- R_f: Risk-free rate
- β_i: Beta of asset i
- $E(R_m)$: Expected return of the market
- $E(R_m) - R_f$: Market risk premium

Visualization: Security Market Line (SML)

The relationship described by CAPM can be visualized through the **Security Market Line (SML)**, which plots the expected return of assets as a function of their beta values. The **SML** is a straight line with:

Y-axis intercept: represents the risk-free rate R_f

Slope of the line: equal to the market risk premium $(E(R_m)-R_f)$

Assets **above the SML** are considered **undervalued** (they offer a return higher than the risk they present), while assets **below the SML** are **overvalued**.

Incorporating a Risk-Free Asset

Based on the previous example with three assets (Stock A, Stock B, and Bond C), we now introduce a **risk-free asset** (e.g., a Treasury bond) to illustrate CAPM and the SML.

Assumptions:

Risk-Free Rate (R_f): 3%

Market Return ($E(R_m)$): 10%

Asset Betas:

Stock A: β_A=1.2

Stock B: β_B =0.8

Bond C: β_C =0.3

Calculation of Expected Returns with CAPM

$$E(R_A) = 3\% + 1{,}2 \times (10\% - 3\%) = 11{,}4\%$$

$$E(R_B) = 3\% + 0{,}8 \times (10\% - 3\%) = 8{,}6\%$$

$$E(R_C) = 3\% + 0{,}3 \times (10\% - 3\%) = 5{,}1\%$$

Constructing the SML Graph

To view the **SML**:

Plot the risk-free asset: at point β=0, with a return of 3%

Plot the market portfolio: at the point β=1, with a return of 10%

Draw the SML: connecting these two points with a straight line

Now plot the individual assets based on their betas and expected returns:

1. **Stock A:**
   - $E(R_A) = 3\% + 1.2 \times (10\% - 3\%) = 11.4\%$
2. **Stock B:**
   - $E(R_B) = 3\% + 0.8 \times (10\% - 3\%) = 8.6\%$
3. **Bond C:**
   - $E(R_C) = 3\% + 0.3 \times (10\% - 3\%) = 5.1\%$

Each asset **should be aligned with the SML** if it is **fairly valued** according to CAPM.

Security Market Line (SML) - CAPM

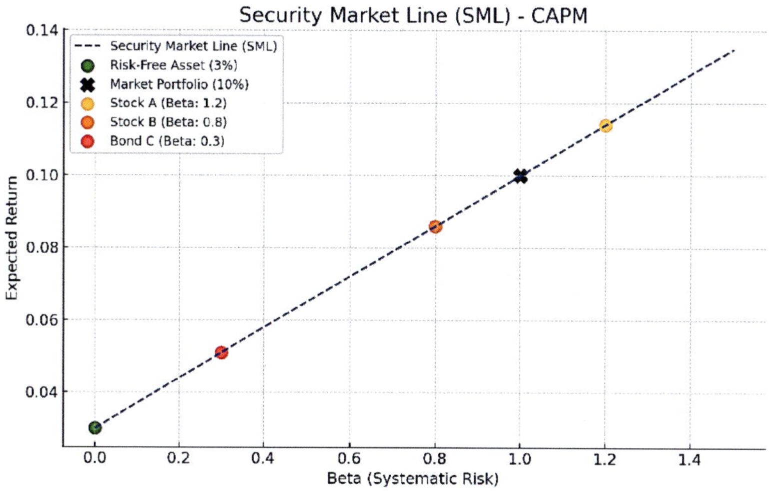

The blue dotted line represents the **SML** (Security Market Line), showing the relationship between **Beta** (systematic risk) and expected return.

- The green dot represents the **Risk-Free Asset** (3%) with **Beta = 0**.
- The black "X" marks the **Market Portfolio** (10%) with **Beta = 1**.
- Individual assets (Stock A, Stock B, and Bond C) are plotted according to their **Beta** values and expected returns.

This visualization illustrates how **CAPM** (Capital Asset Pricing Model) determines the appropriate return for different levels of systematic risk and helps investors assess whether assets are correctly priced.

Tying It All Together: Valuation, Risk, and Return

CAPM provides a framework for assessing whether an asset offers **an adequate return for its level of systematic risk**.

By comparing the expected return of the asset with the SML:

If it is **above the SML** → the asset is **undervalued** (great for buying)

If it is **below the SML** → the asset is **overvalued** (less attractive)

This approach helps investors **make informed decisions**, balancing risk and return, ensuring that **each asset contributes efficiently to the overall performance of the portfolio**.

MPT and CAPM: Connecting the Efficient Frontier with the SML

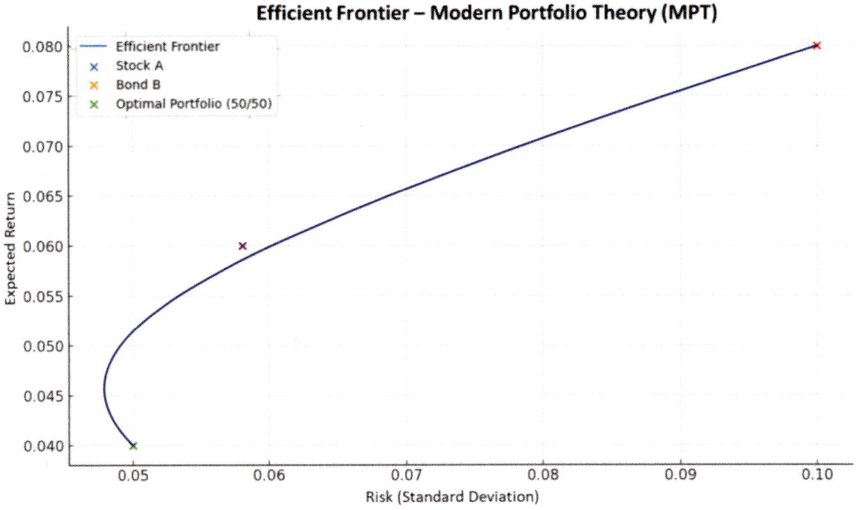

Here is the **Efficient Frontier** chart based on the Modern Portfolio Theory (MPT) example:

- **Stock A**: Expected return of 8%, risk of 10%
- **Bond B**: Expected return of 4%, risk of 5%

- **Optimal 50/50 portfolio**: 6% return with approximately 5.81% risk

The blue line represents all possible combinations between the two assets, highlighting how diversification can **reduce risk for the same return**, or **increase return while keeping risk constant**.

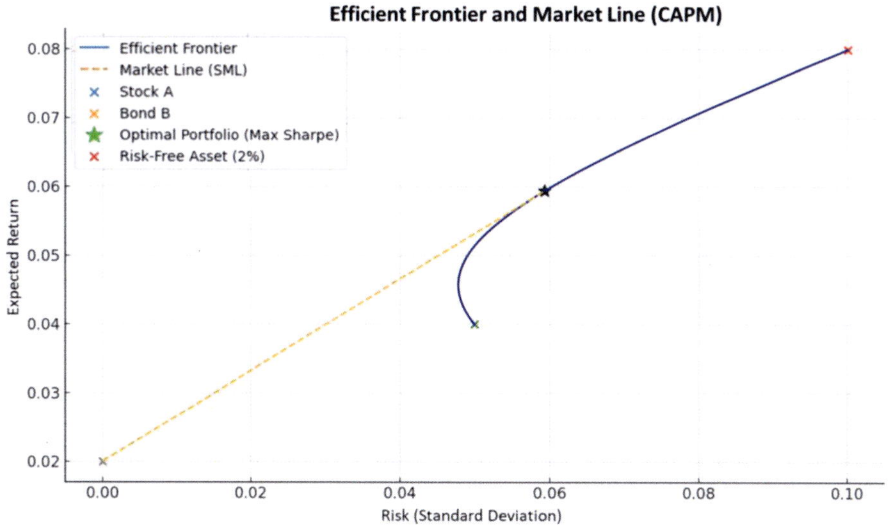

Here is the updated graph with the **Efficient Frontier** and the **Security Market Line (SML)** of the **CAPM** model:

- The **black star** represents the **optimal portfolio with the highest Sharpe ratio**, i.e., the best balance between return and risk.
- The **orange dotted line** shows the **market line (SML)**, starting from **the risk-free asset (2%)** to the portfolio with the highest Sharpe ratio.
- This line represents all **efficient combinations between risky assets and the risk-free asset**.

In CAPM, assets above the SML are **undervalued** (great for buying), while those below are **overvalued** (less attractive).

Here are the **expected returns by the CAPM model** for fictitious assets based on the optimal portfolio identified above:

Asset	Beta	Expected Return (CAPM)
Stock X	1.2	6.73%
Stock Y	0.8	5.15%
Stock Z	1.5	7.91%

Interpretation:

- **Stock Z**, with a beta of 1.5, is more volatile than the market and requires a higher return as compensation.
- **Stock Y**, with a beta of 0.8, is more defensive, and therefore its required return is lower.
- These returns represent the **minimum return required by the investor** to assume the risk of each asset, based on market risk and the risk-free rate.

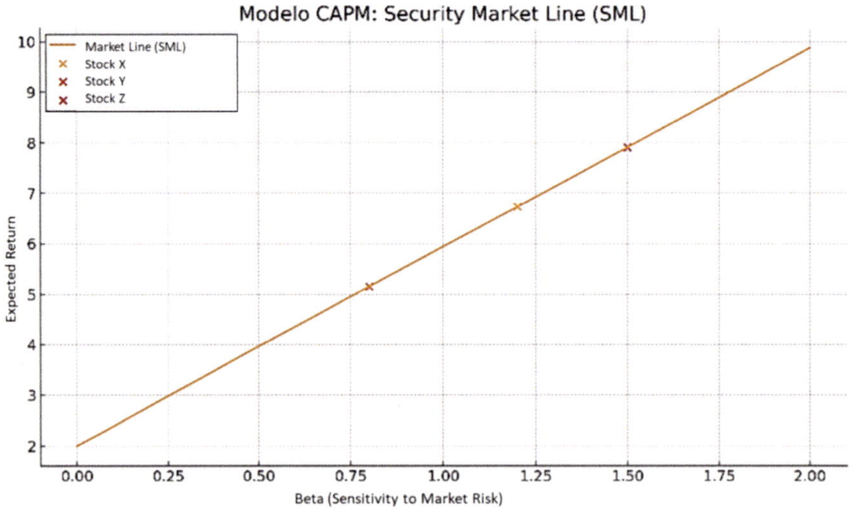

Here is the **Security Market Line (SML)** graph from the **CAPM** model, with the fictitious assets Stock X, Y, and Z positioned according to their respective **betas** and **expected returns**.

Visual Interpretation:

- The **orange line** represents the **SML**, which shows the fair expected return for any asset, given its beta.
- The **colored dots** show where the assets are in relation to the line:
    - If a point is **above the SML**, the asset may be **undervalued** (delivering more return than the risk would justify).
    - If it is **below the SML**, it may be **overvalued** (delivering less return for the risk assumed).

Example with US Market Stocks

If you want to see this analysis applied in practice, we can use real US market stocks as an example. CAPM allows us to estimate the expected return on an asset based on its level of systematic risk (beta), the risk-free rate (such as US Treasury bonds), and the market risk premium. With these variables, we can assess whether these stocks are offering a fair return relative to the risk they present.

Let's apply the **Capital Asset Pricing Model (CAPM)** to estimate the expected return on **Apple (AAPL)**, **Microsoft (MSFT)**, and **Alphabet (GOOGL)** stocks. CAPM is a tool that relates the expected return on an asset to its systematic risk (beta), considering the risk-free rate and the market risk premium.

CAPM formula:

$$E(R_i) = R_f + \beta_i \times (E(R_m) - R_f)$$

Where:

- $E(R_i)$: Expected return of asset i
- R_f: Risk-free rate
- β_i: Beta of asset i
- $E(R_m)$: Expected return of the market
- $E(R_m) - R_f$: Market risk premium

Step 1: Collect the necessary data

- **Risk-free rate (R_f)**: Generally, the yield on 10-year U.S. Treasury bonds is used as a proxy. Let's assume this rate is **3%**.

- **Expected market return ($E(R_m)$)**: Historically, the U.S. stock market has had an average annual return of around **10%**.

- **Market risk premium ($E(R_m) - R_f$)**: Difference between the expected market return and the risk-free rate. In this case, 10% - 3% = 7%.

- **Beta (β)**: Measures the sensitivity of a stock's return relative to the market. Beta values can be found on financial websites or in analysis reports. For this example, we will use the following hypothetical betas:

    - Apple (β_{AAPL}): **1.20**
    - Microsoft (β_{MSFT}): **1.05**
    - Alphabet (β_{GOOGL}): **1.10**

Step 2: Calculate the expected return for each stock using CAPM

1. **Apple (AAPL):**

$$E(R_{\text{AAPL}}) = 3\% + 1,20 \times 7\% = 3\% + 8,4\% = 11,4\%$$

2. **Microsoft (MSFT):**

$$E(R_{\text{MSFT}}) = 3\% + 1,05 \times 7\% = 3\% + 7,35\% = 10,35\%$$

3. **Alphabet (GOOGL):**

$$E(R_{\text{GOOGL}}) = 3\% + 1,10 \times 7\% = 3\% + 7,7\% = 10,7\%$$

Interpretation of Results:

- **Apple (AAPL)**: With a beta of 1.20, the stock is more volatile than the market. The expected return of 11.4% reflects this greater sensitivity to market variations.
- **Microsoft (MSFT)**: With a beta of 1.05, the stock has slightly higher volatility than the market. The expected return is 10.35%.
- **Alphabet (GOOGL)**: With a beta of 1.10, the stock is slightly more volatile than the market, with an expected return of 10.7%.

Important Considerations:

- **Beta**: A beta greater than 1 indicates that the stock tends to amplify market movements, while a beta less than 1 suggests less sensitivity to market fluctuations.
- **Limitations of CAPM**: Although useful, CAPM is based on several assumptions, such as market efficiency and the constancy of beta over time, which is not always the case in practice.
- **Complementary Analysis**: It is essential to consider other factors, such as company fundamentals, economic conditions, and industry outlook, when making investment decisions.

Conclusion:

CAPM provides an estimate of expected return based on the systematic risk of each stock. However, investment decisions should be based on a comprehensive analysis that includes multiple factors beyond beta and expected return.

Chapter 13. [Passive] Passive Investing with Index ETFs

Passive Investing with Index ETFs: The Simple and Efficient Way to Invest

In the world of investing, there are two main approaches to building wealth in the stock market: **active investing** and **passive investing**.

- **Active investing** involves selective stock picking, fundamental and technical analysis, and frequent buying and selling decisions to try to outperform the market. This approach requires time, knowledge, discipline, and a deep understanding of how the financial market works.
- **Passive investing**, on the other hand, seeks to track market performance efficiently and at low cost by investing in broad indices through **ETFs (Exchange-Traded Funds)**.

Passive investing is an ideal solution for **busy people, non-financial professionals, and investors who want a simple, long-term approach** without having to spend hours analyzing financial statements or trying to predict the next big market move.

Why Passive Investing with Index ETFs?

Investing through index ETFs has become one of the most popular strategies for individual and institutional investors. This approach is supported by academic studies showing that most active managers **are unable to consistently outperform the market over the long term**, especially after accounting for fees and operating costs.

The advantages of passive investing include:

Low Cost: Index ETFs have much lower management fees than actively managed funds, maximizing net returns for investors.

Simplicity: There is no need to select individual stocks; simply invest in an ETF that tracks a broadly diversified index.

Instant Diversification: With a single ETF, investors can gain exposure to hundreds or even thousands of stocks from different sectors and countries.

Lower Risk of Error: Since the investment tracks an index, investors do not run the risk of choosing the wrong stocks or making hasty decisions based on emotions.

Competitive Performance: Studies show that, in the long term, most passive investors outperform most active managers, mainly due to lower costs and less market timing error.

Who is Passive Investing Ideal for?

Passive investing is highly recommended for:

- Busy professionals who don't have time to analyze stocks.
- People who want to invest safely without needing advanced technical knowledge.
- Investors who seek a long-term approach and believe in global economic growth.
- Those who want to minimize costs and maximize net returns.

The Role of Index ETFs in an Investor's Portfolio

Index ETFs are designed to track the performance of benchmark indices, such as:

- **S&P 500 (SPY, VOO, IVV)** – Represents the 500 largest companies in the US.

- **Nasdaq 100 (QQQ)** – Exposure to leading technology and innovation companies.
- **Russell 2000 (IWM)** – Tracking small-cap companies in the US.
- **MSCI World (URTH, VT)** – Global diversification with stocks from various countries.

Conclusion: Investing Smartly and Efficiently

Passive investing through index ETFs allows anyone to **access global stock market growth in a simple, diversified, and efficient way**. For those who don't want to spend time analyzing companies, following financial news daily, or taking unnecessary risks, index ETFs are an extremely powerful solution.

In the next few topics, we will explore **how to choose the best ETFs, which indices to follow, how to combine different ETFs in your portfolio, and how to optimize passive returns over time**. But before that, let's also discuss two major problems with passive investing in market indices that you, as a smart investor, need to be aware of.

The Two Major Problems with Passive Index Investing

Passive investing through index ETFs has revolutionized the way investors allocate their resources. It offers **simplicity, low cost, and superior performance to most active investors in the long term**. However, despite its advantages, this strategy **has two major problems** that many investors ignore.

The popular belief that passive investing is **"safe" or "risk-free"** is **false**. There are significant risks that can seriously compromise long-term results.

1. Systemic Risk Is Still Present—And It Is Devastating

One of the great attractions of index ETFs is diversification, which reduces **unsystematic risk** (the individual risk of each company). However, there is one risk that **even the best diversification in the world cannot eliminate**: **systemic risk**.

- **Systemic risk affects the entire market.** It cannot be reduced simply by diversifying assets.
- **Each market crisis destroys trillions of dollars in equity.** Passive investors, who follow a "buy and hold" strategy, **are completely exposed to these declines**.
- **Passivity does not mean safety.** During the 2008 financial crisis, the S&P 500 fell **more than 50%**, taking years to recover. During the 2020 pandemic crash, the market plummeted nearly **30% in a matter of weeks**.

While investing in an index ETF **may seem less risky than trying to select individual stocks, it does not protect against crises and severe market declines**. This is a classic mistake made by investors who think that passive investing is "risk-free" or low-risk.

2. Relatively Low Absolute Returns in the Long Term

Market indices, such as **the S&P 500 and Nasdaq 100**, outperform most active investors over the long term. However, **absolute returns are still relatively low** compared to extremely well-done active investing (and a good dose of luck).

The S&P 500 has an average annual return of around 10% to 12% over the long term. While this is higher than the returns of many active funds and investors, **there are ways to optimize this return** without significantly increasing risk.

For investors who want to accelerate their wealth growth, relying solely on a passive strategy **may not be enough**.

The Solution: The SMIGRM Method

To solve these two major problems with passive investing, **I developed the SMIGRM method**, which was presented in **Chapter 8**.

SMIGRM introduces **two fundamental innovations** that make passive investing **much more powerful, secure, and efficient**:

1. SMIGRM Functions as a Market Crash Detector

- SMIGRM uses an advanced quantitative model to detect **early signs of severe market declines**.
- When a crash is approaching, the system alerts investors to **reduce their exposure to the market and seek safety in more stable assets**.
- This protects investors' assets from devastating declines and accelerates capital recovery.

2. SMIGRM Maximizes Risk-Adjusted Returns

- SMIGRM employs **context-dependent dynamic asset allocation** to ensure that investors **only take risks when it is advantageous to do so**.
- Instead of simply accepting average index returns, **SMIGRM dynamically adjusts portfolio allocation** to capture higher returns **without disproportionately increasing risk**.
- The result? **Significantly higher returns without compromising investor safety**.

The SMIGRM method **transforms passive investing into a more sophisticated, secure, and highly profitable model**. It solves the two main problems of passive investing and puts investors **in control of their financial future**.

The Top 10 Indexes for Passive Investors

For investors who wish to follow the passive investment strategy with index ETFs, below are the **top 10 indices** available to retail investors.

Index	ETF Ticker	AUM (Approximate)
S&P 500	SPY, VOO, IVV	$ 450 billion
Nasdaq 100	QQQ	$ 200 billion
DJIA	DIA	$ 30 billion
Russell 2000 (small cap)	IWM	$ 50 billion
MSCI World (global market)	URTH	$ 10 billion
FTSE Emerging Markets	VWO	$ 80 billion
S&P 400 (mid cap)	MDY	$ 15 billion
S&P 600 (small cap)	IJR	$ 10 billion
MSCI EAFE (Europe, Asia Pacific, excluding USA and Canada)	EFA	$ 50 billion
Total Stock Market (U.S. Stock Market)	VTI	$ 300 billion

Note: There are several ETFs that track the same index. For the **S&P 500**, for example, the largest ETF is **SPY**, but there are also **VOO (Vanguard) and IVV (iShares)**, which have lower fees.

These indices are **perfect for building a passive portfolio**, ensuring **exposure to different sectors and global markets**.

Conclusion: Passive Investing is Powerful, But It Can Be Even Better

Passive index investing is **one of the smartest and most effective strategies for long-term investors**. However, as seen in this chapter, **it is not perfect**.

- **Systemic risk remains present and can cause large losses during market crises**.
- **Long-term returns are relatively low** for those seeking accelerated asset growth.

The **good news** is that **SMIGRM solves these problems** by **offering protection against crashes and optimizing risk-adjusted returns.**

Learning how **to implement SMIGRM in practice** will result **in a more efficient, secure, and profitable passive portfolio**.

Chapter 14. Performance Indicators

Return-Risk Ratio: Understanding Investment Efficiency

The return-risk ratio is a critical metric for assessing how effectively an investment compensates for the level of risk assumed. Many investors ignore this concept, often pursuing returns without considering whether the associated risk is justified. Understanding these relationships enables informed decision-making and portfolio optimization.

1. Sharpe Ratio

Definition:
The Sharpe Ratio measures the excess return per unit of total risk, where risk is quantified by **standard deviation**. It assesses how much an investment compensates for its volatility.

Formula:

$$\text{Sharpe Ratio} = \frac{\text{Portfolio Return} - \text{Risk-Free Rate}}{\text{Portfolio Standard Deviation}}$$

Interpretation:

- A higher Sharpe Ratio indicates **better risk-adjusted returns**.
- Values above 1 are considered good, above 2 excellent, and above 3 exceptional.

Advantages:

- Easy to calculate and widely used.
- Takes into account both the return and the total risk of the investment.

Disadvantages:

- Penalizes positive and negative volatility equally, which may not reflect the reality of investor preferences.

---

2. Sortino Ratio

Definition:

The Sortino Ratio is an adjusted version of the Sharpe Ratio, which only considers **downside risk** (negative volatility), making it more suitable for risk-averse investors.

Formula:

$$\text{Sortino Ratio} = \frac{\text{Portfolio Return} - \text{Risk-Free Rate}}{\text{Downside Deviation}}$$

Interpretation:

- It measures the return per unit of negative risk, offering a more realistic assessment for those concerned about losses.
- The higher the index, the better the protection against declines.

Advantages:

- Considers only negative volatility (declines).
- More aligned with risk-adjusted return analysis.

Disadvantages:

- Requires calculation of **the standard deviation of declines**, which is more complex.

---

3. Return on Maximum Drawdown (RoMaD)

Definition:
RoMaD measures the return obtained in relation to **the largest cumulative decline** in the portfolio (from peak to trough).

Formula:

$$\text{RoMaD} = \frac{\text{Portfolio Return}}{\text{Maximum Drawdown}}$$

Interpretation:

- Indicates an investment's ability to **withstand large losses**.
- The higher the RoMaD, the better the performance in periods of high negative volatility.

Advantages:

- Focus on portfolio resilience in times of crisis.
- Reflects the **worst**-case **scenario**.

Disadvantages:

- Ignores small fluctuations, which can still impact investors.

---

4. Ulcer Index

Definition:
The Ulcer Index measures **the depth and duration** of drawdowns in the portfolio, making it an effective long-term risk metric.

Formula (conceptual):
The square of the daily drawdown percentage relative to the previous peak is calculated, and then the average of the values over time is taken.

$$\text{Ulcer Index} = \sqrt{\frac{1}{N}\sum_{i=1}^{N}(\text{Drawdown}_i)^2}$$

Interpretation:

- A lower value indicates less severe and shorter-lasting declines.
- Very useful for **long-term investors** seeking stability.

Advantages:

- It assesses not only the depth but also the recovery time from declines.
- Shows the stability of the portfolio in turbulent periods.

Disadvantages:

- More complex to calculate than other indices.

---

5. Information Ratio

Definition:
The Information Ratio measures the excess return of an investment over a benchmark, adjusted for **tracking error** (standard deviation of the difference between the returns of the portfolio and the benchmark).

Formula:

$$\text{Information Ratio} = \frac{\text{Portfolio Return} - \text{Benchmark Return}}{\text{Tracking Error}}$$

Interpretation:

- It assesses how well the manager has outperformed the benchmark, considering the **consistency of performance**.

- The higher the index, the better the performance adjusted to the benchmark.

Advantages:

- Very useful for evaluating **active managers**.
- Focuses on **the consistency of performance** relative to the market.

Disadvantages:

- Requires a clear and well-defined benchmark to be effective.

Why Risk-Return Ratios Matter

- Objective Evaluation: They allow investors to compare investments on a standardized basis, regardless of return levels.
- Focus on Efficiency: These metrics emphasize not only returns, but how they are achieved efficiently in relation to risk.
- Risk Awareness: They help investors identify whether they are taking on excessive risk for insufficient reward, preventing reckless decisions.

Risk-return ratios such as the Sharpe Ratio, Sortino Ratio, RoMaD, Ulcer Ratio, and Information Ratio offer valuable insights into investment performance. Each has its unique strengths and is suited to different investor objectives and risk preferences. By incorporating these metrics, investors can make more informed decisions, align portfolios with their risk tolerance, and achieve more consistent long-term success.

Illustrative Numerical Example

Here is an **illustrative chart** comparing five risk-adjusted return metrics with hypothetical values. It shows how different indices, such as **Sharpe**, **Sortino**, **RoMaD**, **Ulcer Index**, and **Information Ratio**, can be used to evaluate a portfolio's performance.

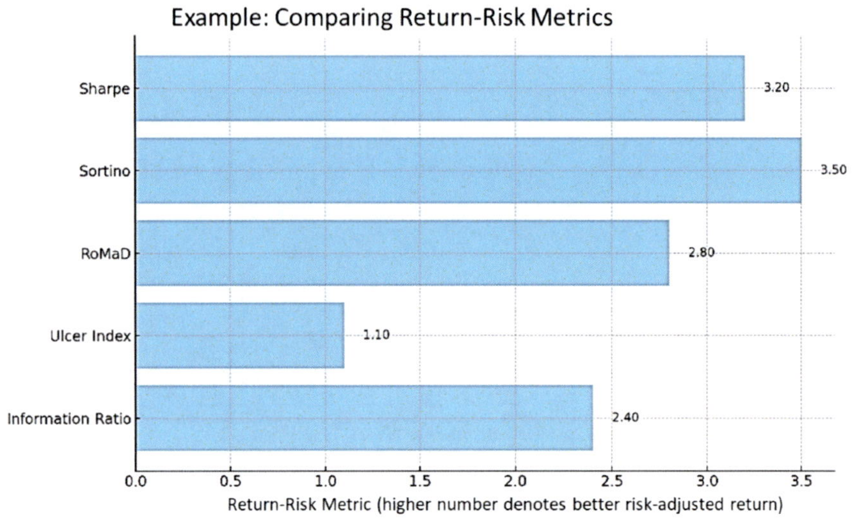

Let's analyze each of the **key risk-adjusted return metrics** based on market best practices and benchmarks widely accepted by professional analysts and managers. The idea here is to help you interpret the values as:

- **Ideal Level**: Excellent risk-adjusted performance
- **Acceptable Range**: Good or reasonable performance
- **Unacceptable Range**: Unsatisfactory performance, requires attention

1. Sharpe Ratio

Interpretation ranges:

- ✅ **> 2.0** — Excellent: the investment compensates very well for the risk assumed
- 🟡 **1.0 to 2.0** — Acceptable: good balance between risk and return
- 🔴 **< 1.0** — Poor: the risk may be too high in relation to the return

Graph value: 3.2
Interpretation: Excellent performance adjusted for total risk

---

2. Sortino ratio

Interpretation ranges:

- ✅ **> 2.0** — Excellent protection against downside risk
- 🟡 **1.0 to 2.0** — Good protection, but with some exposure
- 🔴 **< 1.0** — Return does not adequately compensate for downside risks

Graph value: 3.5
Interpretation: Excellent return adjusted for negative risk (fall)

---

3. RoMaD (Return on Maximum Drawdown)

Interpretation ranges:

- ✅ **> 2.0** — Excellent return vs. worst historical decline
- 🟡 **1.0 to 2.0** — Reasonable: tolerable, but could be optimized
- 🔴 **< 1.0** — Insufficient: drawdown was too high in relation to return

Graph value: 2.8
Interpretation: Very good — high return relative to the largest loss

---

4. Ulcer Index

Note: In this case, **the lower** the better!

Interpretation ranges:

- ✅ **< 5** — Low stress: minor declines and rapid recovery
- 🟡 **5 to 10** — Moderate volatility: tolerable, but should be monitored
- 🔴 **> 10** — Stressful: deep and prolonged drawdowns

Chart value: 1.1
Interpretation: Excellent — smooth and short-lived drawdowns

---

5. Information Ratio

Interpretation ranges:

- ✅ **> 1.0** — Excellent performance above the benchmark
- 🟡 **0.4 to 1.0** — Fair: some alpha generated, with consistency
- 🔴 **< 0.4** — Poor: little consistency or performance below the benchmark

Graph value: 2.4
Interpretation: Excellent consistency and outperforming the benchmark

---

General Summary of Chart Results:

Based on the illustrative values:

- The analyzed portfolio would have excellent risk-adjusted performance, both in terms of total risk and negative risk metrics.
- Historical drawdowns were not severe, and the portfolio demonstrated resilience.
- The manager or strategy consistently outperformed the benchmark.

The Greatest Advantage Brought by SMIGRM: The Return-Risk Ratio and Performance

In Chapter 8, we describe the SMIGRM Method. By avoiding serious corrections and crashes, SMIGRM allows capital to be better preserved when risks rise rapidly and excessively in the market. One of the biggest consequences on long-term investment results is the risk-return ratio. Investment risk is clearly reduced with SMIGRM and is easily visualized in the drastically reduced drawdowns when using the method.

Why are drawdowns so important? The reason is simple. Investors' investment plans often fail and are thrown out the window when drawdowns become unbearable. Even the most aggressive investor begins to throw in the towel when accumulated losses begin to exceed 20, 30, 40, or 50%! It is human nature, and at some point, they have to stop. And they are right to stop. It is foolish and crazy to continue insisting.

But with SMIGRM, this scenario is unlikely to materialize because SMIGRM would have already guided the investor to exit the market and reduce their risk exposure much earlier.

RoMaD (Return over Maximum Drawdown) is our preferred performance metric for this reason.

We have proven in practice, day after day, month after month, and year after year, that SMIGRM boosts the RoMaD of investments, making them much more efficient. In other words, **SMIGRM maximizes returns and minimizes risk in the risk-return ratio**. And that is exactly what every investor should aim for.

Chapter 15. Dividend Aristocrats: Stocks for Dividend Income

Dividend Aristocrats are a select group of stocks that **have a consistent history of paying and increasing dividends over decades**. These companies belong to **the S&P 500** and have a history of **increasing their dividends annually for at least 25 consecutive years**. This demonstrates **financial resilience, strong cash generation, and commitment to shareholders**.

Criteria for being a Dividend Aristocrat:

- Must be part of the **S&P 500**.
- Have increased dividends **for at least 25 consecutive years**.
- Maintain a **minimum market value** (usually above $3 billion).
- Have sufficient liquidity to be traded regularly.

Companies that meet these criteria are often **mature and established companies** operating in defensive sectors such as **consumer staples, healthcare, and utilities**.

Why Invest in Dividend Aristocrats?

For investors focused on **passive income**, Dividend Aristocrats are **strategic assets** because they offer:

- **Stable Income Stream** – As these companies **increase dividends annually**, investors can count on a predictable cash flow.
- **Protection Against Inflation** – With dividends growing over time, the income generated keeps pace with the rising cost of living.
- **Lower Volatility** – Dividend Aristocrats tend to be **less volatile**, as they are solid, profitable companies.

- **Dividend Reinvestment** – Reinvesting dividends increases the power of **compound interest**, accelerating capital growth.
- **Crisis Resistance** – During market crises, many of these companies continue to pay dividends, protecting investors.

Disadvantages and Risks of Dividend Aristocrats

- **Limited Growth** – These are **mature** companies that do not grow as quickly as **growth** stocks.
- **Sensitivity to Interest Rates** – When interest rates rise, investors may prefer **fixed-income securities** over dividend stocks.
- **Dividend Cuts** – Although rare among aristocrats, **dividend cuts** can occur in times of extreme crisis.
- **Variable Yield** – Some companies **have lower yields** and may not be the best options for those seeking high immediate returns.

Examples of Dividend Aristocrats

Here are **10 Dividend Aristocrats** from different sectors, with their approximate dividend **yields** and the length of time they have been paying dividends without interruption:

Company	Sector	Dividend Yield (Approximate)	Years Growing Dividends
Procter & Gamble (PG)	Consumer	2.4%	+65 years
Coca-Cola (KO)	Consumer	3.1%	+60 years
Johnson & Johnson (JNJ)	Healthcare	2.8%	+60 years
McDonald's (MCD)	Food	2.2%	+45 years
Pepsico (PEP)	Consumer	2.77%	+50 years
3M Company (MMM)	Industrial	5.7%	+60 years
Colgate-Palmolive (CL)	Consumer	2.5%	+60 years
ExxonMobile (XOM)	Energy	3.5%	+40 years

Walgreens Boots Alliance (WBA)	Pharmaceutical	6.5%	+45 years
Caterpillar (CAT)	Industrial	2.0%	+30 years

Note: Dividend yields are approximate and vary based on the stock price and the company's payment decisions.

Conclusion: Dividend Aristocrats Are a Smart Strategy for Passive Income

Dividend Aristocrats are a powerful choice for **investors seeking a reliable and growing source of income over time**. With a history of stable growth, resilience to crises, and a strong reputation in the market, these stocks can be **the cornerstone of a dividend-based investment portfolio**.

However, **it is essential to evaluate not only the dividend yield but also the sustainability of payments**, ensuring that the chosen companies will continue to grow and generate profits in the long term.

S&P 500 Dividend Aristocrats Index

Did you know that there is an index called **the S&P 500 Dividend Aristocrats Index?** Published by S&P Global, the index tracks the performance of S&P 500 companies that have increased their dividends every year for the past 25 consecutive years. The Index treats each constituent as a separate component asset, regardless of its size, weighting each company equally.

There are ETFs that replicate the index, such as the **ProShares S&P 500 Dividend Aristocrats ETF (NOBL)**.

Currently, there are **69 Dividend Aristocrats in the S&P 500**, but there are more than **100 U.S. companies** with a history of increasing dividends for 25 years or more. However, some are not part of the index because they are not components of **the S&P 500**, such as **Enterprise Products Partners (EPD)**, an MLP (Master Limited Partnership) with **26 years of consecutive dividend increases**.

David Harrell's article, published in **Morningstar** on February 11, 2025, explores the characteristics and benefits of **the S&P 500 Dividend Aristocrats Index**, as well as its limitations. Below is a summary of the main points covered:

Unique Characteristics of the S&P 500 Dividend Aristocrats Index

The article highlights some of the index's unique features:

Dividend calculation takes into account the total annual amount paid—that is, a company can maintain its streak of increases even if it does not raise its dividend quarterly, as long as it increases the payment at some point during the year.

Companies less than 25 years old can enter the index – If they are listed on the S&P 500 and meet the dividend criteria throughout their existence, they can become aristocrats before reaching 25 years as a company.

Benefits of Dividend Aristocrats

Dividend Aristocrats are **mature**, **financially sound** companies with robust earnings to fund and increase dividends on a regular basis. In addition, their long history of dividend growth indicates **management focused on shareholder value**, even in times of economic crisis.

One example is **ExxonMobil (XOM)**, which in 2020 increased its debt to maintain and modestly raise its dividend during the crisis caused by the pandemic.

Sectors with Greater Representation

The **consumer staples** sector has the largest presence in the index, with **16** aristocrat **companies**, including **Coca-Cola (KO), PepsiCo (PEP), and Procter & Gamble (PG)**. Other well-represented sectors include:

- **Industrial**: 14 companies.
- **Financial services**: 9 companies.
- **Basic materials and healthcare**: 7 companies each.
- **Utilities**: Only **4 companies** among the 32 in the S&P 500.

This data is surprising, as utility companies traditionally pay high dividends, but few qualify for **aristocrat** status.

Dividend Yields May Be Modest

Despite a consistent history of dividend growth, **not all aristocrat companies offer high dividend yields**. The aristocrat in the S&P 500 with the highest current yield is **Franklin Resources (BEN)**, with a **yield of 6.3%**, but **25 companies in the index have yields below 2%**, and **nine of them pay less than 1%**, such as **West Pharmaceutical Services (WST), which has a yield of only 0.3**%.

Average Dividend Yield of Dividend Aristocrats:

- **Average yield of the 69 aristocrats: 2.5%**
- **Average yield over the last 5 years (excluding Kenvue): 2.3%**
- **Yield of the NOBL ETF (ProShares S&P 500 Dividend Aristocrats): 2.0%**

This indicates that **aristocrat status does not always mean high dividend returns**, making it essential to evaluate each company individually.

Dividend Aristocrats Are Not Immune to Market Risks

Although aristocrat companies are more resilient and have a historical commitment to paying dividends, **no company is risk-free**.

Dividend cuts and suspensions can happen—A long history of dividend increases **does not guarantee** that a company will continue to pay them indefinitely.

Stress test: The 2020 crisis – During the pandemic, **66 S&P 500 companies reduced or suspended their dividends** due to falling demand and the global economic impact. Some did so preventively, while others were forced to reduce dividends after accepting government financial stimulus.

The danger of ignoring other opportunities – While Dividend Aristocrats are solid investments for passive income, **restricting a portfolio to them alone could mean missing out on younger companies with greater potential for dividend growth and appreciation**.

Conclusion: Dividend Aristocrats Are a Strong Option, But Not the Only One

The article concludes that **Dividend Aristocrats are an excellent option for investors seeking passive income and stability**, but that they **are not perfect**.

- **They are mature and resilient companies with a strong commitment to shareholders**.
- **They have a robust history of paying and increasing dividends, even during crises**.

- **They can be used as the basis for a solid dividend portfolio**.
- **They do not guarantee high yields** – Some aristocrat stocks have dividends **below 2%**, which may not be enough for those seeking immediate returns.
- **They are not immune to crises** – Companies may cut dividends even with a long history of growth.
- **They may exclude emerging companies with high growth potential** – Focusing only on aristocrats can cause investors to miss out on good opportunities in new and promising companies.

To maximize returns, **investors should balance aristocrats with other stocks with growing dividends and assets with strong appreciation potential**.

Chapter 16. Advanced Stock Option Strategies

In this chapter, we will discuss a very advanced topic that requires more detailed knowledge and teaching to understand. Don't worry if you find it very difficult, as this is natural for most people. This knowledge is not essential for success on Wall Street. But it is an important addition for those who master options. If you find the reading difficult, you can enroll in our options courses, where we will teach this fascinating topic in much more detail, step by step, so that you can take advantage of this phenomenal tool in your arsenal to further accelerate your wealth building.

Stock options are really powerful tools for investors and traders who want **to protect against risk, generate income, and maximize returns**. Unlike simply buying and selling stocks, options offer greater flexibility in a variety of scenarios, allowing for gains in bull, bear, or even sideways markets.

In this chapter, we will explore the **most popular and advanced stock option strategies**, explaining **how they work, their payoff profiles, the risks involved, and the best times to use them.**

The Most Popular Strategies with Stock Options

1. Covered Call: Generating Income with Stocks You Already Own

How It Works:

A covered call involves **selling a call option on stocks you already own**. In exchange, you receive a **premium**, which adds an extra income stream.

Payoff Profile:

- **Limited profit:** If the stock price rises above the strike price, the shares may be called and you lose additional gains.

- **Partial protection against declines:** The premium received partially reduces losses if the stock declines.

Risks:

- Your shares may be **sold at the strike price**, limiting your upside potential.
- The premium received **does not protect against significant declines in the stock price**.

Best Time to Use:

- When you **own shares and want to generate passive income**.
- When you are **neutral or moderately optimistic** about the stock and do not expect significant appreciation.

Numerical Example:

John owns 100 shares of **Apple (AAPL)**, currently trading at **$180.00**. He wants to generate income without selling his shares. He then **sells a call option with a strike price of $190.00 and a maturity date one month from now**, receiving **$4.00 per share** as a premium.

Possible Outcomes:

If AAPL remains below $190.00:

- John **keeps the $400 premium ($4.00 × 100 shares)** and retains his shares.

If AAPL rises above $190.00:

- The shares will be **sold at $190.00**, and John will earn a **total gain of $1,400 ($10.00 × 100 shares of appreciation + $400 from the option premium).**

If AAPL falls to $170.00:

- John still holds the shares, but the premium received **reduces the net loss to $6.00 per share, instead of $10.00**.

Best use: When the investor is **neutral to moderately optimistic** and wants to generate **passive income**.

2. Cash-Secured Put: Buying Stocks at a Discount

How it works:

The **cash-secured put** strategy involves **selling a put option on a stock you want to buy** while keeping enough cash in your account to purchase it if the option is exercised.

Payoff Profile:

- If the stock remains above the strike price, **you keep the premium received**.
- If it falls below the strike price, **you will buy the stock at a lower net cost (strike price minus the premium received).**

Risks:

- If the stock price falls significantly, you **may be forced to buy it above the market price**.

Best Time to Use:

- When you **want to buy a stock at a discount**.
- When you are **neutral to moderately optimistic** about the stock.

Numerical Example:

Carla wants to buy shares of **Tesla (TSLA)**, which is currently trading at **$220.00**. Instead of buying now, she sells a put option with a strike price **of $210.00**, receiving a premium of **$5.00 per share**.

Possible Outcomes:

If TSLA remains above $210.00:

- The option **expires worthless**, and Carla **keeps the $500 ($5.00 × 100 shares) as profit**.

If TSLA falls below $210.00:

- Carla **is obligated to buy the stock at $210.00**, but since she received a $5.00 premium, **her effective cost was $205.00 per share**.

Best use: For those who want **to buy shares at a discount** but want to be paid while they wait.

3. Protective Put: Protecting Against Losses

How it works:

The **protective put** strategy involves **buying a put option on a stock you already own** to protect yourself against declines in the asset's price.

Payoff Profile:

- If the stock price falls below the strike price, **the option limits your maximum loss.**
- If the stock rises, **you keep the gains, minus the cost of the option premium.**

Risks:

- The main cost is the **premium paid**, which can reduce profits if the stock does not fall.

Best Time to Use:

- When you want **to protect an investment against declines**.
- When you are **optimistic in the long term but concerned about short-term risks**.

Numerical example:

Lucas owns 100 shares of **Microsoft (MSFT)**, currently trading at **$330.00**. He fears a market correction and buys a put option with a strike price **of $320.00,** paying a premium of **$6.00 per share**.

Possible Outcomes:

If MSFT remains above $320.00:

- The option **expires worthless**, and Lucas **loses only the $600 ($6.00 × 100 shares) paid in premium**.

If MSFT falls to $300.00:

- Lucas can exercise his put option and **sell his shares at $320.00**, limiting his loss to **only $10.00 per share, instead of $30.00**.

Best use: To **protect positions** against severe declines without having to sell the shares.

4. Long Straddle: Profiting from Large Movements (Betting on Volatility)

How it works:

A **long straddle** involves **buying a call option and a put option at the same strike price and expiration date**. Profit occurs if the stock moves sharply in either direction.

Payoff Profile:

- If the stock rises or falls sharply, **one of the options will offset the losses of the other and generate a profit**.
- If the stock remains stable, **both options lose value and the strategy generates a loss**.

Risks:

- **Time decay (Theta):** If the stock does not move enough, the options will lose value.
- **High cost:** Premiums are expensive, especially when implied volatility is high.

Best Time to Use:

- When you expect a **big move but don't know which way** (example: before balance sheets or macroeconomic events).
- When volatility **is still low**, making premiums cheaper.

Numerical Example:

Marcos expects **NVIDIA (NVDA)** shares to move significantly after the next earnings report. The stock is trading at **$500.00**, so he buys:

- **A call option with a strike price of $500.00** paying **$20.00**.
- **A put option with a strike price of $500.00,** paying **$18.00**.

Total cost: **$38.00 per share ($3,800 for 100 shares).**

Possible outcomes:

If NVDA rises to $550.00:

- The call option **is worth $50.00**, the put option **becomes worthless**, and Marcos has a net profit of **$12.00 per share ($1,200 in total).**

If NVDA falls to $450.00:

- The put option **is worth $50.00**, the call option **is worthless**, and Marcos has the same profit of **$12.00 per share**.

If NVDA stays close to $500.00:

- Both options lose value and Marcos **loses money.**

Best use: When **strong volatility** is expected without knowing the direction.

5. Iron Condor: Generating Income in Stable Markets

How it works:

The **iron condor** combines **a put spread sale and a call spread sale**, profiting when the asset remains within a price range.

Payoff Profile:

- If the asset price remains between the strike prices, **all options expire worthless and you keep the premium received**.
- If there is a large price movement, **you may incur a loss**.

Risks:

- If the asset moves outside the comfort zone, you **may lose the difference between the strike prices minus the premium received**.

Best Time to Use:

- When you **expect low volatility** and the asset to remain within a price range.
- When you want **to generate recurring income with limited risk**.

Numerical Example:

Fernanda believes that **S&P 500 ETF (SPY)** shares will remain between **$420.00 and $440.00** next month. So she sets up an **Iron Condor**:

- **She sells a call with a strike price of $440.00 and buys a call with a strike price of $445.00.**
- **She sells a put with a strike price of $420.00 and buys a put with a strike price of $415.00.**
- She receives a **net premium of $2.00 per share ($200 for 100 shares).**

Possible Outcomes:

If SPY remains between $420 and $440:

- All options **expire worthless,** and Fernanda **keeps the $200 premium she received**.

If SPY exceeds $440 or falls below $420:

- She may **suffer a limited loss** of up to **$300**.

Best use: When **low volatility and a sideways market** are expected.

6. Butterfly Spread: Precise Bet on Stability

How it works:

A **butterfly spread** consists of **buying a call at a lower strike price, selling two calls at an average price, and buying a call at a higher price**.

Payoff Profile:

- The **maximum profit** occurs if the asset closes exactly at the middle strike price.
- The **maximum risk** is limited to the cost of entering the trade.

Risks:

- If the asset moves too far in either direction, **the cost of the trade may be lost**.

Best Time to Use:

- When you expect **low volatility** and want to bet that the price will remain within a specific range.

Final Considerations: Choosing the Best Strategy

Stock options offer numerous ways to optimize investments, **but each strategy has a specific purpose**.

- If you **want to generate passive income**, use **covered calls or iron condors**.
- If you want **to protect your portfolio**, opt for **protective puts**.
- If you expect **sharp movements**, adopt **long straddles**.
- If you believe in **low volatility**, try **iron condors or butterfly spreads**.

Mastering these **advanced strategies** will allow you to **invest more accurately, reduce risk, and maximize your returns**. However, it is essential to understand the **trade-offs between risk and reward** before implementing them.

Combining Option Strategies for an Even More Efficient Portfolio

Now that you have mastered the **key advanced options strategies**, it's time to take it a step further. **What if we could combine these strategies to further optimize portfolio returns, reducing risk and maximizing gains?**

The secret to an **efficient portfolio** lies not only in **choosing good stocks**, but in using **different options strategies** to benefit from **various market conditions**. In this chapter, we will explore how these strategies can be combined to create a **robust investment system with greater risk control and high return predictability**.

Strategy 1: Generating Passive Income Safely

Objective: Maximize **passive income** without significantly compromising the portfolio's appreciation potential.

How to Implement?

1. Covered Call Selling on Stocks You Own

- Sell out-of-the-money (OTM) calls on **low-volatility** stocks that you already have in your portfolio.
- Example: If you own **100 shares of Apple (AAPL) at $180**, you can sell a call **with a strike price of $195.00** and a one-month expiration.

2. Sell Puts to Buy Stocks at a Discount

- Choose **high-quality stocks** you want to add to your portfolio and **sell puts at attractive prices.**
- Example: If you want to buy **Tesla (TSLA) at $210.00**, sell puts **with a strike price of $205.00**, guaranteeing an additional discount.

Expected Results:

- **Steady cash flow** from premiums received.
- **Purchase of stocks below market price**, increasing capital efficiency.

Best for: Investors who want **to increase passive income while maintaining exposure to the stock market**.

Strategy 2: Protecting Your Portfolio Against Crises

Objective: Create an **automatic** crash **protection** system without having to completely exit the market.

How to implement?

1. Buy Protection Puts During Times of High Valuation

- After sharp market rallies, buy puts to protect profits.
- Example: Did the S&P 500 (SPY) rise from **$410 to $440** in three months? **Buy puts with a strike price of $430.00** to protect against a possible correction.

2. Finance Protection by Selling Calls (Collar Strategy)

- To **reduce the cost of the protective put**, sell calls on the same asset, creating a **Collar Trade**.
- Example: If you buy a **protective** put **for $5.00**, you can sell an OTM call for **$3.00**, reducing the net cost of protection.

Expected Results:

- **Reduction of the impact of crashes**, ensuring that large declines do not compromise the portfolio.
- **Profit protection in times of high volatility**.

Best for: Conservative investors who want protection against market declines.

Strategy 3: Betting on Volatility Without Choosing a Direction

Objective: To profit from large movements without having to predict whether the market will rise or fall.

How to implement?

1. Long Straddle on Key Events

- Buy **a call and a put at the same strike price** before high-impact events (e.g., balance sheets, Fed decisions).
- Example: Nvidia (NVDA) **before earnings** → purchase of **call and put at a strike price of $500.00**.

2. Conversion to Iron Condor After the Event

- If the asset price has not moved much, convert the **Long Straddle** into an **Iron Condor** by selling additional calls and puts to recover the premium.

Expected Results:

- **High profit if the market moves significantly in either direction**.
- **Minimization of losses if volatility decreases** with the conversion to Iron Condor.

Best for: Traders looking to **profit from volatility without having to predict the right side of the market**.

Strategy 4: Creating a Personal "Hedge Fund"

Objective: Implement a **hedge fund-like protection structure**, leveraging advanced options tactics.

How to Implement?

1. Use Iron Condors to Capture Low Volatility Income

- Choose assets that trade in **predictable price ranges** and trade iron condors monthly.
- Example: SPY fluctuates between **$420 and $440 → sell an Iron Condor with strikes at $415 and $445**.

2. Use Butterfly Spreads to Profit from Small Movements

- For highly stable stocks, **butterfly strategies can generate well-defined profits**.
- Example: If **Microsoft (MSFT) is consolidating at $320.00**, set up a **Butterfly at $320.00**.

3. Finance Protection with Short-Term Option Sales

- To ensure continuous protection without high costs, use **revenue from short option sales to finance long-term protection**.

Expected Results:

- **Active crisis protection structure**, similar to large hedge funds.
- **Income generation with structured trades**, minimizing directional risk.

Best for: Advanced investors who want **to manage risk professionally**.

Conclusion: Building an Optimized Portfolio with Options

By combining different options strategies, you can build a **more efficient, resilient, and profitable portfolio**. Here is a **summary of which strategy to use for each objective**:

Objective	Best Strategy
Passive Income Generation	Short Covered Calls + Short Protective Puts
Protection Against Crashes	Protective Puts + Collar Strategy
Profit from Volatility	Long Straddle + Conversion to Iron Condor
Create Your Own Hedge Fund	Iron Condors + Butterfly Spreads + Sale of Options to Finance the Strategy

With these combinations, your portfolio **will become more stable and efficient**, **maximizing returns while controlling risk**.

Risk Management in Options: Essential Principles and Analysis of the "Greeks"

Options are powerful tools for investors, but they can also be **highly sensitive to various market factors**, making **risk management** an essential component for success.

One of the most critical aspects of options pricing and risk management is **volatility**, and traders use a set of metrics called **"Greeks"** to measure and control the risks of their positions. In this chapter, we will understand how these elements influence trading strategies and decisions.

The Importance of Volatility in Options Pricing and Risk Management

Volatility is one of the most critical factors in options pricing, as it determines the **probability that the price of the underlying asset will reach certain levels before the option expires**.

Types of Volatility and Their Impacts

Historical Volatility: Measures past fluctuations in the asset's price. The higher the historical volatility, the more likely the asset is to continue to experience large variations.

Implied Volatility (IV): Measures the market's future expectations regarding the asset's volatility. The **higher the IV, the more expensive the options are**, as the market expects large movements.

Conclusion:

- If **implied volatility rises**, options **become more expensive**.
- If **implied volatility falls**, options **become cheaper**.
- Strategies that **sell options (such as Iron Condors and Covered Calls)** benefit when volatility **falls**.
- Strategies that **buy options (such as Straddles and Strangles)** profit when volatility **rises**.

Now that we understand volatility, let's explore **the "Greeks,"** which help investors manage their positions effectively.

The Greeks and Their Role in Options Risk Management

The Greeks are metrics used to measure the impact of different variables on option pricing. They help traders understand how their contracts may behave in response to changes in asset price, time, and market conditions.

Let's take a closer look at each one:

Delta (Δ) – Measuring Sensitivity to Asset Price

What is it?
Delta measures **how much the price of an option changes in relation to a $1.00 change in the underlying asset**.

How does it work?

- A **Delta of 0.50** means that if the asset rises **by $1.00**, the option will increase in value **by $0.50**.
- Calls have **a positive Delta** (from 0 to 1).
- Puts have **a negative Delta** (from -1 to 0).

Practical interpretation:

- If a **call has a Delta of 0.80**, it behaves **as if you owned 80 shares of the underlying asset**.
- If a **put has a Delta of -0.30**, it means that **it moves like -30 shares of the underlying asset**.

Used for:

- Measuring the directional exposure of a position.
- Adjust strategies with hedging.

Gamma (Γ) – Measuring Delta Acceleration

What is it?
Gamma measures **how much Delta changes when the asset price rises or falls by $1.00**.

How does it work?

- If Delta increases **from 0.50 to 0.60** as the stock rises by $1.00, then **Gamma is 0.10**.
- The **higher the Gamma**, the faster Delta changes.

Practical interpretation:

- **At-the-money (ATM)** options have **higher Gamma** because they are close to the decision point.
- **Deep-in-the-money (ITM) or deep-out-of-the-money (OTM)** options have **lower Gamma**.

Used for:

- Assessing **the risk of sudden movements in the underlying asset**.
- Adjusting strategies in volatile markets.

Theta (Θ) – The Effect of Time on Option Value

What is it?
Theta measures **the loss of value of the option over time (time decay)**.

How does it work?

- A Theta of **-0.05** means that the option loses **$0.05 per day**, all else being equal.
- ATM options lose value **faster** than ITM or OTM options.

Practical interpretation:

- **Option sellers (e.g., Iron Condors, Credit Spreads)** profit from **high Theta**.
- **Option buyers (e.g., Long Calls, Straddles)** lose money with **high Theta**.

Used for:

- Choosing **the best time to sell or buy options**.
- Maximizing time exposure in credit strategies.

Vega (ν) – Volatility Sensitivity

What is it?
Vega measures **the impact of changes in implied volatility on the price of an option**.

How does it work?

- If Vega is **0.10**, then for every 1% increase in implied volatility, the option will gain **$0.10** in value.

Practical interpretation:

- **Long-term** options have **high Vega**.
- **High volatility → more expensive options**.
- **Low volatility → cheaper options**.

Used for:

- Adjusting positions in highly volatile markets.
- Choosing the best time to enter or exit trades.

Rho (ρ) – Interest Rate Sensitivity

What is it?

Rho measures **the impact of changes in interest rates on the price of the option.**

How does it work?

- If Rho is **0.05**, then a **1%** increase **in the interest rate** will cause the option to rise **by $0.05**.

Practical interpretation:

- Calls have **positive Rho** (they benefit from rate increases).
- Puts have **negative Rho** (they lose value when rates rise).

Used for:

- Adjusting portfolios in variable interest rate environments.

Omega (Ω) – Option Elasticity

What is it?

Omega measures **the percentage change in the option price for each 1% change in the underlying asset**.

How does it work?

- If an option has an Omega of **2.5**, it means that a **1%** increase **in the asset price** results in a **2.5%** increase **in the option price**.

Used for:

- Determining **leverage opportunities in options**.

Conclusion: Using the Greeks to Manage Risk

Summary of the Functions of the Greeks:

Greek	**Main Function**
Delta (Δ)	Sensitivity to asset price
Gamma (Γ)	Change in Delta rate
Theta (Θ)	Time decay of the option
Vega (ν)	Sensitivity to volatility
Rho (ρ)	Sensitivity to interest rates
Omega (Ω)	Option elasticity

Understanding these metrics allows **for more precise control of option strategies, reducing risk and maximizing returns**.

Chapter 17 – From 1900 to 2025: The U.S. Economy and Its Impact on the Stock Market

(A Brief History to the Present Day)

The United States has built the world's largest economy over the past 120 years, weathering **wars, crises, economic booms, technological revolutions, and structural changes** that have shaped its trajectory. To understand the dynamics of the US economy and its reflection in the financial market, it is essential to analyze the **main economic cycles**, the evolution of **inflation and interest rates**, and the impact on **the stock market, especially the S&P 500 index**.

Below, we explore the main economic periods in the US, divided by decades and presidencies.

1900-1919: Industrial Growth and World War I

Presidents: William McKinley (1897-1901), Theodore Roosevelt (1901-1909), William Taft (1909-1913), Woodrow Wilson (1913-1921)

- **Expansion of the Industrial Revolution:** The early 20th century was marked by strong industrialization and population growth. Railroad, steel, and oil companies grew exponentially.
- **Creation of the Federal Reserve (Fed) in 1913:** The US central bank was established to stabilize the financial system.
- **World War I (1914-1918):** The US entered the war in 1917, boosting the industrial and military sectors.
- **Inflation and Post-War Economic Boom:** With the end of the war, the economy expanded rapidly, but inflation rose to **20% in 1919**.

Impact on the stock market: The stock market grew at the beginning of the century but suffered from banking crises and high inflation after the war.

1920-1929: The Roaring Twenties and the Stock Market Crash

Presidents: Warren Harding (1921-1923), Calvin Coolidge (1923-1929), Herbert Hoover (1929-1933)

- **Decade of rapid growth:** GDP grew, and the US became the world's largest economic power.
- **Euphoria in the financial market:** Speculation led to the formation of a bubble in the stock market.
- **Crash of 1929:** The stock market crash triggered the **Great Depression**.

Market impact: The S&P 500 lost nearly 90% of its value between 1929 and 1932.

1930-1945: The Great Depression and World War II

Presidents: Franklin D. Roosevelt (1933-1945), Harry Truman (1945-1953)

- **Great Depression (1930-1939):** GDP fell 30%, unemployment reached 25%, and deflation dominated the period.
- **New Deal:** The Roosevelt administration intervened with major stimulus programs.
- **World War II (1939-1945):** The US entered the war in 1941, boosting the economy with military spending.

Impact on the market: After the crisis of the 1930s, the war helped to revive the economy and the stock market.

1946-1970: Postwar Expansion and Oil Crisis

Presidents: Dwight Eisenhower (1953-1961), John F. Kennedy (1961-1963), Lyndon Johnson (1963-1969), Richard Nixon (1969-1974)

- **Highest growth in history:** The postwar period saw tremendous expansion in GDP and the middle class.
- **Inflation begins to rise in the 1970s:** The Vietnam War and social spending put pressure on prices.
- **Oil crisis (1973):** The OPEC embargo caused oil prices to quadruple, leading to stagflation.

Market impact: The S&P 500 grew strongly in the 1950s and 1960s but struggled in the 1970s due to high inflation.

1980–1999: Reaganomics, Globalization, and the Internet Bubble

Presidents: Ronald Reagan (1981-1989), George H.W. Bush (1989-1993), Bill Clinton (1993-2001)

- **Deregulation and tax cuts:** The Reagan administration promoted free markets and fought inflation with high interest rates.
- **Globalization and technological growth:** Companies such as Microsoft emerged and transformed the economy.

- **Internet bubble (1999):** Euphoria over startups led to excessive valuation of technology stocks.

Market impact: The S&P 500 grew 1,300% from 1980 to 2000.

2000-2019: Internet bubble, 2008 crisis, and post-crisis expansion

Presidents: George W. Bush (2001-2009), Barack Obama (2009-2017), Donald Trump (2017-2021)

- **Dot-Com Crash (2000-2002):** The internet bubble burst, bringing down the market.
- **2008 Crisis:** The collapse of the real estate and banking sectors led to the biggest financial crisis since 1929.
- **Post-2008 economic expansion:** The S&P 500 grew by more than **400% between 2009 and 2019**.

Market impact: The recovery from the 2008 crisis resulted in **the longest bull market in history**.

2020-2024: Pandemic, Inflation, and Rising Interest Rates

Presidents: Joe Biden (2021-2024)

- **COVID-19 pandemic (2020):** The economy collapsed, and GDP fell 9% in the second quarter of 2020.
- **Massive stimulus:** The Fed cut interest rates to 0% and injected trillions into the economy.
- **Record inflation in 2022:** The excess money in the economy caused inflation to rise to **9%**.

- **Interest rate hikes:** The Fed raised interest rates to curb inflation, impacting stocks and real estate.

Market impact: The S&P 500 experienced high volatility but remained resilient.

2025-Present: Donald Trump's Second Term

President: Donald Trump (2025-present)

- **Inheritance of a Strong Economy:** Upon taking office in January 2025, Trump found a robust economy characterized by consistent economic growth, low unemployment at 4%, and inflation controlled between 2.2% and 2.4%.
- **Economic and Trade Policies:**
    - **Tax Cuts:** Proposals to further reduce corporate taxes in order to stimulate economic growth.
    - **Tariff Increases:** Implementation of tariffs on imports, especially from China, with the aim of protecting domestic industries.
- **Impact on Businesses and Investments:**
    - **Political Uncertainty:** Trade and immigration policies have created an environment of caution among companies, leading to a more conservative stance on investments and expansion.
    - **Review of Sustainability Initiatives:** Some companies have reconsidered their sustainable investment strategies due to changes in environmental and social policies.
- **Financial Markets and Inflation:**

    - **Market Volatility:** Fiscal and trade policies have contributed to volatility in financial markets, with investors adjusting their strategies in light of new economic guidelines.
    - **Inflationary Pressures:** Import tariffs and increased government spending have raised concerns about inflation, prompting the Federal Reserve to consider adjustments to monetary policy.

- **National Debt and Fiscal Deficit:**
    - **Debt Growth:** The combination of tax cuts and increased spending has resulted in a growing fiscal deficit, with the national debt exceeding $36 trillion.
    - **Fiscal Sustainability:** Debates over the need for measures to curb the rise in debt, including possible cuts to social programs and fiscal adjustments.

- **International Relations and Trade:**
    - **Rapprochement with Russia:** Changes in foreign policy, including the reconfiguration of negotiations related to the Russia-Ukraine conflict, have affected traditional alliances and geopolitical dynamics.
    - **Trade Tensions:** The imposition of tariffs and the renegotiation of trade agreements have influenced relations with trading partners and impacted global supply chains.

This period is marked by assertive economic policies that seek to strengthen the domestic economy, but also introduce challenges related to inflation, market volatility, and international relations.

The US Dollar as the Hegemonic Currency

- **Adoption of the dollar as a global currency:** The Bretton Woods Agreement (1944) consolidated the dollar as a store of value.
- **Petrodollar:** Since the 1970s, oil has been traded in dollars, strengthening its hegemony.
- **Global crises increase demand for the dollar:** During crises, investors rush to dollar-denominated assets such as Treasuries.

Market impact: A strong dollar influences exporting companies and impacts the profits of S&P 500 multinationals.

Conclusion: How Do Economic Cycles Affect Stocks?

- **Periods of economic growth** tend to boost stocks as companies earn more profits.
- **Recessions and crises** cause market declines, but are followed by strong recoveries.
- **High inflation and high interest rates** tend to put pressure on the stock market.
- **Periods of economic stimulus** generate booms in financial markets.

The S&P 500 directly reflects the cycles of the U.S. economy, but history shows that, in the long term, the trend continues to be one of growth.

Will the Future Repeat the Past?

Take a look at the chart showing the 150-year history of the S&P500® Index, which represents the U.S. stock market. As you can see, the U.S. stock market really took off after World War II. Note that the growth is even more dramatic than shown in the chart because it is on a logarithmic scale. What explains this impressive and explosive growth?

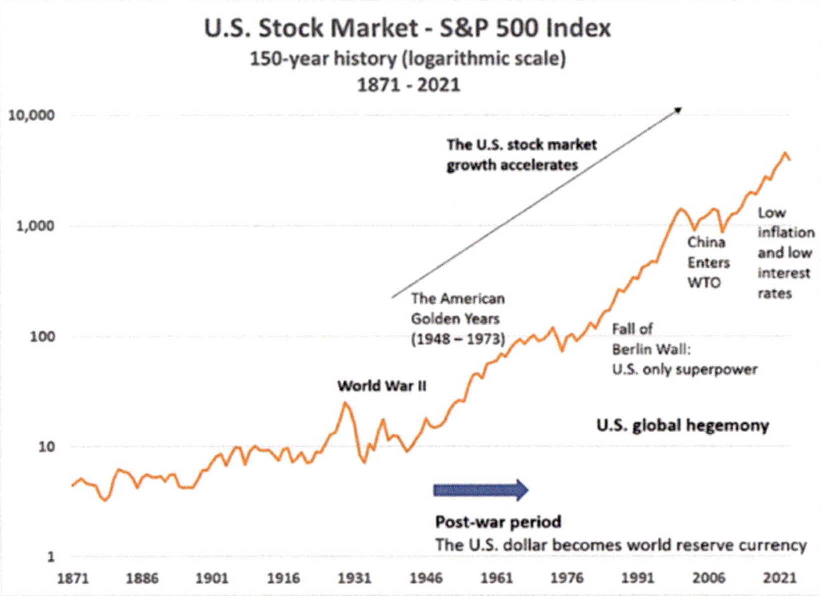

After World War II, the US emerged as the biggest winner in every sense of the word. The US became the world's largest economic engine, the US dollar became the world's reserve currency, American companies dominated the world, and the American world order was established. As a result, the US stock market has invariably reflected the last 80 years of economic growth and abundance, giving the impression that stocks always rise in the long run.

But now, consider this. Times are changing. The entire G-7 club of the world's seven richest nations, which includes the United States, no longer accounts for more than half of the world economy like it once did. That is why the G-20 was introduced. China is now seriously competing with the US in today's high-end industries and tomorrow's most promising industries (AI, quantum computing, new materials, etc.) and winning the race in many areas, such as electric vehicles, green energy, Another indication of this trend can be seen in the number of patents that countries register each year: in 2019 alone, China registered twice as many patents as the US and about 44% of the world's total.

Making money in the US market has been relatively "easy" until now. Today, that is changing. Crashes and corrections have increased since 2018, and average volatility has also increased.

To navigate this brave new world, the need to proactively manage risk and take early action against adverse market movements is greater than ever.

SMIGRM was created at the right time. Investing without a tool that does everything RISP 500™ does for investors in the U.S. stock market is extremely inadvisable in the 21st century.

Chapter 18. Currency Risk Hedging for Global Investors

Currency Uncertainty: The Invisible Risk in Global Investing

Investing across borders opens the door to new opportunities, but it also introduces a layer of risk that many investors overlook: currency fluctuations. When you buy U.S. stocks as a non-U.S. investor, you are not just betting on the performance of the companies you choose. You are also implicitly betting on the value of the U.S. dollar relative to your home currency. A strong dollar can boost your returns, while a weak dollar can diminish them, sometimes dramatically. This dual exposure means that even a well-constructed portfolio can behave unpredictably when exchange rates shift.

History offers vivid examples of this dynamic. In 2017, U.S. equities delivered strong returns in dollar terms, yet many European investors saw their gains cut in half because the euro appreciated sharply against the dollar. Conversely, in 2022, the dollar surged to multi-decade highs as global markets reeled from inflation and geopolitical tensions. Investors in Japan and the United Kingdom enjoyed far higher returns than U.S. investors holding the same stocks, simply because their home currencies weakened. These episodes show how currency movements can overshadow the performance of the underlying assets.

Understanding Currency Exposure

Currency exposure arises whenever your base currency differs from the currency of the assets you hold. For a global investor, this is almost unavoidable. A European buying U.S. stocks is exposed to the EUR/USD exchange rate. A Japanese investor faces the JPY/USD rate. Even investors in countries with relatively stable currencies experience fluctuations that can meaningfully affect their returns.

The direction of the currency pair that benefits the global investor is that the US dollar appreciates in relation to its home currency. This creates a tailwind for the investor's net return in the investor's currency. Conversely, if the investor's home currency appreciates in relation to the US dollar, it creates a headwind for the investor's net return in its home currency.

This exposure can be direct, such as owning U.S. shares or U.S.-listed ETFs, or indirect, such as holding a domestic company that earns a significant portion of its revenue in dollars. A classic example is the Brazilian stock market in the early 2000s. Many of its largest companies were exporters, meaning their earnings were tied to the dollar. As the Brazilian real strengthened sharply between 2003 and 2007, local investors saw the value of those earnings fall in local-currency terms, even though the companies were performing well globally. The mechanics are straightforward: if the dollar weakens against your home currency, your U.S. investments become worth less when converted back. If the dollar strengthens, the opposite occurs.

Should You Hedge?

The decision to hedge currency exposure is ultimately strategic. Hedging can reduce volatility and protect the value of your investments in your home currency. This is especially important for investors with short-term goals or those living in countries where the local currency is prone to large swings. Hedging can also help investors who expect to use their investment proceeds for expenses in their home currency, such as buying a house or funding education.

Historical episodes highlight when hedging becomes essential. During the Asian Financial Crisis of 1997–1998, currencies such as the Thai baht, Indonesian rupiah, and South Korean won collapsed by more than 50 percent. Investors who held unhedged foreign assets saw their portfolios swing wildly in local-currency terms. In contrast, those who hedged their exposure were able to preserve purchasing power during a period of extreme volatility. On the other hand, hedging can limit upside when the dollar strengthens. In 2014–2016, the dollar appreciated sharply as the Federal Reserve began tightening monetary policy. Investors who hedged their U.S. exposure missed out on a significant currency-driven boost to returns.

Therefore, the decision to hedge or not hedge against currency risk is a very personal one. It really depends on the investor's own circumstances, needs, risk tolerance, investment horizon, and goals.

Situations to Consider

One situation in which the investor may decide not to hedge at all is that of a global investor who wants to diversify investments abroad and does not want to repatriate such resources. This investor intends to keep US dollar investments in the United States and has no plans to repatriate its wealth heald abroad. In that case, the "global citizen" investor may consider the U.S. dollar as its own "home" country like any American investor.

Another situation is a very favorable one. Imagine your stock investments in U.S. dollars are so successful that you achieved oversized returns. In that case, which is common for those who follow the SMIGRM Method, investors may not be as much concerned about potential losses from adverse currency fluctuations than those earning small returns. If your stock returns are marginal, even small currency fluctuations that move against you can easily erase your gains.

Tools for Hedging Currency Risk

Investors have access to a wide array of tools to manage currency risk, ranging from simple to highly sophisticated. Hedged equity ETFs are among the most accessible options. These funds automatically neutralize currency movements by using forward contracts, allowing investors to focus solely on the performance of the underlying stocks. A well-known example is the surge in popularity of currency-hedged Japan ETFs in 2013–2015, when the yen depreciated sharply under Abenomics. Investors who used hedged ETFs captured the strong performance of Japanese equities without suffering from the weakening yen.

Currency ETFs and ETNs offer another straightforward approach by providing direct exposure to the U.S. dollar, which can offset the currency component of an equity investment. More advanced investors may turn to FX forwards, which allow precise hedging of a specific amount of currency for a defined period. Futures contracts, available on major exchanges, offer liquidity and transparency but require margin and daily mark-to-market adjustments. Options on currencies provide flexibility by allowing investors to protect against adverse movements while retaining upside potential. Institutional investors often rely on currency swaps for long-term hedging, though these instruments are typically not accessible to retail investors. Even without financial instruments, some investors use natural hedging by aligning their assets and liabilities in the same currency.

Building a Practical Hedge

Creating an effective hedge begins with understanding your exposure. This means identifying how much of your portfolio is denominated in U.S. dollars and how sensitive your financial goals are to currency movements. Once you have a clear picture, you can choose a hedge ratio that aligns with your objectives. A full hedge eliminates currency fluctuations entirely, while a partial hedge balances stability with potential upside. Some investors adopt dynamic hedging strategies that adjust the hedge ratio based on market conditions or volatility.

A practical example comes from pension funds in Canada and Australia, which often hedge between 25 and 50 percent of their foreign equity exposure. This partial-hedge approach reduces volatility without fully eliminating the potential benefits of currency movements. Implementing the hedge requires selecting the right instrument and defining the time horizon. Most hedging tools have expiration dates, which means they must be rolled over periodically. This process introduces additional costs and requires discipline. A well-designed hedge is not a one-time action but an ongoing strategy that evolves with your portfolio and the market environment.

How Investors Around the World Approach Hedging

Investors in different regions face unique challenges when managing currency risk. In Europe, hedging U.S. exposure is often relatively inexpensive due to interest rate differentials, making it an attractive option for reducing volatility. Japanese investors, on the other hand, frequently encounter higher hedging costs because of Japan's historically low interest rates, which can make long-term hedging less appealing. This dynamic was particularly evident in the 2010s, when hedging U.S. exposure from Japan often cost more than 2 percent per year.

Investors in emerging markets may experience far more dramatic currency swings, making hedging a vital part of risk management rather than a discretionary choice. For example, during the 2015 commodity downturn, currencies such as the Brazilian real, Russian ruble, and South African rand depreciated sharply. Investors who held unhedged U.S. assets benefited from the stronger dollar, while those who hedged missed out on a rare period when currency movements worked in their favor. Even investors in countries with currencies pegged to the U.S. dollar must consider the stability of those pegs. The Swiss franc's sudden break from its euro peg in 2015 is a reminder that currency regimes can change abruptly.

The Cost of Hedging

Hedging costs extend beyond transaction fees. The most significant factor is often the interest rate differential between the investor's home country and the United States. This differential influences the pricing of forward contracts and can make hedging either cheap or expensive.

When the U.S. has higher interest rates than the investor's home country, hedging tends to be costly. When the opposite is true, hedging can be relatively inexpensive or even generate a small return.

A clear example occurred in the mid-2010s, when U.S. interest rates were higher than those in Europe and Japan. Hedging U.S. exposure from these regions was expensive, discouraging many investors from doing so. In contrast, during periods when U.S. rates fall below those of other countries, hedging becomes cheaper. Rolling hedges over time introduces additional costs, including bid-ask spreads and potential slippage. Hedged ETFs, while convenient, may experience tracking error if the currency hedge does not perfectly offset exchange rate movements.

Designing a Currency-Hedged Global Portfolio

A global portfolio can incorporate hedging in several ways. Some investors maintain separate hedged and unhedged allocations, adjusting the balance as market conditions change. Others adopt a systematic approach, such as hedging a fixed percentage of their foreign exposure or adjusting the hedge ratio based on volatility. Over long periods, hedged and unhedged portfolios can behave quite differently, especially during times of significant currency movements.

Historical data from the MSCI World Index shows that hedged versions of the index tend to have lower volatility than unhedged versions, particularly for investors whose home currencies are volatile. However, during periods of sustained dollar strength, unhedged portfolios often outperform. The goal is to design a strategy that aligns with your financial objectives, risk tolerance, and time horizon.

Hedging Alternatives for Global Investors

Global investors have access to a wide range of tools to manage currency risk, each designed for different levels of sophistication, cost sensitivity, and investment horizons. Some solutions are simple and automated, requiring no knowledge of derivatives. Others offer precision and flexibility but demand a deeper understanding of financial markets. The choice of instrument depends on the investor's goals, the size of the exposure, and the availability of products in their home market.

One of the most accessible options is the currency-hedged equity ETF. These funds hold the same underlying stocks as their unhedged counterparts but neutralize currency movements by rolling forward contracts. They are ideal for investors who want a set-and-forget solution without dealing with derivatives directly. Currency ETFs and ETNs offer another straightforward approach by providing exposure to the U.S. dollar itself. By holding a dollar-tracking ETF alongside U.S. equities, an investor can offset the currency component of their portfolio.

More advanced investors often turn to FX forwards, which allow them to lock in an exchange rate for a specific amount of currency over a defined period. Forwards are widely used by institutions because they offer precision and can be tailored to the exact size and timing of the exposure. Futures contracts, available on major exchanges, offer similar benefits with greater liquidity and transparency, though they require margin and daily mark-to-market adjustments. Options on currencies provide yet another layer of flexibility, allowing investors to protect against adverse movements while retaining upside potential. These instruments are particularly useful when an investor wants insurance rather than a full hedge.

Institutional investors may also use currency swaps for long-term hedging, especially when managing large or ongoing exposures. Swaps allow two parties to exchange cash flows in different currencies, effectively locking in exchange rates for extended periods. While powerful, swaps are rarely accessible to individual investors. Finally, some investors rely on natural hedging by aligning their assets and liabilities in the same currency. For example, someone earning income in dollars or planning to spend time in the United States may choose not to hedge their U.S. equity exposure at all.

Comparison of Hedging Tools

Hedging Tool	Cost	Complexity	Accessibility	Best For
Currency-Hedged Equity ETFs	Moderate (embedded forward costs)	Low	High in developed markets	Investors wanting simplicity and automation
Currency ETFs / ETNs	Low to moderate (fund fees, spreads)	Low	High in major markets	Investors seeking direct USD exposure without derivatives
FX Forwards	Varies by interest rate differential; often low	Medium	Medium (banks, brokers)	Investors needing precise, customizable hedges
Currency Futures	Low (tight spreads, exchange-traded)	Medium to high (margin, mark-to-market)	High in markets with futures exchanges	Investors comfortable with derivatives and leverage
Currency Options	Moderate to high (option premiums)	High	Medium	Investors seeking protection with upside potential
Currency Swaps	Low to moderate (institutional pricing)	Very high	Low (institutional only)	Large investors with long-term exposures
Natural Hedging	None	Very low	Universal	Investors whose income or expenses are already USD-linked

Hedging Effectiveness Under Different Market Conditions

The effectiveness of a currency hedge depends not only on the instrument used but also on the broader market environment. Exchange rates respond to interest-rate differentials, capital flows, geopolitical events, and shifts in global risk appetite. As a result, a hedge that performs well in one environment may behave very differently in another. Understanding how each hedging tool responds to various market conditions helps investors choose the right approach for their needs.

Periods of strong U.S. dollar appreciation tend to reward unhedged investors, while hedged portfolios may lag because the hedge neutralizes the currency gains. Conversely, when the dollar weakens, hedged portfolios often outperform because they avoid the drag from unfavorable exchange-rate movements. Volatile markets introduce additional considerations: some instruments, such as options, become more expensive when volatility rises, while others, like futures and forwards, remain relatively stable in cost but may require more active management.

The table below compares the effectiveness of major hedging tools across a range of common market environments. It is not meant to be predictive but rather to illustrate how each tool tends to behave under different conditions.

Comparison of Hedging Effectiveness Across Market Conditions

Hedging Tool	Strong USD	Weak USD	High FX Volatility	Stable FX Markets	Rising Interest-Rate Differentials	Falling Interest-Rate Differentials
Currency-Hedged Equity ETFs	Underperform (hedge removes USD gains)	Outperform (hedge removes USD	Effective but roll costs may rise	Highly effective	Costs rise when U.S. rates exceed home	Costs fall when home rates exceed U.S.
Currency ETFs / ETNs	Strong performance	Weak performance	Moderate effectiveness; tracking error	Effective	Benefit when USD yields rise	Weaker when USD yields fall
FX Forwards	Effective hedge but opportunity cost is high	Effective hedge with strong benefit	Very effective; pricing adjusts quickly	Highly effective	Hedging cost increases	Hedging cost decreases
Currency Futures	Effective but may require margin adjustments	Effective with positive impact	Highly effective; deep liquidity helps	Highly effective	Futures pricing reflects rate differentials	Lower cost when differentials
Currency Options	Effective if using puts; upside preserved	Effective if using calls; upside preserved	Very effective but premiums rise sharply	Effective but costlier than forwards	Premiums increase when USD rates rise	Premiums decrease when USD rates fall
Currency Swaps	Effective for long-term hedging	Effective for long-term hedging	Effective but complex to adjust	Very effective for stable exposures	Swap costs rise with U.S. rate advantage	Swap costs fall when home rates rise
Natural Hedging	Neutral; depends on income and expenses	Neutral	Neutral	Neutral	Neutral	Neutral

Most Accessible Hedging Alternatives for Retail Investors

Retail investors generally have access to three categories of hedging tools:

1. Currency-Hedged Equity ETFs (the simplest option)

These ETFs hold U.S. equities but automatically hedge the USD exposure back into the investor's home currency using forward contracts.

2. Currency ETFs / ETNs

These track the value of a currency directly (e.g., USD, EUR, JPY).

Holding a USD ETF can hedge a foreign-currency portfolio, and holding a foreign-currency ETF can hedge USD exposure.

3. Multi-currency ETFs

Some ETFs offer baskets of currencies or allow hedging against broad USD exposure.

These are the easiest tools for retail investors worldwide because they trade like stocks and require no derivatives knowledge.

Currency ETFs and Hedged ETFs by Currency Pair

Below is the global list of the most widely available ETFs for each major USD pair.

Summary: Best Retail-Friendly Hedging Tools

Currency	Best ETF(s)
EUR	FXE, EUFX, HEZU
JPY	FXY, YCS, HEWJ
GBP	FXB
CAD	FXC
AUD	FXA
CHF	FXF
CNY	CYB
MXN	MXN
BRL	BZF

Example: How to hedge a USD 250,000 portfolio using ETFs

Below is a concrete, narrative example you can drop into the book as a boxed case or mini-appendix.

Investor profile and goal

Imagine an investor based in the euro area. Their base currency is EUR, but they hold a U.S. equity portfolio worth USD 250,000, invested in broad U.S. index funds. They are comfortable with equity risk, but they do not want their long-term plan to be derailed by a sharp fall in the U.S. dollar versus the euro. Their goal: hedge most of the USD currency risk using only ETFs—no forwards, no futures.

Step 1: Define the exposure

The investor's foreign-currency exposure is the USD value of their U.S. equity holdings:

- U.S. equity portfolio: USD 250,000
- Base currency: EUR

- FX exposure: effectively "long USD / short EUR" on USD 250,000

They are not trying to hedge stock-market risk—only the currency leg.

Step 2: Choose a hedge ratio

They decide to hedge **80%** of the USD exposure. That gives a good reduction in FX risk while leaving some room for potential upside if the dollar strengthens.

- Hedge ratio: 80%
- Hedge notional: 0.80 × 250,000 = **USD 200,000**

This is the amount of USD exposure they want to neutralize.

Step 3: Pick the ETF approach

There are two ETF-based ways to do this:

1. Switch part of the portfolio into **EUR-hedged U.S. equity ETFs**
2. Keep the existing U.S. equity ETFs and add a **currency ETF** that offsets the USD exposure

For simplicity and clarity, we'll use **EUR-hedged U.S. equity ETFs**.

Suppose the investor currently holds an unhedged S&P 500 ETF in USD. They can:

- Keep USD 50,000 unhedged (20%)
- Move USD 200,000 into an **EUR-hedged U.S. equity ETF** (80%)

Now, 80% of the portfolio's USD exposure is automatically hedged back into euros via the ETF's internal forward contracts.

Step 4: Implement the hedge

In practice, the investor:

- Sells USD 200,000 of the unhedged U.S. equity ETF
- Buys EUR-hedged U.S. equity ETF(s) with the same underlying index exposure, for the same USD amount (or equivalent EUR amount)

After this switch:

- Total U.S. equity exposure: still ~USD 250,000
- Currency profile:
    - 80% in EUR-hedged share classes
    - 20% in unhedged USD share classes

The equity risk is unchanged; the currency risk is largely neutralized.

Step 5: Monitor and rebalance

Over time, two things will move:

- The value of the U.S. equities
- The EUR/USD exchange rate

If the portfolio grows to, say, USD 300,000, the investor may want to keep the 80% hedge ratio. That means:

- Target hedge notional: 0.80 × 300,000 = USD 240,000

- If the hedged ETF portion is now only USD 220,000, they can shift another USD 20,000 from unhedged to hedged ETFs.

A simple rule they might adopt:

- Once a year (or when the hedge ratio drifts by more than, say, 10 percentage points), rebalance between hedged and unhedged ETFs to restore the target hedge ratio.

Step 6: What happens in different scenarios?

1. **Dollar weakens sharply vs. euro**
    - Unhedged portion (20%) suffers from FX losses.
    - Hedged portion (80%) is largely insulated; returns reflect mainly equity performance.
    - Overall portfolio is much less hurt by the weaker dollar than a fully unhedged portfolio.
2. **Dollar strengthens sharply vs. euro**
    - Unhedged portion benefits from FX gains.
    - Hedged portion does not participate in the currency upside.
    - The investor still captures some of the dollar strength via the 20% unhedged slice.
3. **FX stays roughly stable**
    - The hedge neither helps nor hurts much.

- The main cost is the ongoing expense ratio and embedded hedge cost in the ETF, which the investor accepts as the price of reduced FX uncertainty.

Step 7: Variations for other base currencies

The same logic works for other investors:

- A Japanese investor can combine unhedged U.S. equity ETFs with **JPY-hedged U.S. equity ETFs**.
- A British investor can use **GBP-hedged** share classes.
- A Canadian or Australian investor can use **CAD- or AUD-hedged** versions where available, or pair unhedged U.S. equity ETFs with local-currency hedged products.

The mechanics are identical: decide the hedge ratio, shift that proportion of the portfolio into hedged share classes, and rebalance periodically.

Conclusion: A Smarter Way to Invest Globally

Currency risk is an inherent part of global investing, but it does not have to be a source of uncertainty. Hedging provides a way to manage this risk and bring greater stability to your portfolio. For some investors, it offers clarity and peace of mind. For others, it may introduce unnecessary complexity. The most effective approach is one that reflects your personal circumstances and long-term goals. With a thoughtful strategy and the right tools, you can navigate currency fluctuations confidently and focus on building wealth across borders.

Investors who outperform as stock investors using solid risk management tools like SMIGRM based on the RISP 500™ indicator, typically experience currency risk as a lesser concern than regular global investors. But still, heging currency risk may still be a good idea, especially when the U.S. dollar experience a period of weakness.

Chapter 19. Home Trading: Access global markets from home

Investing in today's digital age offers unparalleled convenience, allowing people to access global financial markets from the comfort of their homes. With just a few keystrokes and mouse clicks, you can trade stocks, exchange-traded funds (ETFs), mutual funds, and options.

There are many trading platforms on the market, and they are usually provided by the US brokerage firms where you open your accounts. For illustrative purposes only (without recommending one or the other), let's take an example of the platform provided by Charles Schwab, which is the thinkorswim® trading platform. It provides comprehensive tools to facilitate these transactions. Thinkorswim® is very popular in the United States.

Step-by-Step Guide to Trading with Charles Schwab and thinkorswim®:

1. **Open and Fund Your Brokerage Account:**
    - Registration: Visit the Charles Schwab website to open a brokerage account.
    - Funding: Link your bank account to deposit funds into your brokerage account.
2. **Access the Trading Platform:**
    - Charles Schwab Website: Log in to your account at schwab.com.
    - thinkorswim® Platform: Download and install the thinkorswim® platform, now available to Schwab clients.
3. **Trading Stocks and ETFs:**

- **Using the Schwab website:**
  - Navigate to the "Trade" tab and select "All-In-One Trade Ticket."
  - Enter the symbol of the stock or ETF you want to trade.
  - Choose "Buy" or "Sell," specify the quantity, select the order type (e.g., market or limit), and set the time.
  - Review your order and confirm to execute the trade.
- **Using thinkorswim®:**
  - Open the platform and navigate to the "Trade" tab.
  - Enter the symbol of the desired stock or ETF.
  - Configure the order details: stock (buy/sell), quantity, order type, and expiration time.
  - Review and submit the order.

4. **Mutual Fund Trading:**
   - **Using the Schwab website:**
     - Go to the "Trade" tab and select "Mutual Funds."
     - Enter the mutual fund symbol or search by name.
     - Specify the investment amount, review the order, and submit.

5. **Options Trading:**
    - **Approval:** Make sure your account is approved for options trading. You can request approval for options through your Schwab account.
    - **Using the Schwab website:**
        - Navigate to the "Trade" tab and select "Options."
        - Enter the underlying stock symbol and choose your desired options strategy.
        - Select the options contract, including the expiration date and strike price.
        - Specify the action (buy/sell), quantity, order type, and time.
        - Review and submit the order.
    - **Using thinkorswim®:**
        - Open the platform and go to the "Trade" tab.
        - Enter the symbol of the underlying asset and access the options chain.
        - Select the desired option, configure the order details, review, and submit.
6. **Trade Monitoring and Management:**
    - **Portfolio Review:** Use the "Accounts" tab on the Schwab website or the "Monitor" tab in thinkorswim® to track your positions and performance.
    - **Order Status:** Check the status of your orders and make modifications or cancellations as needed.

Additional Resources:

- **Educational Materials:** Both Schwab and thinkorswim® offer extensive educational content to enhance your trading knowledge.
- **Customer Support:** Access 24/7 support for any questions related to the platform.

By embracing these platforms, you can actively participate in the financial markets, making informed investment decisions with ease and confidence.

Chapter 20. Opportunity Brought by Life-Changing Knowledge

The Right Knowledge Transforms Lives

Congratulations on reading! You have just taken a huge step toward a new reality for yourself, expanding your horizons in a way that will certainly make a significant difference in your life. It is not often that we encounter such a powerful opportunity in life that can change lives. As we know, money is not everything in life, but money can solve a large part of the problems we face in life, right? Who doesn't want to make their hard-earned money work hard for them by multiplying their wealth? Accelerating wealth growth means shortening the distance of the journey so that financial goals can be achieved faster.

But what good is it if it's not done safely? If for every three steps you take forward, you have to take two (or more) steps back, which is what happens when you encounter a financial crisis with a stock market crash along the way (which we've seen happen at least once every decade), your journey will be cut short and you'll probably never reach the promised land. This phenomenon is what happens to most people who try their luck on the stock market. It was precisely to solve this very serious problem that plagues all investors on the planet that SMIGRM was created!

If we have a limitation in our lives, that limitation is TIME. We all have a biological clock that starts ticking as soon as we are born. By the time we start walking on our own two feet and earning our own money, and putting it to work for us, perhaps at least 20 years have gone by? That is, if we have had the sharp and disciplined mindset to start investing early, which unfortunately is not the case for most people. At 20 years of age, most people's focus is still on other things, such as studies, sports, dating, and earning money by finding a good job, etc. At that age, little is known about investing, and the initial base is still very small. The reality is that by the time we learn from the cold, hard reality of the markets and discover the right formula for investing intelligently and safely, at least another decade of our lives will have gone by, right? With so much misinformation, from the media itself, biased to serve the big corporate interests of the financial industry, to false gurus on the internet, and all kinds of conflicting and mismatched information causing confusion, it's really not easy! For all these reasons, for many people, the right knowledge will only be acquired at the age of 40 or 50. Conclusion: everyone needs a safe and reliable method to help accelerate wealth formation safely. This formula also needs to be easy to apply, so that even people without financial training can implement it without great effort or expenditure of time. This book was created precisely to fill this gap in people's financial lives and enable them to achieve this goal more easily, safely, and quickly.

As soon as you take the first steps on this journey, it will become clear to you that reading this book was more than just consuming information; it was embarking on a learning journey that has the potential to transform your financial life forever. You have allowed yourself to explore a new world full of possibilities, and now you have in your hands the knowledge you need to **accelerate the growth of your wealth safely, diversifying in the largest stock market on the planet**.

The truth is that most people go through their entire lives without ever discovering these opportunities, trapped in a limited financial system and to beliefs that prevent them from expanding their horizons. But you did things differently. You opened your eyes to a new reality and took responsibility for building a solid financial future **by investing intelligently and strategically in the US stock market**.

Breaking Down Complex Knowledge

Throughout this journey, we have explored in depth all the essential aspects so that you can invest with confidence in the world's largest stock market. We began by laying the foundation for success on **Wall Street**, highlighting the importance of **preparation, the right mindset, and investor psychology** (Chapters 1 and 2). After all, **before any technical strategy, it is essential to develop the right mindset to deal with the challenges and opportunities that the market offers**.

Next, we took a deep dive into **the U.S. stock market** (Chapter 3). Knowing the environment in which you are investing is crucial to making more informed decisions. We also analyzed the role of the **Federal Reserve (Fed)** and **economic indicators** (Chapter 4), as these factors directly influence asset prices and market direction.

With this structured foundation, we moved on to one of the most important pillars of any successful investor: **risk management** (Chapter 5). Without a clear risk management plan, even the best strategy can lead to disastrous results. This is where you began to understand the importance of anticipating problems and protecting your capital against adverse fluctuations.

We deepened this knowledge even further by studying the **VIX (Volatility Index) and the options market** (Chapter 6), powerful tools for understanding volatility and using derivatives to your advantage. We also discussed **contextual dynamic allocation** (Chapter 7), which is essential for optimizing your portfolio and adjusting your risk exposure as the market scenario changes.

Then we introduced the **SMIGRM (Stock Market Investing Guided by Risk Management) Method** (Chapter 8), the key differentiator that **allows you to accelerate the growth of your wealth easily and safely, outperforming most professional managers**. This method incorporates everything we have learned so far: **risk analysis, dynamic allocation, and protection against large losses, while accelerating wealth during bull markets, resulting in maximization of long-term returns**.

Next, we addressed the **two main investment approaches: active and passive** (Chapter 9). For those who want an active approach, we covered the concepts of **fundamental analysis, valuation, and technical analysis** (Chapter 10), as well as strategies for **active allocation and portfolio construction** (Chapter 11) and the theoretical basis of **Modern Portfolio Theory** (Chapter 12). For those who prefer a passive approach, we discussed **investments in index ETFs** (Chapter 13). We then conclude this section with a very important discussion on **performance indicators** that help measure your results, as this is the only way you will know if you are heading in the right direction and at the right speed so that you can make adjustments or even change your method if necessary (Chapter 14).

In addition, we explored **dividend stocks** (Chapter 15) for those seeking passive income in US dollars, and more advanced strategies, such as **stock options** (Chapter 16). To give you a broad overview of the past history of the U.S. stock market in the broader context of the U.S. economy's trajectory since the year 1900, we prepared a timeline for you to see the evolution and sequence of major events (Chapter 17). Since all cross-border investments entail currency risk, we dedicated some discussion and ideas on how retail investors may hedge against US dollar depreciation (Chapter 18).

But investing in the US is not just about buying assets—it is also about accessing the market in the most efficient, inexpensive, and secure way. That is why we added a quick guide to **home trading** (Chapter 19), teaching you how to trade directly from the US without relying on intermediaries.

All of this leads to a single goal: to accelerate your wealth growth more easily and safely.

Each concept presented, each strategy discussed, and each tool shared has a clear purpose: **to equip you with the knowledge and means**

necessary to invest safely and with high performance in the U.S. stock market.

The **SMIGRM method** is what **sets us apart**, as it combines **intelligent risk management, proven strategies, and an objective decision-making system**, allowing you to **outperform the market and protect your wealth without having to spend hours studying or trying to guess where the market is headed**.

Now, the decision is in your hands. You already have the knowledge and the tools. **The next step is action.** The powerful American market is within your reach—and with it, a real chance to accelerate your financial trajectory. **Your new future starts now.**

Addressing Common Concerns and Reinforcing Your Confidence

Throughout this book, we have presented a tested and validated approach to accelerating the growth of your wealth more **easily, quickly, and safely** in the largest stock market on the planet. However, it is n ly natural to have questions and concerns before taking the next step. Here, we will address the main concerns that may be on your mind—and show why **none of them should prevent you from taking advantage of this great opportunity**.

📌 **"I don't have time, my work and routine are very busy."**

That's exactly why this book was written! We know that many busy people want to invest efficiently, but can't spend hours analyzing the market.

✅ **The solution:** For those who really don't have time, we've created the **SMIGRM Super-Abbreviated Shortcut**, which **only** requires **1 to 5 minutes a day**. You can simply follow two easy steps:

1. **Adopt the passive investment philosophy with index ETFs**, ensuring exposure to the US market with minimal management requirements.
2. **Subscribe to RISP 500™, our risk indicator based on the SMIGRM Method**, which indicates the best times to be in or out of the market.

This approach **is** much cheaper than paying financial advisors and generates much higher returns. If you can spend 5 minutes on your cell phone per day, you can already execute this strategy.

📌 **"I don't have enough confidence to execute it on my own."**

Confidence comes with practice. Think about how you learned to ride a bike or drive a car. At first, it seemed difficult, but after a few tries, it became natural. The same is true for investing.

✅ **The solution:** If fear is an obstacle, you can start with the **SMIGRM Super-Abbreviated Shortcut**. It simplifies everything, allowing you to follow the method without having to make complex decisions. **Even without experience, you can achieve excellent results without stress.**

📌 **"It sounds too good to be true. How do I know that the SMIGRM Method really works?"**

Skepticism is natural—and healthy! After all, there are many empty promises circulating in the market.

✅ **The solution: SMIGRM's results are 100% verifiable and public!**

- Since **2022**, we have been posting the results of **eight SMIGRM-based strategies daily** on **Facebook and X**.
- All results are **recorded with the date and time**, proving their authenticity.
- Unlike methods that rely solely on **backtesting**, SMIGRM **demonstrates its effectiveness live, in real time.**

In other words, there is no way to cheat – the numbers are there for anyone to see and confirm. **The best way to overcome skepticism is <u>not</u> through testimonials but through concrete evidence. And we have that evidence for everyone to see and check: www.facebook.com/risp500 or www.X.com/risp500.**

📌 **"What if I fail?"**

The fear of failure is common, but it usually comes from **the unknown**.

✅ **The solution:** Knowledge eliminates fear. Think of the first humans when they encountered fire: a mixture of fear and fascination. But once they understood how it worked, they began to use it to cook, keep warm, and evolve. The same is true with investments.

- This book, **courses, and strategic advisory programs** were created precisely to help you **master this knowledge**, step by step.
- In addition, **SMIGRM's Super-Abbreviated Shortcut** drastically reduces complexity, facilitating implementation and ensuring **security in execution**.

There is no reason to fear something **you can learn to control**.

📌 **"There's a lot of information to process. I don't know if I can learn all this."**

We know that investing in the US can seem challenging for those who have never done it before.

✅ **The solution:**

- The book was written for **those who already have some experience with investing in their country** and want to expand into a new market.
- But for those who want an **even easier and more interactive learning experience, we will offer courses and strategic advisory programs**.
- In these strategic advisory sessions, learning will be **progressive**, allowing more complex concepts to be absorbed **in a natural and interactive way, focused on execution and achieving results**.

In other words, you **don't have to learn everything at once**. The path has been designed so that you **can evolve at your own pace**.

📌 **"What if the author isn't reliable? How can I know that they really know what they're talking about?"**

This is one of the **most important** objections—and a completely valid one! The market is full of fake gurus and course sellers who have never had real experience in the financial sector.

✅ **The solution: Here's what sets this book and its author apart from any other "expert" on the market:**

◆ **Education at one of the best schools in the world:** The author graduated from the **prestigious Wharton School in the US**.

◆ **Over 25 years of real experience in the US:** Unlike many "gurus" who have never lived or worked in the United States, the author has lived in the country for **over two decades** and knows the market inside out.

◆ **Career in prestigious financial institutions in the US, Brazil, and China:** He has worked as **a trader, portfolio manager, risk manager, and derivatives specialist**.

◆ **Management of large fortunes:** During global financial crises, he was responsible for managing **more than $10 billion** in assets for his employers.

◆ **Public and verifiable track record:** Unlike fake experts who live off theories, **the author developed and implemented the SMIGRM Method over 10 years, proving its effectiveness in practice**.

✅ **Conclusion:** You are learning from someone **who has been on the battlefield**, who has gone through **real financial crises**, managed billions, and **now shares that knowledge with you. If anyone is truly qualified to teach this, it is him.**

🚀 **Conclusion: Nothing Can Stop You from Getting Started Now!**

Now that we've addressed the main objections, the final question remains: **what's still stopping you from taking the next step?**

✓ Don't have time? → SMIGRM's Super-Abbreviated Shortcut solves this in **1 to 5 minutes a day**.

✓ **Lacking confidence?** → Confidence comes with practice, and the method makes it easy to execute.
✓ **Are you skeptical?** → The results are **public and verifiable**.
✓ **Afraid of failure?** → Knowledge eliminates fear.
✓ **Think it's too much information?** → The book, courses, and mentoring were designed to **simplify** learning.
✓ **Do you have doubts about the author?** → His track record speaks for itself.

Now it's up to you. **Your assets, your financial future, and your freedom are within your reach.** You already have all the tools you need to grow and invest with confidence in the largest stock market on the planet.

Don't let this opportunity pass you by. Get started now.

Real-Life Stories of Life Transformation with the SMIGRM Method

What sets a successful investor apart from someone who just "tries their luck" in the market is the existence of a **proven method**. Stefan J. and Rachel W. are just two examples of how **SMIGRM has changed lives**, providing security, consistency, and financial freedom.

📌 Stefan J.: A German Doctor Who Found Financial Security Amid Uncertainty

The story of **Stefan J.**, a 42-year-old German doctor living in Frankfurt, is an impressive testament to the power of SMIGRM. A devoted father of two girls, Stefan has always had a busy life between his work, his patients, and his family. For years, he invested his savings through a financial advisor on the German and American stock investments, but with mixed results, like most other investors.

With the deterioration of the German economy due to the prolonged war in Ukraine, concern for his family's financial future became a red flag. Losses from his investments began to worry him about his retirement plans and his daughters' future. The problem? He didn't have time to study possible solutions. After changing advisors, he felt that it was not really helpful because it's always the same old mainstream strategies. None of the plans presented gave him the peace of mind he was looking for.

When Stefan learned about SMIGRM, something changed. Despite his exhausting routine, he decided he needed to take action—and he acted quickly. He studied the methodology with discipline, applied SMIGRM immediately, and in a short time, his results began to appear. He managed to recover not only his previous losses, but finally found a safe path to growing his wealth faster than he ever imagined possible.

His testimony speaks for itself:

"I really have no words to describe this feeling of accomplishment but only to thank you. You are a lifesaver, Professor Shauy. Literally. This SMIGRM thing works like magic. Now I am confident all my goals will be reached. Thank you."

📌 **Rachel W.: From Skeptical and Disillusioned to Confident and Successful as a Stock Investor**

Rachel W., 39, a resident of Atlanta, Georgia, accountant, and single mother of an 11-year-old boy, always had a good understanding of finance, but the stock market was like a big casino to her, where the big players got even richer at the expense of the little guys.

While still in college, she tried investing in stocks, but her experience was frustrating and disastrous. The disappointment was so great that she never bought another stock again. For her, the stock market was neither fair nor did it make sense.

But after her divorce, her financial reality changed, and this worried her deeply. Now, despite having an excellent salary, as the sole provider for her family, Rachel knew she needed to do something different to ensure a better future for herself and her son. But fear prevented her from taking the first step. And the worst part was that in her search for a way out, Rachel fell for scams twice. She purchased an expensive course and mentoring program from fake gurus she met on YouTube and Instagram. The first made no difference in her results. The second caused her to lose a lot of money, and when she confronted the guru, he blamed the market and blamed her for not following his recommendations to the letter. Disappointed, Rachel thought about giving up for good.

That's when she learned about SMIGRM through a friend in the financial market, who was also a former student of mine. Although skeptical at first, she decided to give it a try. The results spoke for themselves. In just a few weeks, she began to gain confidence, seeing in practice that the method really works.

Her testimonial makes clear the impact of this change:

"SMIGRM gave me the confidence I never really had. I was very skeptical at first because I've been cheated before. But the impressive results I have using SMIGRM are the source of my newly discovered confidence."

📌 What Do These Stories Have in Common?

The cases of Stefan and Rachel are no exception. **Many other investors have had similar experiences.** Think about it:

- Opening an account with a broker, transferring money, and buying stocks is something anyone can do. It can be done in a matter of hours.
- But achieving consistent success, month after month, year after year, is another story. It requires a method—a proven method.
- SMIGRM is not just any method. It has been tested, refined, and validated over the years, offering a clear and safe path to accelerate wealth building easily, quickly, and safely.

If you're hesitant, I understand. Trying to invest money in another country can be nerve-wracking the first time around. What if you don't see the results you expected? The fear of making mistakes, losing money, not knowing if you're making the right decisions. The insecurity of entering a market that seems dominated by giants, where the rules of the game are not always clear, in addition to a foreign language. Maybe you've tried investing in the US stock market before and were disappointed. Or maybe you never took the first step because you simply didn't know where to start. But one thing is certain: you are not alone. I have seen many people face these same difficulties — and I know there is a way to change this reality. Just as I helped Stefan and Rachel, just as I have helped so many other investors around the world, I can help you too. Together, we can rewrite your financial history and create a future of prosperity, security, and freedom.

Now, the decision is in your hands. What to do with everything you've learned? The best strategy, the most efficient method, and the right tools are worthless if they are not put into practice. But the good news is that you don't have to do it alone. Marcelo, Stefan, and Rachel took the first step, and they are already changing their lives. Now it's finally your turn!

Next Steps for Definitive Acceleration of Results

This book was written to give you an introduction and overview of the investment environment in the United States, a foundational theoretical basis, and practical tools to start taking the first step today. We introduce the SMIGRM Method and the RISP 500 risk indicator so that you are well supported and guided from day one. However, the book cannot teach you everything, or it would easily be 10,000 pages long (better to bind it as an encyclopedia, in that case!). In order to give depth to each of the topics taught in this book, each chapter could become another book or books. For example, we discussed fundamental analysis, chart analysis, *valuation*, etc., but we did not teach any of these methods in sufficient depth in the book. To really teach fundamental analysis, we would have to at least teach a little about *financial statements* and accounting, such as balance sheet analysis and income statements. It is not uncommon to find books on fundamental analysis that are 500 pages or more. In other words, it would be impossible to teach everything in a single book. My goal with this book is to provide you with a comprehensive introduction covering the most diverse aspects you need to know before buying stocks in the United States, if you want to be successful in your endeavor.

More Educational Opportunities

We acknowledge that different people have different learning styles. Some like to learn from reading books. Others prefer to attend lectures, in person or online. Yet others, especially those who are past the basic stuff, don't want any courses but want guidance, personally or in a group setting. For these folks, they need someone to give them specific directions, help them with implementation, and provide feedback to help them achieve the results they want. The reality in education is that everyone has different needs and different favorite learning styles.

Besides writing books, we are also committed to produce content for new courses and advanced strategic advisory programs to help students delve deeper into the techniques presented throughout the book plus offering interactive follow-up so they can achieve results more accurately and quickly. The focus is always on practical execution and achieving concrete objectives — whether they are specific short-term goals (such as how to read economic indicators, how to operate strategies with options, or how to boost results by exploiting trading opportunities that arise occasionally, etc.) or broader, long-term goals (such as becoming a full-fledged Wall Street investor, or achieving financial freedom faster, etc.).

The courses and advisory programs will provide much greater breadth and depth to truly transfer the knowledge built up over at least three decades of work in the field.

The **Sovereign Global Wealth** strategic advisory program, focused on guidance, implementation, feedback, and achieving results, is a prime example.

Epilogue: The Next Phase of Global Wall Street

As investors look ahead, one reality is becoming increasingly clear: the global economic landscape is undergoing a structural transformation. The 21st century will no longer be defined by a single dominant engine of growth, but by the emergence of a more complex, multipolar system.

Today, the United States remains the world's largest and most influential capital market, offering unmatched depth, liquidity, and innovation. At the same time, China has established itself as a central pillar of global economic expansion. While its capital markets remain relatively smaller and less accessible compared to the U.S., this imbalance is unlikely to persist indefinitely. Projections suggest that China's economy may surpass that of the United States between 2030 and 2050, in US dollar terms, reshaping the global balance of economic power.

Already, the United States and China together account for nearly half of global GDP. Looking further ahead, the composition of global growth will continue to evolve, with emerging markets, regional blocs, and resource-driven economies playing an increasingly important role. The relative share of the G7 countries is expected to gradually decline, giving way to a broader distribution of economic influence across regions such as BRICS nations and other emerging economies.

In addition, demographics trends in advanced economies and the gradual encroachment of AI and robotics in daily life and at work will forever change society and disrupt everything with far-reaching consequences and impact on financial markets around the world.

In this environment, static investment approaches and the old playbook are unlikely to remain effective. Global investors will need to become more adaptive – capable of reallocating capital across geographies, asset classes, and macro regimes as conditions change – quickly and decisively. Success will depend not only on identifying opportunities, but on understanding when and where to deploy capital with precision.

To meet these challenges, a new framework is currently being developed: the **G2 Macro Allocator**. This approach is designed to help investors navigate the two primary engines of global growth—the United States and China—while incorporating broader allocation opportunities across emerging markets, regional blocs, and real assets such as metals and commodities. By integrating macroeconomic indicators and real-time signals, the framework aims to support tactical allocation decisions across shifting global conditions.

The objective is straightforward: to provide investors with a more agile, globally integrated approach to capital allocation—one that reflects the realities of a changing world.

As the investment landscape continues to evolve, those who remain disciplined, informed, and adaptable will be best positioned to capitalize on the opportunities ahead.

Gratitude

I hope I have managed to meet your expectations when you started reading this book. My goal was to empower you and open new horizons so that you can definitely accelerate your journey to build the wealth you want in a fast, easy, and safe way. Writing the book took months, but I hope I have managed to deliver real value to you. I also hope that you can make good use of what you have learned here to transform your life, achieving your dream of financial freedom, a peaceful retirement, or any other financial goal you have in mind.

I would like to offer my sincere words of gratitude for your trust. After "talking" so much, I now want to hear what you have to say. I only ask that you leave me your honest review as feedback to help me improve as an author and communicator. I really value what you think! I would greatly appreciate your review on Amazon:

https://www.Amazon.com/review/create-review?&asin=https://www.amazon.com/dp/196069118X

Your contribution will guide my next steps in creating better content, making changes, improving, and better helping everyone.

Thank you!

Sidney Shauy, MBA

Author's Books

Author's books available on Amazon or through the website:

www.Engineering-Finance.com

Bibliographic References

In writing this book, we consulted multiple sources of information:

- Risk Scientific LLC – RISP 500™
- Stock Market Investing Guided by Risk Management, by Sidney Shauy and Rodrigo Bittencourt Shauy (2024)
- Achieving Wealth Preservation with High Returns, by Sidney Shauy (2024)
- Wall Street para Brasileiros (Portuguese version, 2025)
- Fire Your Stock Analyst, by Harry Domash
- Wealth Management, by Harold R. Evensky
- Spiraling Up, by Steven Medland
- Finance, Barron Business Review Series
- S&P Dow Jones Indices – S&P 500®
- RiskMetrics – MSCI Technical Paper
- S&P 500 Daily Risk Control 5% Index
- @RISK – Percentile Settings
- Investopedia
- Wikipedia
- Morningstar
- U.S. Securities and Exchange Commission (SEC)
- Federal Reserve, FOMC
- MSCI, RiskMetrics
- NASDAQ and NYSE
- Dartmouth College
- Business Insider
- The Guardian
- AP News
- Cinco Dias, El Pais
- The Australian
- The Times UK
- InfoMoney

Made in United States
Orlando, FL
04 November 2026

90201111R00236